THE RISE AND RISE OF CHARLTON ATHLETIC

For baby Aidan, who arrived late,
and made a real impression, as they say in football . . .

MAINSTREAM *SPORT*

THE RISE AND RISE OF CHARLTON ATHLETIC

FROM PORTOKABINS TO PORTO CAPTAINS

MICK COLLINS

MAINSTREAM
PUBLISHING

EDINBURGH AND LONDON

First published in Great Britain in 2002 by
MAINSTREAM PUBLISHING (EDINBURGH) LTD
7 Albany Street
Edinburgh EH1 3UG

ISBN 1 84018 765 4

Revised and updated, 2003

A catalogue record for this book is available from the British Library

Typeset in Berkeley and Copperplate

Printed in Great Britain by
Cox & Wyman Ltd

ACKNOWLEDGEMENTS

Thanks are due in all directions and for all sorts of reasons, but, with apologies to anyone temporarily overlooked, the people listed below are the ones without whom the book would never have been finished, and in some cases, started.

On the professional front, without the decent midfield three of Neville Maw, Colin Cameron and Tom Morris, the book would have floundered long ago. Thanks also to Bill Campbell, who showed great faith in the face of scant evidence. It was much appreciated.

As far as my friends are concerned, thanks to Charlie Connelly, who generously proffered sensible, valuable advice and pints of 'council lager' in equally welcome amounts. I'm also indebted to Jeanette Earl, the best press officer in the Premiership (sorry Paul, not even close), as well as Matt Wright, handbook editor and Budball World Champion, no less – my cap is doffed. Also to Jon Lucas, the finest painter and decorator on the radio – evidently a very hard act to follow. Personally, huge thanks are also due to all those who let me moan on about my difficult job, without pointing out what an extraordinarily lucky man I was.

Thanks to all the staff at Charlton Athletic, from the players, who deserve the praise they get, to the people behind the scenes, who don't get the praise they deserve.

Thanks to all those who gave their time to speak to a lone figure, armed only with a notepad, Dictaphone and a cheerfully befuddled expression – Steve Brown, Ian Cartwright, Alan Curbishley, Mervyn Day,

Tony Evans, Ben Hayes, Alan Honey, Andy Hunt, Mark Kinsella, Keith Peacock, Kevin Portch, Chris Powell, Colin 'Paddy' Powell, John Robinson, Glynn Snodin, Steve Sutherland, David Tall, Ben Tegg and Mike Wadd, and, in the early days, Rick Everitt, Richard Murray, Martin Simons and Peter Varney. Without their observations, mine would mean even less than they already do.

To the Far Canal, the only other team in my life, may the search for line and length continue, and to Uncle Tim, for causing me to miss a punch-up, and gain a lifetime of glorious footballing fanaticism. I'd make an exception if you decided to change your mind, and start supporting a proper team, you know . . .

As far as my family are concerned, a huge debt of thanks goes to my mum and dad, for a lifetime of love and support, sensible advice and a well-stocked fridge. Thanks also to Dot and Brian, for always enquiring about the progress of the book, despite the fact that, by the end of Chapter 3, my answers usually consisted of exhausted grunts.

Finally, and most importantly, all my love and thanks to my wife, Cas for more reasons than could properly be recorded here. Also, to my daughters, Honor and Amy, one of whom said 'Daddy does good cuddles and watches football'. May their priorities always remain so well ordered.

CONTENTS

Introduction

AN INTERESTING DECADE . . .

It wasn't, when you look back on it, a very promising way to start a lifelong relationship. My uncle took me down to The Valley to watch Charlton play Maidstone in the FA Cup. It was an evening game, so I would imagine that part of my excitement derived from the fact that I was 'up late on a school night'. It was, so I have been told, a terrible game of football. Again, I have to admit to not remembering much of the detail. Like most eight year olds, I was more excited by the atmosphere and the surroundings than the tactical subtleties on the pitch. Anyway, I'm reliably informed that, on that particular night, there weren't many tactical subtleties to appreciate.

With about five minutes remaining, the uncle who had taken me could finally take no more. He was, I suppose, more of a purist than a dyed-in-the-wool Charlton fan. In fact, he only took me along because I insisted that it was Charlton I wanted to see, even at that early age possessing an innate wariness and suspicion as far as Millwall were concerned. He knew his football though, and the untidy spectacle unfolding throughout the course of the evening had left him far from impressed.

'Come on, time to go home. This is rubbish. It's not worth watching.'

As we left the ground there was a huge roar, which I don't think was directed at us. The problem was, that from our position, about a hundred yards the wrong side of the turnstiles, we weren't entirely sure at what it was directed. Missing a winning goal would have been hard to take, in fact, after the game we'd endured, missing any goal would have been hard to take. We needn't have worried, we hadn't missed a goal. Nothing as trivial as a goal . . .

Oh no. We'd missed Derek Hales and Mike Flanagan getting sent off for having a punch-up in the middle of the pitch. Two players from the same side – my side – were knocking lumps out of each other in front of a paying audience. Well, a paying audience two short of its original number, because we were heading onto Floyd Road and back home. I can say in all honesty that I've never been able to leave a game early since.

I'd told all my friends that I was going to the match, and they were all going to want to know about this punch-up, which was obviously going to create headlines all over the place. I didn't know whether to lie, or just try and pretend I'd seen it, hoping to bluff it out. I couldn't make a joke out of the fact that I'd missed it, because at eight years of age, that level of irony was still way beyond me.

From that moment onwards, I was smitten. The way in which I'd missed the action summed up my relationship with my new team. I expected little, and still frequently left disappointed, but at least I knew where I stood. My compass was set, and for the rest of my life any triumphs would be all the better as a result of the sinking feeling I still associate with that early visit.

As for the uncle who sounded that hasty retreat? He lives in Ireland now. When I'm feeling particularly bitter about the night in question, which these days is only once or twice a week at most, it still doesn't seem nearly far enough away. Football gets to you like that, and Charlton, in my thoroughly biased opinion, get to you more than most clubs.

This book seeks to tell the story of my club's extraordinary last decade. There are some who will have read the tale of our first meeting, and concluded that I must be mad to want anything more to do with Charlton. There have been times when they would have undoubtedly been right, but the highs have comprehensively outweighed the lows, albeit that the balance hasn't been fully tilted to my advantage until the last few years. It remains, however, a story with both an absurd number of twists in its plot, and some rather unexpected destinations.

There are endless ways of demonstrating the progress we've made over the last decade, since we returned home to The Valley, but some comparisons are starker than others, and footballing comparisons are maybe easier to grasp than financial ones. When he first took over as joint manager of the club with Steve Gritt, Alan Curbishley remembers looking out his office window at a squad of 'about 14 players'. In the run-up to the 2002 World Cup finals, no fewer than 13 Charlton players represented their countries.

Wherever you looked, a Charlton player was getting involved in the biggest tournament of the lot. A quick glance down the squad list on the back of the programme told the tale of the extent to which the club had become both cosmopolitan and successful.

The ball had really got rolling with victory in the First Division play-off final at Wembley in 1998. Admittedly, no victory at that stage of the season is ever going to be remembered with anything other than hysterical affection by the fans, given that it provides a short-cut through to English football's promised land – the Premiership – but even then, we felt the need to leave our mark. It was strangely in keeping with the Charlton way of doing things that we concluded that this, by itself, wasn't quite exciting enough.

In the process of beating Sunderland, we considered the dramatic potential of simply letting our resident Wearsider, Clive Mendonca, score a hat-trick against his home-town side, and then decided that we could do much better than that. After two and a half hours, eight goals, three Charlton equalisers, and thirteen successive penalty kicks slotted away, Michael Gray scuffed a left-footed prod into the waiting body of Sasa Ilic, and we were in the Premiership.

Satisfied that this represented all the drama we could ever take in the space of one football-club-supporting lifetime, we staggered slowly and unsteadily back to SE7, and pondered what would happen next. It was easily the most extraordinary afternoon anyone could ever have hoped to witness in the course of supporting his or her team. I would have enjoyed it had I been watching it on television with no involvement with either side. As it was, sitting there at Wembley, intermittently praying and cursing as the afternoon wore on, there were points where it got so fraught, I wished I didn't have an opinion one way or the other.

I'll always look back at that afternoon and think of the place warmly. The atmosphere, the colour, the explosion of emotion at the end and the churning of the stomach throughout – all of it viewed with a rose-tinted hue. In truth, the whole place smelt of stagnant urine while the feet of the man sitting squashed behind me were coming close to performing some kind of intimate examination of my nether regions.

When a light breeze carried away the stench of the 'sanitation', the charming odour of fried onions sought to leave a lingering reminder of our national stadium. It should have provided an early warning to us about the importance of ignoring reputations – people were still trying to tell us what a great stadium it was, even after we'd been there and experienced the squalor for ourselves.

The first season in the Premiership was wonderful, but we were wide-eyed, unready for what was to come, and acted as if we expected our invitation to be revoked at any moment. We had a thrilling, if frequently heartbreaking year, but ultimately found that those two wonderful clichés 'grit and determination' weren't enough to survive. There were some memorable moments and an astonishing victory at Villa Park in the penultimate weekend of the season almost convinced us that the impossible was about to happen, but defeat against Sheffield Wednesday in the last game sent us down. Let's face it, if you lose to Sheffield Wednesday, you deserve to go down . . .

In any event, the new First Division season opened with yet another Mendonca hat-trick at The Valley, and we just seemed to go from strength to strength. There was a run of 13 successive winning games throughout the post-Christmas and New Year period, leaving us on the brink not only of winning the title, but lapping the rest of the field. We still managed to add a twist though. Week after week we'd turn up to see the victory which finally made things safe, only for the wheels to fall off in dramatic fashion.

It was almost as if, in the midst of triumph, we were being reminded not to get carried away. Fittingly perhaps, we ended up winning it on a day when we weren't playing, thanks to a Manchester City stumble. After a bit more indecision, we finally went on to win the title. At Blackburn. After half-a-dozen attempts to do it in front of a home crowd, we managed to wait for about as distant an away fixture as we were to face all year, before tumbling gratefully over the finishing line.

If we had been running the marathon, they would have wrapped us up in one of those silver blankets and left us staggering around the Mall, like an undercooked and overtired turkey. Come to think of it, that would have been a more dignified end to the season, but we got over it, and spent the summer looking forward to fresh, if slightly daunting, challenges.

In our first season back in the top flight, despite rarely dropping out of the top half of the table, we still didn't get taken all that seriously. We waved around copies of the Premiership table, of course, but that always had Ipswich a few places in front, leaving Charlton permanently contesting for second place as far as the 'plucky newcomers' headlines were concerned.

We celebrated a draw against Manchester United so hard that we even found ourselves producing a video of the game. That's right, we produced a video of a draw. I told you we were still coming to terms with success.

We produced loads of colourful brochures about our facilities, which had a habit of talking about the 'lovely' views of the Thames Barrier. Lovely, that is, if your definition of the word includes the phrase 'just beyond the solid half a mile of grey industrial estate'. No, to all intents and purposes, we were acting like a Premiership football club, apart from the fact that, behind the headlines and glossy pamphlets, there was still a slight problem. We suffered from a paralysing combination of an excess of modesty and a habit of staring around in wonderment, wondering if it was all a bit of a dream.

It was better than it used to be, though. Suddenly, announcing yourself as a Charlton fan held less terror than the first trip to your feet to announce yourself at an Alcoholics Anonymous meeting. Finally, I could say it without fear of mockery. The fact is, I'm a Charlton fan. Always have been, always will be. Didn't get a say in the matter, and didn't want one either. As far as I'm concerned, growing up and finding out that you support Charlton feels like winning the lottery. Oh, and you don't have to tick the box for 'No Publicity'. Well, not any more.

Now, that might not stand up to much objective evaluation or scrutiny. Indeed, many will find it very hard to understand. Why Charlton? To be perfectly honest, though, it's never occurred to me that there might even be a question relating to whom I support.

Supporting a football team isn't like buying a house. You don't get to consider how nice the area is, or whether you like the neighbours. It's not like buying a car, because you don't get a choice about the colour, or even whether it's going to still be running five years from now. No, it's not a conscious thing, or a deliberate act of selection. It's just there as part of me.

The majority of football fans are the same, in that they can't really put their finger on the precise reason they support their club. I mean, they can offer forward the standard 'Well, they're my local team', or the occasional 'My dad brought me to watch a match when I was a kid', but beyond that, they are not, thankfully, a group prone to overmuch self-indulgent self-analysis.

I've always thought the deal was a particularly straightforward one. You support a team, you stick by them and you pray for good times. The ones supporting sides for whom the good times are rare and trivial moan about the lack of success, while those whose sides win trophies as an annual occurrence, moan about the new fans – the 'hangers-on'. In truth, the major things uniting football fans are an ability to moan at even the greatest triumph, and a fear that it's never going to be this good again.

It's the heady mix of fear and celebration that makes the game, for supporters at least, what it is. The inescapable churning feeling in the stomach, the explosion of celebration, and the muscle-tightening and fist-clenching moment of triumph, before disappointment causes you to slump back into your seat and stare blankly.

It's what makes it harder to understand those who 'change' clubs. Players do it, of course, but we never really believe that they're in it for anything much more than the money anyway. We allow ourselves a temporary suspension of reality when they punch the air, run over to the stands and kiss the nylon badge on their nylon shirt, but, deep down, we know it's all a bit of an act. Paul Ince, for example, has kissed badges in front of different fans, at different grounds and for different sides, all over Europe, and fair play to him.

For fans though, it's different. How can you possibly wake up as a child and discover that you've fallen in love with Fulham, only to grow older, and switch your allegiance over to, say, Chelsea? What sort of football fan could do something like that? Someone who was prepared to accept strange looks from real fans for the rest of time, obviously. You can't drop what you believe in and pick up a different side, just because it suits you. Well, I suppose you could, but it's amazing how much credibility that stroll down the Kings Road could cost you, especially when it's your allegiance that's being taken for a wander.

No, realistically you just can't do that, because supporting a club isn't a logical decision. Football is about emotion – not corporate packages, or brands, or mascots, or sponsors. Or indeed, any of the other fripperies and sideshows which assemble alongside the modern game to feed. The need to bring money into the game is inescapable, but as any fan knows, once the whistle blows, it is all thrust promptly and rightfully back into its place – behind the emotion of the day.

Even the dullest sides in the world have inspired a degree of passion at one time or another. In among the mundane, run-of-the-mill seasons, which gently amalgamate to form their histories, there have been moments of tension and excitement. There have been periods of success, which have led their terraces to burst into a staccato chorus of 'We Are Going Up' and equally, the one vital result in amid a sea of disappointment which leads its sister-song, the defiant 'We Are Staying Up'.

Relegation isn't as bad as it gets though, not by a long chalk. The worst situation in football imposes itself on the supporters, only when the money men have got it thoroughly wrong. Most of the time, football fans are concerned with how Saturday's result will go, how the team will line up, whether the ref will be any good, and whether there will be a queue for the bar.

Very occasionally, all of this is threatened. Every now and then, a club takes one step too many backwards and finds itself staring over its shoulder, down a financial precipice from which there is no return. Suddenly, the result, the team and the bar don't really matter. We just want them to still be there next week.

Charlton have been there, we've played that tricky away leg in the bankruptcy courts, and we've not just survived, but prospered. The effects leave their mark though, and once you've experienced that, you tend not to take anything else for granted. The fear of conceding a late goal is rather put into perspective by the fear of having to note down your most difficult opponent as the Official Receiver.

Over the course of the last 20 years, other clubs have dallied with the prospect of relegation, the relative picnic of a loss of form, and the occasional wave of hooligan-induced tabloid loathing. Very few though, have stared down the barrel of bankruptcy and wondered if the accountants were feeling trigger-happy today. We have.

It's not a situation with which we've really come to terms, because it still feels a bit remote. We are, as I've suggested, laden with an admirable degree of self doubt and well armed with a lethal arsenal of self-depreciating humour. We can reel off a list of our worst-ever players far more happily than a roll of honour of our best. That's just in our nature; it's the way we are.

We sit there cheerfully, watching our side produce results which nobody expects, amused and occasionally irritated by the response we get from the outside world. Like a member of the chorus line stepping forwards and taking over the closing number, there's still a feeling that we're behaving like upstarts.

When success really came knocking, on one view, it caused us more confusion than when mere chaos reigned. At least in the bleak old days we knew to expect the worst and look upon anything else as a bonus. Suddenly, it's not even a question of whether the glass is half full or half empty – it's almost over-flowing, and it can get to be a bit disconcerting.

We didn't imagine it would ever be like this, not when we were in court, waiting to see if they'd closed us down. Not when we got that piece of paper saying next week we'd be playing at Selhurst Park. When we arrived back at The Valley, we thought the limit of our expectations had been reached.

Winning at Wembley caused a fair bit of head-scratching, while prospering in the Premiership has made the most miserable amongst us wonder how it could possibly get any better. And then, just when we swore we could see the glass ceiling above us, just when we were convinced there weren't mountains left to climb, half the squad went and got picked for the World Cup. Suddenly, I can't imagine why I'm ever surprised any more. This is Charlton. Even if it's not plausible, anything is possible.

The problem is, that to the outsider, and even to be honest, after reading back through the last decade, to the established fan, it doesn't seem all that extraordinary. Admittedly, we're a football club that has risen while many others have sunk, and we've bucked a financial trend which seems set to be seeping dozens of clubs gently towards their doom, but surely it's not all that unusual?

Well, I'd hazard the suggestion that it's not only unusual (as Tom Jones nearly sang), but unique. There's a touch of disbelief among the fans, principally and reasonably enough, during some of our more unbelievable episodes, but even outside of that, we've gone through much of the journey in a state of dazed cheerfulness.

What makes Charlton different is that they've matched a hard-fought battle for survival off the pitch, with a steady growth and development on it. With no hugely wealthy benefactor, and with a fan elected onto the board, we cut an unlikely presence in the Premiership, where doing things 'properly' seems to become less common with each passing season.

It's always a proud boast to claim that your club is ahead of its time, albeit that it's usually a hollow and slightly questionable claim. Crystal Palace were the team of the 1980s, QPR and Luton had plastic pitches, while Swansea have got a psychopathic swan as a mascot. On top of that, every year, the third round of the FA Cup sees a publicity-hungry lower-league side bringing a ballet teacher into training, explaining that in a few years' time, everyone will be doing it.

It's a contagious disease, being ahead of the game, and at Charlton we went down with a strain that was very nearly terminal. In the 1980s we had a board of directors who were determined to show that they were entirely capable of ensuring Charlton left an enduring mark on the game. Unfortunately, they seemed to want us to leave a mark by leaving the game. Forever.

Fifteen years before the collapse of a subscription-based television channel brought the lower reaches of the game to its knees, we'd already tried our best to go broke. Although we'd seen Accrington Stanley claim the proud title of undisputed front runners in the field of imprudent financial management, we seemed to set out determined to at least claim the silver medal. With arms wide open and faces wreathed in smiles, our board of directors led us skipping towards the abyss. Surely, no one before or since has ever invited bankruptcy with quite so much zeal?

In September 1985, fans turning up at The Valley to watch Charlton face Crystal Palace found an extra piece of paper included with their programme. It announced that the club was leaving The Valley, and that as of a fortnight's time, it would share a ground with that afternoon's opponents – Palace.

It didn't quite add 'and if you'll all be good enough not to moan at this, the dismissal of your history and heritage, and move along nicely, halfway around south London to your new home, that would be much appreciated' but other than that, it was just about as glib and trite as you could ever hope for.

Short of putting up a large, cartoon sign, pointing in the other direction, bearing the legend 'They went thatta way . . .', it's hard to see a more efficient way of killing the club. There wasn't exactly a lot to behold on the pitch as it was, but at least we all knew where it was. Suddenly, they were taking it somewhere else, and expecting us to follow.

To enter the football administrator's top ten bad decisions obviously takes an incredible effort, but the Charlton directors had shown that they were prepared to give it a go. All logic dictated that it was a footballing suicide note. A magnificently ridiculous gesture, and the logical extension, for a football club director at least, of an age-old childhood retort. Oh yes, it was their ground, and they were taking it home. Except they weren't – it was our home, and they were shutting it, but I think you get the basic idea. Which was more than they seemed to.

A lot has happened since then. As you walk along the front of The Valley today, it's hard to imagine that it wasn't always like this. It's nice and new, the glass is shiny and the queues to swap the location of your season tickets are several deep, remaining a constant sight throughout the course of the late-June afternoons. The irony is fading, but still apparent, in a ground where you once could have split the terrace in half and discussed a 'my half, your half' arrangement with the only other bloke likely to be standing on it.

Where a shambolic organisation had allowed itself to drift into aimless financial chaos, a well-managed football club, both on and off the pitch, has risen from the ruins. The ground holds just under 27,000 people, the team is stocked with internationals from around the globe, and the people at the helm seem to have considerably more idea of how to survive and prosper in an increasingly businesslike game than their eccentric forefathers.

But, as can be demonstrated and described to you by virtually anyone in the ground, in any one of a thousand different ways, it wasn't always like this.

If football isn't about memories and emotions, then it's not really about much at all. Football is recent history brought into pin-sharp focus. The sensation of hairs rising on the back of your neck when a great moment of the past is discussed. The slight misting of the eyes and the cheerfully blank gaze into the middle distance – that's what football is about.

In my mind, football grounds are places for dreams, emotions and glory, not bills, debts and interest payments – they belong to grey and dull everyday life, not the loud and colourful world which exists inside those red, wrought-iron gates. Unfortunately, for my chances of becoming a Charlton chairman in the year 2002, though, that's just not a very sensible way to approach running a football club, where financial matters have to be considered and dealt with the same as for any other business.

These days, the right person running the financial side of the show is just about as vital as having the right man wearing the number-nine shirt. At Charlton, we've come to accept that more than most, simply because we saw what it was like when there wasn't anyone to fill the role. Speaking for myself, though, I can still do without all that financial stuff in too much detail. I'll get all wrapped up in the emotion and excitement, and leave someone else to worry exactly how all the bills are being paid.

I'm not ungrateful, but I just don't feel like I need to know. I've placed my trust in people, and they seem to be doing the job just fine, thank you very much. It might not be the greatest analogy in the world, but it's like being at the end of the runway, just before take-off. I don't need the person next to me to start explaining how this big chunk of metal gets into the air and, more importantly, how it stays there.

I've invested a deal of great faith in the pilot, and he seems to be just the chap to get me to my destination safely. What I don't know, quite honestly, can't hurt me, and I don't think I'm alone in approaching it like that. Where I might be unique, is that financial details fill me with the same degree of foreboding – especially when they intrude upon things like football. You can do courses to deal with a fear of flying, though, and I'm not sure they exist to help you come to terms with a fear of finance – more's the pity.

At heart, I'll always be a wide-eyed dreamer when placed anywhere near a football ground, and when it's my ground, I'm even worse.

Explain to me very loosely how much we need to generate to survive, or how much we've got to spend on players, and I'll do my best to follow. Give me too much detail though, and I'll stop listening. Children don't want to know who's inside the Mickey Mouse costume when they go to Disneyland, and I don't want normal life intruding when I step inside a football ground.

In the 1970s, however, my sort of approach would have led to me being considered a visionary and a man of the people. My nonchalant and emotional outbursts would have seen me carried shoulder high through the streets, en route to my enthronement as chairman. A sort of Mark Goldberg figure, 20 years before my time. I'd probably have remained a heroic figure right up until the point where I bankrupted the club.

Thankfully, and due in no small part to the fact that I was about 15 years old when it all went wrong, I was never asked to take on the job. There have been quite enough people who think like me running football clubs, and their cavalier approach to real life has created havoc all over the league. The people who did take on the task managed to forge a remarkable bond between the fans in the boardroom and the fans in the stands. Maybe all that flowery rhetoric wasn't as good a way of running the club as a modicum of solid financial planning.

Having endured problems and heartbreaks, which would have seen most clubs consigned to a footnote in the *Rothmans Annual* and the rubbish bin of history, Charlton survived. The wounds of that battle for survival, however, ran deeper than many of us were prepared to admit. Caught in some kind of post-traumatic state, and maybe made overly humble as a result of our experiences, we weren't sure how to start greeting success.

It's a curious situation, and the reasons for it could be discussed and debated endlessly. What is certain is that this odd blend of fans, with a receptive board of directors, a talented manager and a squad of players who relish, rather than shirk from, a challenge, have achieved minor miracles.

Charlton Athletic may not be the first name to trip off the tongue when discussing footballing achievements, but theirs deserves a place among other, more notable candidates. Without mortgaging their future, selling their soul or alienating their fans, they have pulled themselves back from the brink of disaster, and now stand safely among the most famous football clubs in the land.

Having come back to a ground sculpted from scaffolding and planks, stretching around just three-quarters of the pitch, they have a stadium of which to be proud. Where once they relied on Portakabins to form everything from dressing-rooms to boardrooms, they now have state-of-the art 'suites' and the gloriously incongruously named 'Conference and Banqueting' department to run them.

We once sold Robert Lee to Newcastle because we needed the money to pay the wages, and we couldn't fight off the demands of a 'big club'. Last year, we saw Porto captain Jorge Costa come to The Valley, because he said it improved his chances of getting to the World Cup finals. Porto of all places!

The vision of my club reaching out a benevolent hand to a giant of European football, and offering to help him get somewhere his own club couldn't manage, is one that will stay with me for a very long time. My recollection may be a little bit biased, but after the decade we've had, I'm not letting reality intrude to dull the edges of the memory.

This book charts that rise, through the eyes of those involved on the pitch, off it, in the stands and beyond. Oh, and also from the perspective of a man who had his first ever visit to The Valley cut short.

'It's not worth watching'?

Some prediction that proved to be . . .

1

'AND IT BECOMES THE PERFECT START . . .'

To describe Charlton's tale as a rags-to-riches story is to underestimate and misrepresent the extent of our troubles by some considerable distance. To adopt a cod northern accent, and paraphrase the classic *Monty Python* sketch: 'We used t' dream of 'avin' rags. You were lucky . . .'

I suppose, if we're being precise, we should describe it as a riches-to-rags-to-riches story, given the successes of half a century ago, but for the vast majority of fans, the successes really do belong firmly in the history books, having happened before they were born. For them, Charlton had endured a dismal period which seemed to last for the best part of an ice age, followed by a glorious upturn in fortunes, where each season passes in, or at least what feels like, about 45 minutes.

Whether we actually have an interest in it or not, the distant past seems to be a thing of huge fascination for some fans, and at Charlton it's no different. I remember being on a radio programme once, where the topic of conversation was the finest players ever to play for the club. It never got broadcast nationally – I can't imagine why. Someone came on the line, sounding no older than 30 at the absolute outside, and proceeded to put the case on behalf of a chap by the name of Seth Plum.

Now, I can honestly say that I've got nothing against Seth. More honestly still, I can state, with the evidence of history behind me, that I've never met him. To be honest, and surrendering any right I ever had to be considered any sort of Charlton historian, the only reason his name rang a bell with me at all was because its vague comedic value left it lodged in a remote corner of my brain. It turned out, after a quick scoot through a book in the corner of the studio, that he had been our first England international, so I listened as the man on the telephone put his case across.

It wasn't until halfway through the conversation that the penny dropped. The chap on the phone was warming to his theme, and explaining how well Seth could cross a ball, and how nimble he was.

'He, er, played his last game in 1924, didn't he?' I asked, in that tone you really hope will disguise the fact that you're reading it straight out of a book.

'Yes, 1924, that's right,' replied our cheery caller, barely breaking stride as he continued on into Seth's defensive qualities.

'And he died in 1969, I believe?' I offered, gaining in confidence that he might actually think I knew these things off the top of my head. In fact, I was getting a bit scared that people might think I did know these sort of things, but I had to press onwards.

'Yes, I believe so,' replied the Seth fan club, hesitating not a fraction.

I didn't have the heart to make the obvious point – what good would it have done? The man had died a year before I was born – so at least I hadn't pretended that I'd ever spoken to him, and he played his last game for Charlton round about the time my grandad was born. Despite this, here was someone of about my age, giving what appeared to be, or at least was intended to sound like, an eye-witness account of the player's talents.

From that moment onwards, I refused to be surprised at football's ability both to cast its eyes backwards and re-invent the past, convincing itself that everything was better in the good old days. In fact, there will undoubtedly be someone reading this, complaining bitterly that I've got no respect for the past, and cursing the fact that the club has gone bad from the top downwards, because of all these people intent on looking forwards all the time.

It's not actually true, I can see the benefits of many of the things that happened in the past. I think the onset of commercialisation of the game is a necessary evil, rather than the force for good that some people would have us believe. I think that there is a cynicism about much of the modern game, which wasn't always there, and I think money has got a lot to do with that.

I also know that the extraordinary wages collected by players have turned the game into something of a financial freak-show. People on their way to very averagely paid jobs discuss the 'hundred-grand-a-week' players, and do it in an almost abstract way. The money is so ridiculous, it bears no resemblance to real life. Players don't get the bus to work any more, and they almost certainly never will again. They don't live 'down my street', they live behind gates and at the end of driveways, and it's a change that may never be reversed.

It's all a sign of progress, though, and the fact that it's happening at Charlton – although to a lesser degree than elsewhere – is a sign that something is being done correctly. The desire to look back and reminisce is a powerful one, but it also distracts from the task in hand.

In the wake of the move back to The Valley, the Charlton board could have sat back, accepted the plaudits and raised yet another toast to themselves. Nobody would have blamed them, and the feelgood factor would have guaranteed a vast pool of forgiveness in any event. It would have been a disaster though. Such was the precarious foothold Charlton had secured on the bottom rung of the ladder to safety, the club, of course, would have slid back into trouble twice as easily and about ten times as fast as the rate at which they had just escaped.

The reality was, thankfully slightly different. We had escaped from the shipwreck, paddled to shore, and smiled to ourselves at our good fortune in escaping with our lives. Now, we had to find something to live off, or face much the same fate as we did before, only via a slightly different route. It was like that film where Tom Hanks gets washed up on a beach. In fact, now I come to think of it, Hanks' character bore an uncanny resemblance to Stuart Balmer, who threw himself around the centre of the Charlton defence for several of the early seasons back at The Valley. I knew that we'd work that back round to Charlton, if we had faith and stayed with it . . .

This is not to say, of course, that there aren't certain pieces of history we don't all look back on from time to time – the problem is becoming obsessed with it, and wallowing in it, rather than having a healthy regard for it. For many it's the play-off final, while for others it's a far more anonymous game, which has personal significance for reasons that may seem utterly insignificant to anyone else. For anyone who was anywhere near the club, either emotionally or geographically, the first game back – the starting point for this book – has a very special resonance.

Once Curbishley had finished prowling around the dressing-room, delivering his team talk on that famous December afternoon, his side went out to claim a result which now seems inevitable, and back then, seemed virtually impossible. Having won just once in their previous ten league outings, Curbishley could have been forgiven for thinking that three o'clock was going to mark the end of the celebrations, and the start of another gloomy afternoon. It might have been spent in a setting whose familiarity would have more than made up for the defeat, but his side needed to start picking up a few results from somewhere, and the visit of Portsmouth wasn't, on the face of it, a promising prospect.

We needn't have worried. With an exuberant crowd still looking around and regaining their bearings once again, the gods smiled down. The words of the late Brian Moore still cause a smile and a surge of emotion. Although principally a Gillingham fan, Moore retained a huge affection for Charlton, and understood the club in a way few, if any, other television commentators of the time could claim.

The footage of him sitting in a temporary wooden shelter, held aloft by a sea of scaffolding on an otherwise deserted terrace, is an enduring image. In fact, the sheer volume of scaffolding around the place that day is something we'll never forget. Every time Curbishley and the rest of the tracksuited inhabitants of the dugout leapt forward in excitement, it looked like a five-a-side team trying to escape from a building site. It was an extraordinary day, and Moore's excited, yet perfectly measured response to events seven minutes into the game will live with the fans for many years to come.

He is, and will continue to be, hugely missed, and his voice, along with the smell of roast beef, Courage Best and Hamlet cigars will always effortlessly and happily transport me back to the Sunday lunchtimes of the mid-'70s. It is for that one, perfectly judged piece of description, however, that Brian Moore will always be prominent in my memory.

> Gritt . . . towards Leaburn. He's certainly got the pace and the power. Finding Pitcher . . . and a shot, and a goal! By Walsh, for Charlton! And it becomes the perfect start . . .
>
> Well, they've dreamed about this for so long, after seven long years of playing at Selhurst and playing at Upton Park, they're back home in the finest possible style.

I believed, as all supporters do, and children do more fervently than most, that my team was unique. I probably still hung onto that terrace-based belief that we really were 'by far the greatest team the world has ever seen'. All right, I didn't think we were the best by far, but I knew deep down that we were edging it by a nose against anyone else in the world. Did you ever see any scaffolding at the Bernabeu, the Stadio delle Alpi, Old Trafford or the San Siro? Is there, as a child, anything more exciting than a huge pile of scaffolding? I rest my case – nobody else came close.

Despite my unapologetically biased memories, there is a desperate need for insight from someone who can look back on those days and retain some kind of grasp on reality, as I plainly can't. As with any such situation, there were some people better placed to comment than others. Having played at the ground in a decent side in front of reasonably decent gates, Colin Powell, known universally as Paddy, had seen some glorious days and nights there. After striding down the wing for many years, retirement from the game saw him plodding down it, pushing a lawnmower, as he become the groundsman. After having enjoyed the extraordinary moment of marking the lines back out onto the pitch for the first time in seven years, he knew of the mundane day-to-day reality.

> I knew it wasn't going to be easy, and to be honest, it's hardly the best way for a groundsman to show what he can do, working under the conditions that we did. But, even when it was hard back then in those early days back here, nobody who understood anything about the club would have had it any other way. Nothing changes, either. I get nervous on match-days, partly for the result and partly because of the pitch, and hoping it will be OK. I still get a buzz coming down here though, even after all the years I've spent here. It's a special place.
>
> I played practically all my professional career here, so it's obviously a place close to my heart. In fact, when you come to think of it, if you can get up in the morning and look forward to going to work, then you know you're working in a fairly special place. Despite all the mickey taking, and a lot of the moaning that happens at any workplace, I couldn't deny for a minute that this is unlike any other football ground I've ever been to.

Powell isn't alone in his way of thinking, and he's also not the only player from the club's recent history to retain his links with this little corner of south London. He's also not the only one to have a slightly 'off-beam' reason for remembering it so fondly.

Mark Robson is now employed as the assistant director of the club's youth academy, conveying strategies and formations to young players with the same boyish enthusiasm with which he once scampered around the Charlton midfield. In terms of the future prospects of the club, though, his most important run might not have even been on a football pitch, as Curbishley recalls:

> We were playing over at West Ham, and the coach got stuck in terrible traffic about a mile short of the ground. We were going to

get whacked with a fine for not handing the team sheet in on time, and to be honest, we wouldn't have had the money to pay it – we could only just afford to pay the wages, and I mean only just as well.

I had to send Robbo off on a little jog through the streets of West Ham to hand the team sheet to the ref before the half-past-one deadline. It was like a parks team: he had to explain that the rest of his mates were on the way, but that they'd got stuck in traffic, but we should still be all right for a three o' clock kick off.

It weren't the greatest preparation for a game ever, but you have to do what you have to do in circumstances like that. It's memories like that which make me wander around this place sometimes, see how far we've come and how good the ground looks, and have a little smile to myself. People laugh when you call it a funny old game, but I don't know how else you describe something like that!

In some ways, I can see that the desire to laugh at something deeply depressing and bleak stems out of a sort of relief that the whole episode is now consigned to history. On a far more serious level, there are still older people, who talk fondly about the good times they had during the war, seemingly unwilling to recall the reality of fear, tragedy and death. It seems to be a human defence mechanism, on every level from the most serious – war – to the most trivial – football – to subsequently make light of your plight.

The truth, as far as I can remember it, is that life at Charlton, in the immediate wake of our return at least, wasn't anything to look back on too fondly. The combination of not having to travel across the river every week, and actually being back at a place we thought of as home, were however, considerable consolations. The trips to West Ham seem to crop up in virtually every story you hear told about those days, and not only from the fans.

Gary Nelson played more than 750 professional football matches, a few hundred of them for Charlton, before settling into an impressive post-football career with the Professional Footballers' Association and as a broadcaster. Rarely showing any signs of being ruffled while on the pitch, Nelson recalls that, back in the early 1990s, events off it were frequently rather more difficult to deal with.

Having been brought to the club while they resided at Upton Park, he experienced the joys of travelling through the Blackwall Tunnel on more occasions than he would care to remember.

'That was the pattern of things at Upton Park – you never knew if you were facing a fine or a non-appearance. The traffic was horrendous, week after week.'

Now, these are men who earned their living while receiving vast amounts of adulation, in front of thousands of people. When they score goals, whole grounds start singing out their name, and when they achieve something even more significant, they claim a place in our memories forever. How bad must that journey have been, to keep cropping up time and time again in people's reminiscences of the time?

The thing was that if returning home was like a giant early Christmas present, the rest of the campaign wasn't really much to write home about. The third round of one cup and the second round of another aren't really the heady heights, and as fans, we found ourselves looking around at the ground, celebrating the fact that we were back, and, if we're all being honest, wondering where we went from here.

I remember walking out of the back of the west stand after one game, having been beaten, trying to hop my way around the Lake Windermere-sized puddles which were appearing across the expanse of mud and gravel. I eventually gave up trying to avoid the puddles in order to concentrate on bracing myself against the torrent of water falling from the temporary roof of the (very) temporary stand. We weren't all that good, and while it was better to be not very good at The Valley than to be halfway decent at Selhurst Park, I could see that the attraction of merely being back home was not going to sustain us forever.

We were, however, setting ourselves up for a managerial quote, which was to be repeated over and over again as the years passed by. Whenever he is asked to describe how far the club has come, or how much of a transformation has occurred, Curbishley harks back to the state of the ground, and our lack of a full complement of stands. Unfortunately, he suffers from the same disease as everyone else around the club, in that he doesn't stop to think that not everyone is as familiar with our plight as we are.

'You want to know how far we've come? Well, how do you start to describe it? Blimey. I tell you what, I can remember when there was only three sides at this place, that shows you how far we've come.'

I must have heard him say it a hundred times, and every single rendition has left at least one of the journalists looking utterly baffled. You can see the thought process in action, as they stare out in search of an explanation. It was a Norwegian chap who eventually asked me the question, politely whispering in my ear after the manager had moved onto his next subject.

'I know they shared with Palace, and then they shared with West Ham, and Wimbledon share with Palace now, but three sides? At The Valley? I can't remember that . . .'

Sometimes, I felt moved to explain that he meant three stands, not three teams, but I must confess, after the first 50 or so recitations, I started to consider it a personal joke, a small, mirth-inducing perk of the job. Curbs, on the other hand, didn't stop to see their reaction, but strode off with the deep conviction that he'd eradicated all confusion and cleared the matter up for them. I wonder why he thought they all looked more confused afterwards than they did before? If I was predisposed not to like him, it would have become a cause of major irritation by now, blown out of all proportion. As it is, I smile as soon as he gets to the 'I remember when there was only . . .' bit.

It's hard, as a fan, not to like the manager. If the leaps and bounds undertaken by Richard Murray, Martin Simons and the rest of the board are virtually unparalleled in the British game, the development of the side over the last few years has more than kept pace. Working with a transfer budget so small that it could get lost down the back of the sofa at the United, Chelsea and Arsenals of this world, he has constructed a team which holds its own in the top flight.

'Paddy' Powell, who has enjoyed as close a view as anyone of the developments at the club over recent years, is under no illusions as to how much credit belongs to the manager:

> He's done fantastically well, and his record speaks for itself. He also signs good players which is the hallmark of a good manager. He rarely picks up anyone who doesn't become a consistently good player. He also doesn't panic when the side get beaten, which is very important.
>
> Things seem to go in cycles with Charlton teams. The Peter Shirtliff side definitely had a lot of strong points, and I think Lennie Lawrence was only a couple of signings away from building a really good team. For actual commitment, and ability, though, this side are a bit special.
>
> The thing is that they play the game the way I think it's meant to be played. They stick in there when it's not going so well, and they stretch out and expand teams when they get the chance.

It's not a bad tribute, especially from a man who played the game in such an attractive way himself – it's the sort of compliment you grade mentally, depending on your opinion of the player who offered it. If

Vinnie Jones acclaims someone as a talented ball player, you tend to take it with a pinch of salt, but if George Best said it, it's a slightly different matter. Paddy Powell might not quite have reached George's orbit, but for a generation of Charlton fans, he played the game 'properly'.

The season which ended in 1993, and saw our return home, finished with the side in 12th place in Division One, while the two which followed saw a rise to 11th followed by a fall back to 15th. It didn't actually seem all that exciting at the time, and to be honest, looking back at the figures now, that's not a memory laden with too much injustice.

I'm not usually given to overmuch study of the league table, but as someone helped set out all the figures in a club handbook, it seemed rude not to have a quick glance to check that my instincts were sound and my memory accurate. Over the course of those three years, we not only finished resolutely 'mid-table' every single year, we managed to score precisely two more goals than we conceded, and one year even managed to win exactly as many games as we lost.

That is not, even if you get Ruud Gullit to say in his most beguiling and suave manner, 'sexy football'. Most of the time, we'd have finished up about the same if we'd sat down with all the other clubs at the start of the year, and agreed not to bother playing any games, but to split the points and go straight to the pub. I'll try and remember all that, the next time someone tells me that it's boring being a mid-table Premiership side, and it was better a decade ago, when it was ups and downs all the way . . .

There were high points in amongst all the mediocre offerings, in the form of a couple of cheerfully distracting cup runs, one of which took us to Anfield for a fifth-round clash, while the other led to Old Trafford, a round further still into the competition. Both games ended in defeat, although for a club routinely dispatched from the FA Cup by the end of January, the fixtures were welcome diversions from the norm.

What was remarkable, and set the tone for a continued relationship between the club and the fans unlike anywhere else in the country, was the fact that, despite the frequently less than enthralling fare being served up, the crowds continued to grow.

A campaign was launched, with vast amounts of work undertaken by the supporters' club, to slowly try and raise the size of the crowd. As the ground expanded slowly, the results of 'Target 10,000' began to bear fruit. From an average crowd of just over 7,000 in the first year back, further seating, and continued efforts to increase the number of people actually attending games, saw a rise of a further thousand people in the next season.

Despite a decidedly average season, and the sale of Scott Minto to Chelsea to help ensure the ongoing slow-but-steady recovery of the club's finances, interest in Charlton continued to grow. The average crowd for the 1994–95 season topped 10,000 for the first time since the turn of the previous decade, and for only the second time since the late '70s. By the middle of the 1990s, Charlton were seeing their healthiest gates for almost 20 years.

In hindsight, while there might have been moments when things were starting to feel like something of an anti-climax, Charlton's graph was continuing to rise with a steady certainty. If, and it seems most unlikely, there was still anyone who thought the previous board's decision to leave The Valley had been a wise one, the figures were making more of a mockery of their arguments with each passing season.

If the Valley Party had been a vital force in ensuring the club's return, and arguably its continuing existence, the Target 10,000 scheme was proving to be just as effective in making sure that the return home was not the last step of the journey, but one of the first. The achievement should have been granted more of an audience over the years, but it happened at a place where the extraordinary was becoming less unexpected with each passing season . . .

2

RED, WHITE AND IN THE BLACK

While the mid-'80s trick of managing to lose our home may have marked Charlton Athletic out as front runners, it wasn't a trend we really expected anyone else to pick up on. A few other clubs, most notably Wimbledon, have faced a similar fate, but, generally, football clubs ride the storm, stay where they are, and a wealthy benefactor comes galloping over the horizon to save the day.

Had Charles Dickens not decided that David Copperfield was to make the acquaintance of the exuberantly optimistic financial mind of Wilkins Micawber, football would surely have had to invent him. When pressed on financial matters, Micawber would explain that: 'Until something turns up (which I am, I may say, hourly expecting), I have nothing to bestow but advice.'

It is a sentiment proffered with increasing frequency in the world of professional football, usually by the prospective buyer of a once-proud club, fallen on hard times. It's not even limited to the smaller clubs. Hands up at the back anyone who remembers Michael Knighton, juggling the ball in front of the Stretford End in full Manchester United kit, shortly before announcing that he wasn't going to buy the club after all?

It's unfortunate that Knighton managed to do that really, because nobody else is ever going to be daft enough to let someone pull that sort of stunt again. No football club will ever again let someone get away with such a display, or at least not before the cheque's safely in the account. It's like letting the people who want to buy your house start repainting your front room before the sale has been completed. What do you mean, I've got too much faith in the amount of common sense at the average football club as far as money is concerned?

Michael Knighton never made his way down the M6 to join us at The Valley, and that's a cross we'll just have to bear as best we can. We never had to deal with the Wilkins Micawber school of economics either, or at least not once we'd actually got back home. There's certainly an argument that it was exactly that system of financial forward planning that caused us to leave in the first place. It proved to be our undoing simply because, while the board 'hourly expected' it, nothing did happen to 'turn up'.

By the time the club had returned home, there had been a change, both in the nature of the people in charge, and in the attitude of the fans. An expectation hung about the place, but an expectation interwoven with reality. To a degree, dreams had already come true, in that we were back playing football at a ground we had almost given up for dead. What we all realised though, was that it could so easily go wrong – 'going bust' wasn't a phrase uttered with the light-heartedness apparent at other grounds, because we'd been there and stared it in the face.

The intimate nature of the run-in that we'd had with bankruptcy forced us into realising how we'd nearly become football supporters without a club to support. In spectating terms, it was a bit like coming to terms with your own mortality. Having grown used to scraping through and living to fight another day, we really couldn't have cut it much finer – one London radio station had already announced that we had been closed down.

Having fought and battled though, after campaigning and cajoling, we eventually found ourselves back home, staring around, frequently through slightly misty eyes, and wondering what would happened next. I can remember when my eldest daughter was born and it was a vaguely similar sort of feeling I was now experiencing. We brought her home, and for the first time in several days, we were on our own, without thrilled relatives or attentive nurses, and with the rapidly growing realisation that it was now all up to us.

On the Sunday morning after the first game back, Charlton's board of directors would have been forgiven for feeling much the same. The celebrations had been heartfelt and prolonged, the result had gone our way and there was still the faint scent of euphoria lingering in the air. As it cleared though, there was still a club in a financially vulnerable state that was going to need a lot of nursing before it came close to being fully grown. While there were happy memories, and enough stories to fuel hundreds of cheery, beery reminiscences, there was still pressure in all directions.

Looking around the ground today, it seems hard to believe that those days were only a decade ago. The fans take a pride in the journey we've undertaken and you only have to look at the speed of the recent development at the ground to appreciate that the acceleration onwards and upwards continues to this day.

Surely life's a bit of a walk in the park now, and maybe even our memories of those bleak years have become exaggerated – footballing fisherman's tales? Richard Murray, now the chairman of Charlton Athletic plc's board, recalls the reality:

> I am a fan, and when we score, anyone who looks into the directors' box will see that I'm jumping as high as anyone. It's a bit different nowadays though, because we are running a very big business here and there are big consequences attached to all the decisions we take. I can assure you though, in the days at West Ham or Crystal Palace, we'd enjoy the result just as much, but we'd drive home knowing that we had to sell Robert Lee, or someone like that, just to pay the bills. That was real stress.

For the last decade, Murray has been seeing through the smoke and mirrors which seek to obscure a clear view of football finances. It comes as little surprise to anyone connected with the club that his involvement has coincided with such a stunning period. In the view of the fans, and in stark contrast to some other clubs, the chairman is the reason for, rather than the beneficiary of, this success.

His manager has little doubt why it has all come about, and he certainly doesn't seek to corner the lion's share of the credit for himself. 'Whether you're talking about this football club or any other, it's very important that we all understand where we're going, and me and Richard have got that,' says Curbishley. 'I think our expectation levels match each other and that's vitally important.'

It would appear safe to say, on the strength of that quote alone, that Alan Curbishley has something of a special relationship with Murray. After all, are football managers usually meant to say things like that about their chairmen? It's not exactly adopting the finest traditions of the halcyon days of Doug Ellis and John Gregory or the non-cheery banter of Ken Bates and, well, anyone he's ever employed. Curbishley, speaking from a position of solidity which hardly requires him to dish out extravagant praise, does so anyway – he could be the first football manager in history to say what he actually thinks about his boss, while he's still in the job. And stay in it.

> I couldn't work for a better chairman – and I've had a couple of opportunities to go somewhere else and see what it's like, but Richard is definitely the main reason I haven't moved. He lets me get on with it, and we both know pretty much where we're trying to go, and at what pace we're trying to get there.

Curbishley and Murray are undoubtedly close, speaking most days on the phone, and frequently meeting face to face. It is maybe a mark of Murray's desire to stay out of the limelight that the meetings tend to be conducted after training, late in the afternoon at The Valley, well away from the Sparrows Lane training ground and the rest of the squad.

I have watched Curbishley in close proximity to Murray on many occasions over the course of the last three years and never once saw the manager looking other than totally relaxed in his chairman's company. Compared to the tight-lipped, monosyllabic responses elicited from some Premiership managers when asked to discuss their chairman, theirs is plainly a relaxed relationship, based on a considerable degree of mutual respect.

What is certain is that Murray and his fellow directors have adopted a policy of investing in the club and accepting that, in the short term at least, the financial rewards are unlikely to appear. It's a policy that is rare, if not unique in the top flight of English football. Peter Varney, the club's chief executive, and a long-term friend of Murray, is under no illusions as to the extent of the chairman's contribution:

> He's never made money from the club, and in fact he's only ever put it in and probably lost it. Last season in the space of one week there were three sets of accounts came out. One chairman paid himself £600,000 with a £400,000 bonus, and the other two got a £250,000 bonus because their sides stayed in the Premiership. We stayed in the Premiership as well, but Richard didn't award himself a pay-out.

The absence of 'pay-outs' underpins Charlton's careful approach to financing themselves. They don't pay a dividend out to their shareholders at the end of the financial year, and with the vast majority of shares in the ownership of the members of the board, this virtually ensures that only 'true fans' will be interested in seeking a place around the boardroom table. It's hardly a guaranteed way of making money after all, and almost all the members of the current board have achieved a degree of success in businesses outside football.

Martin Simons, for example, who acts as football club chairman, enjoyed a lucrative career in the oil business before joining the board in 1991, the same year as Murray. A hugely likeable figure, he strolls around the place, red-faced and beaming, cigar in hand and an immediately evident and thoroughly justified sense of satisfaction at what the club has achieved.

Rarely happier than when talking about his side over a pint of bitter, you couldn't convey the impression that he was enjoying himself any more clearly if you made him wear a T-shirt with 'I'm having a bloody good time' emblazoned on the front. Quite apart from having pumped a considerable amount of money into Charlton Athletic, he turns out at a multitude of community events and other functions to represent the club, demolishing with each passing remark any preconceptions about football chairmen being self-important, stand-offish types.

> I agreed to put some money in and come on board in 1991. It was extremely tough back then. There's a mystique about football clubs that there's more money than there really is. You come on board, and you're realistic about, well, to be honest, if I'd known how bad it was when I first came on board, if I'd known the full extent of it, I really would never have had anything to do with it. They were on the verge of bankruptcy. In hindsight, I don't regret it because it all worked out, but it could have very easily gone the other way, and I would have regretted that severely.
>
> In those days, we just didn't have the money we needed to survive. All the directors would be talking at half-time and at the end of the game, not about the game but about who was going to put their hand in their pocket this week and try to pay the wages.
>
> You'd get people saying, 'Well, I'll pay them this week, but then that's my lot.' It really was a case of having a whip round among the board to pay the wages. If we hadn't got back to The Valley, we wouldn't have been in existence, and it's as simple as that.

I remember standing outside Highbury in November 2001, just after we had pulled off a 4–2 victory over the eventual Premiership champions.

It had been an extraordinary afternoon, and as I walked out of the press entrance, the Charlton team coach was parked in front of the main entrance, waiting for the players to emerge and surrounded by a few hundred very happy fans.

Nobody had told Simons that he was about to stroll out into a mob of fans, and it would be fair to say that he might already have disposed of a celebratory drink or two. The chairman was greeted with a cheer, and responded with a stunned look around him, a bit of blinking to get used to the sunlight and a beam the size of a jumbo jet's wingspan.

It's a smile that has been earned at a hefty financial price, but not one that would give you the impression that he would even hesitate to pay all over again. It told an interesting tale of the nature of the relationship Charlton fans have with the people who run their club.

Peter Varney appreciates that, for all the ridiculously long hours he puts into being chief executive of the club he supported as a boy, without the financial backing of those people, he wouldn't have Charlton as an employer. The club's recovery has been down to solid planning and careful growth, while their survival has required the sort of direct action Murray, Simons, and others alongside them were prepared to take. Murray now devotes the major share of his working week to the club, in a bid to ensure that the next stage in its development passes off smoothly, and Varney is quick to appreciate the value of his dedication.

> None of what's happened could have taken place without Richard. If you look back all those years – and Richard knows all about it because he was one of those who had to put his hand in his pocket just to pay the wages – to be sitting there while you're doing that and to say I've got a plan to turn this stadium into a 27,000 venue, with a team packed with the best players you can get, you'd have been forgiven for suggesting that he should be popping off to see the psychiatrist.

Varney, it transpires, is not the first person in Murray's life to make that particular suggestion – a point the chairman cheerfully accepts:

> Whenever I go and see my accountant, it all passes quite smoothly, until we get around to the subject of Charlton Athletic, when he begins to suggest that I go and see a psychiatrist. He thinks it's my financial blind spot, and he might be right, but I wouldn't have it any other way!

Throughout the Premiership, there are examples of clubs where boards of directors hide from the fans, and a few instances where chairmen have arrived at grounds with bodyguards to keep them safe from antagonised supporters. Murray, Simons and their fellow directors have different concerns – pats on, rather than knives to, the back seem to be the order of the day.

At the end of each season, they are invited out onto the pitch and stroll around a lap of honour, applauding, and being applauded by, the fans. They even oversee a system whereby a supporter gets voted onto the board for a two-year period to become the fans' representative.

Known as the VIP director, the representative puts the views of the supporters, and ensures that the views of the board are reported back accurately to the remainder of the fan-base. Therein lies the reason why the fans and the board work in partnership so effectively – they actually do things to make it a partnership, rather than just describing it as such. At Chelsea they wanted to put their fans behind an electric fence, at Charlton they install a fan in the boardroom. Spot the difference?

All this, however, shouldn't leave the impression that there haven't been problems along the way. The club was, as I have said, and the fans can well remember, deeply financially wounded upon its return to The Valley, and needed careful handling to get back on its feet. They were precarious days, although with the considerable benefit of hindsight, they provided the foundations for what was to follow.

The idea of cutting our cloth accordingly was grasped more readily than at many other clubs, who stored potentially fatal financial problems up for themselves, waiting for years in some cases, before learning the full impact of their plight. The multi-million-pound striker, who was going to score the goals that would propel them to the big time, didn't score the goals. The high-profile manager, the man who could help the club to make that final leap forwards, couldn't. Most dangerous of all, the chairman, who had the vision to announce a clever financial restructuring in order to generate millions, yet didn't transpire to be quite all he had made himself out to be.

The ethos of building carefully, and making sure that the club is secure from the bottom upwards, is one that appears to leave a mark on almost everyone who comes into contact with the place. Glynn Snodin coaches the reserves, and has exported his chirpy Yorkshire observations on the game to more than a dozen clubs over the years, both very rich and very poor. He makes no bones about the value of the way in which Charlton have gone about their development.

'When we get some more stands built, and we get 30,000 or 40,000 in the ground,' he says, 'we'll not just be a big side in the Premiership, but we'll be a big side with foundations that have been built in the right way.'

Doing things in the 'right way' seems to be one of the prevailing sentiments whenever Charlton are discussed. While Snodin is emphatic in his conviction that Charlton's way really is the right way, Varney goes a step further and identifies why he feels that this is the case:

> While I do things off the pitch with my team, and Alan does things off the pitch with his team, someone has got to come in and really be a leader in order for the whole thing to work. That's what Richard has done. Someone had to have the vision to see where we were, to take us to where we are now, and to have the courage to look ahead to the future and draw up the plans and the route to take us to where he really believes we can get to.

All of it rings true, but, then again, all of it would ring true to me. The odd thing is that despite my bias towards them, and despite the fact that I'm always going to be prone to exaggerating their achievements, so many people agree with me. What is slightly more frightening is that the way in which they've set about it seems so simple. If a financial half-wit like me can understand why it works, why isn't everyone else sorting out their problems with such apparent ease?

The Charlton experiment seems to stem from a simple premise. Only people who were really genuine fans were admitted onto the board, and the money which was paid to secure those places is better viewed as a donation than an investment. Spending hundreds of thousands of pounds to obtain a stake in a football club worth (at the time) virtually nothing, is not the sort of action readily embraced by those in search of a quick buck.

I'm really not sure that, as a fan, I'm entitled to want all that much more than for my club to develop ever onwards, moving from strength to strength, but what has happened at The Valley is, even by those standards, a considerable bonus. While Murray is undoubtedly viewed with great respect, it has been earned with hard work which has seen a firm band of trust created between him and the fans. When he does go, his legacy will be a carefully thought out and implemented plan, which will benefit us long after his departure. Not every club can say the same thing.

I don't suppose Reading fans feel a real sense of connection with Mr Madejski, despite his cash, and I can't really believe that the late Jack

Walker claimed as much affection at Blackburn as Murray seems to at Charlton, despite having bought them a Premiership title. As I say, that residual fear at the back of your mind comes into play – the nagging voice that keeps asking you what's going to happen if the chairman pulls out and takes his money with him.

Strangely enough, or maybe not so strangely at all, the fact that we did it by the 'long route' has become something of a source of extra pride for Charlton fans and some of the longer-serving players alike. John Robinson came to the club in the year they returned to The Valley and has thrown himself whole-heartedly into everything ever since. When asked what makes us special, he gives one of those answers which could have been designed to leave the fans grinning in appreciation:

> They really are like no other set of supporters in the country. When I first came here from Brighton I had the option of going to three other clubs, but Curbs sold this place to me entirely on the strength of the fans. When fans have to dip into their own pockets to stump up the money to get the club back to The Valley, you know you're talking about something that you wouldn't get anywhere else.
>
> The club was already heading the right way when I got here, but the progress since then has been staggering. A few years back, as I say, it was the return to The Valley, then it was the rebuilding of the ground, then the same process but this time on the team. When we went down, we didn't really have to sell anyone for financial reasons. The next year we signed a huge sponsorship deal. There's not many clubs that can look back on steady progress like that.
>
> We got more season-ticket holders after relegation to the First Division than we did when we were in the Premiership the first time around. That's solid growth and that's a sign of the strength of the club. Years ago there were three or four thousand turning up, then the club lost the ground and it looked like things would never turn around. The fans got up and decided to do something about it rather than just moaning about it and that's where the upturn in the club's fortunes came about.
>
> No one has wandered past The Valley with a huge wad of cash and slung it in our direction. We didn't have a Jack Walker figure slinging money at all our problems. You can trace back, step by step, how we have got to where we are today and it wasn't

through hand-outs. This club is built on very solid foundations now. What happens on the field is far from the whole story.

If the lines about wealthy benefactors, and our lack of them, are pure, aggressive Robinson, the sentiments and mentions of 'solid foundations' are yet further echoes of how Charlton came to be where they are now. When you think of it, it's a fairly strange thing for a set of supporters to be proud of. It's mostly a question of prudent financial management, resisting the option of the 'quick fix' and the instant signing of cheques to alleviate your problems.

These are not things the average football fan wishes to see too much of. At 99 per cent of clubs, the end of the season is greeted with demands to 'spend big' during the summer, fuelled by the massed ranks of agents and sports journalists with pages to fill and nothing with which to fill them. Transfer stories are the sporting version of horoscopes, crosswords and a letters page. They fill the space, and require minimal input from the journalists.

At The Valley, however, the fans all seem to be in possession of an indecent amount of knowledge about how much money we've got to spend, and where it might best be targeted. If one fan raises his head above the parapet, demanding that we make the signing which all the papers are suggesting, several others start to ask him how we're going to afford the wages, and why we'd want to buy now, when the price is obviously inflated by 'paper talk'. It's like a cross between a supporters' club and a financial advisors' support group, but that's the way we seem to have developed.

We certainly get some of our sense of caution from Murray, but there's a large chunk of it that comes from a man more frequently in the limelight. In the financially lunatic world of the Premiership, the manager certainly hasn't lost sight of the reality of the situation:

> It's not an even playing field when one club can go £100 million in debt, and another can spend £60 million in just over a season – it just can't be. At this football club, though, we can honestly say that while we all might be ready to move on at some stage, we'll all look back at this place gladly. We've all learned a few lessons about what you can achieve when you do things properly, and given the state some of the bigger names seem to be in, maybe it's not such a bad thing, the way it's happened to us.

Maybe it's not. After all, there are plenty of grounds around the country, filled with fans who sing their demands to 'sack the board' every week. At The Valley, if any of us turned the corner and walked into one of the directors, we'd be more likely to ask for an autograph, or slap them on the back. Or just get all tongue-tied in their presence and mumble something indecipherable while going red and looking like an idiot. Unfortunately, I know exactly which one I'd probably end up doing. I've never been good in those type of situations . . .

Shortly before that famous first game back, Curbishley was giving a team talk, trying to ignore the television camera stuck in the corner of the dressing-room, recording the event for posterity. To call it a dressing-room is, in fact, to give it airs and graces. It was one of the Portakabins that remained part of life at The Valley for about another eight years after the return was made.

Elbowing his way around the limited space, he tried to combine winding up his side with keeping them calm, afraid that the occasion would either cause them to freeze, or hurtle around like headless chickens. It's a delicate balancing act at the best of times, but the tape tells the tale of a mood judged almost to perfection.

> I want you to keep the tempo, make sure you're setting the tempo and doing it on your terms. After the first five minutes, make sure you keep it going – run to corners, run to throw-ins and run to freekicks. Get the ball in their box, make them do some defending, and give this crowd something to cheer about.

As far as a statement of intent goes, it wasn't a bad effort. Curbishley appears to have been abiding by his own team talk for much of the last ten years. The tempo has been high and the crowd have had things to cheer, and he's certainly kept things going. There have been a few sides made to do a bit of defending as well.

The return to The Valley, and the subsequent growth of the club, has happened in the midst of a strange set of circumstances. While, on the face of it, the financial questions being set don't seem to be particularly tricky ones, we seem to be one of the few clubs getting them right. I've heard longer financial speeches and explanations from the likes of Ken Bates than I ever have from Richard Murray, and yet when I look at the financial predicament faced by their respective clubs, I'm forced to conclude that the shorter answer was closer to being the right one.

That's not the culture anymore, though, at least as far as finance is concerned. I listened keenly to the radio one morning, while a man whose company made video recorders, or satellite receivers, or some such piece of technology, explained why things had been a touch tricky of late.

'I think, looking back on things, one of our problems was that the unit price at which the items were retailing was insufficient to recoup the cost of manufacture and development which went into their creation.'

Now, as has been made sparklingly clear already, I'm not much of an economist, and I'm sure there were other factors to be taken into account, but I think I understand his problem: he was selling them for less than they cost him to make. Most of us learned that this wasn't a good idea from the school tuck shop, or another such early brush with commerce, but if he's an example of the far-sightedness of British business, maybe football should be grateful for what it's got. Charlton should certainly be, and indeed are, extraordinarily grateful for the bonus they received when it came to their senior management.

So, leaving the subject where we greeted it, more than a hundred years ago, Wilkins Micawber seems to have put his finger on the problem: 'Annual income twenty pounds, annual expenditure nineteen nineteen and six, result happiness. Annual income twenty pounds, annual expenditure twenty pounds ought and six, result misery.'

Charlton haven't just been lucky – they've resisted making 'vanity' purchases, and stayed true to their original plan for survival. Others have floundered, caught in a vicious circle of spending more than they earn, like gamblers chasing a loss. If only Dickens had tried his hand flogging video recorders, football might be in a healthier state today than the one in which it finds itself.

And that's not a conclusion you reach every day.

3

UP FROM THE RUINS

At first glance, The Valley of today offers precious few hints as to the story surrounding its redevelopment. The geography of the place has changed very slightly, with stands expanding backwards and access routes changing here and there, but essentially, the ground occupies the same space it always did.

Tucked away just above the Woolwich Road, no more than three or four hundred yards from the River Thames, the contours of the land somehow contrive to disguise the ground from view, almost until you have walked into it. Once upon a time, probably no more than a year ago, it was even more carefully camouflaged, but the extension at one end of the ground leaves the silver steel framework of the roof structure visible from all directions.

Once inside, it seems remarkable that the ground isn't immediately visible from all vantage points. The slopes up and away on all sides are dotted with houses, yet somehow the development below remains hidden from the small streets winding down to the river. There are one or two spots which allow a view down into the stadium, but, otherwise, the natural contours of the land and the placement of the buildings in the immediate vicinity have ensured that, on three sides at least, the ground remains extraordinarily secluded.

Before the extension of the north stand, the roof of the old 'covered end', which was little more than a glorified cattle shed, lay below the sightlines from the road behind, and ensured almost total anonymity. Now, the rear of the stadium rises high into the sky, ensuring that people arriving on trains from Woolwich and travelling along the 'lower road' are given a clear hint as to what lies just behind them.

You can imagine the effect it had on local estate agents, even if, quite rightly, you can't quite dredge up anything resembling sympathy for them. As long as there wasn't a match on, the sharp-suited one could have strolled the unsuspecting purchaser around practically any part of Charlton without being forced to cough up to the fact that there was a Premiership football ground down the road.

Now, even the least determined of questioners might manage to ask what the great big thing over there, with all the red seats around the lawn and the big silver bits sticking out of the roof was.

Strangely enough, the ease with which The Valley is swallowed up by its surroundings could, in some way, be brought forward as one of the reasons why the club's exile was so lengthy. If it had stood on a prime location, in the centre of town and with easy and ample views stretching over it, the sight of its slow descent into dereliction would undoubtedly have caused more concern than was otherwise the case. Tucked away in a corner and largely shielded from view, it probably wasn't seen by enough people to cause widescale offence – and suffered as a result.

It's ironic really. While it was a 'working' football ground, it was seen by too few people to keep it in business, and when it slipped into the role of a 'resting' ground, it was seen by too few to cause extreme offence. As each day went by, with the paint flaking, the floorboards rotting, the weeds thriving and the steel rusting, it was looking less like a much-loved and missed home and more like the eventual symbol of Charlton's demise.

I went walking down there on several occasions while they were away, not so much in a genuine attempt to find anything meaningful from the experience, but in that way teenagers have of trudging around mournfully, trying to convince themselves that no one else has ever had it so bad. Unfortunately, I didn't find anything there which really changed my mood one way or another.

The stands were so empty and so derelict that it was virtually impossible to imagine them packed and noisy. The vast terrace looked worse still, with green leaves protruding from every spare inch. Imagine that huge, concrete external sewer, where they had the car race in *Grease*, only without the blue skies and Olivia Newton-John, and you've sort of got the picture. It didn't make me feel any sadder about the state of things, because it wasn't close enough to how I remembered it to cause my brain to make the necessary emotional link.

It's a bit like when I see palaeontologists picking over piles of bones and getting all excited by what the animal must have looked like. I can appreciate that the jigsaw puzzle in front of them used to be a huge beast of some kind, and also that what they're doing really is terribly clever, but it doesn't look like an animal to me. I'm sorry, I know that years of study have gone into allowing them to explain how this was a dinosaur of some description, but it just looks like a pile of bones to me. In the same way, The Valley, when deserted, overgrown and derelict, didn't cause the ghosts of years gone by to whisper in my ears. Thank God they didn't rely on me to get us back there – I just couldn't see how it was going to happen.

There are times now, however, when I'll stroll around the place and look up at the banks of red seats, and the extraordinary green-ness of the grass, and I can see every game that's been there for the last half a dozen years or so. I can replay every bit of action with a chilling precision. If you wanted me to show you how John Robinson equalised against Manchester United, I'd not only show you where he stood to score the goal, I'd be able to trace the celebratory scamper he made in its aftermath.

Dean Kiely's penalty save against Arsenal? In front of the south stand, going left, halfway up, left hand out, palmed over the top – then he pushed Scott Parker away from an attempted celebration and told him to get on with defending the corner. I could show you where Mark Kinsella ran before Nicky Weaver brought him down for the penalty that made it 4–0 in our first game back in the Premiership (inside right channel, waving at the linesman, pointing out just how onside he was, since you ask).

My point is this – the 'new' ground speaks to me, it holds memories, maybe even the ones that go back before large chunks of it were built. If I want to remember my first game there, I can place myself in relation to the new, two-tiered west stand, even though it wasn't built until 18 years after I followed my uncle so prematurely out of the ground. When I looked up at the old grandstand, although it was precisely the same structure from which I'd watched, it brought back nothing, because it had no connection with football anymore.

It was just a shell and a ramshackle one at that. These days, you get people doing all sorts of things with deconsecrated chapels and churches, turning them into anything from flats to recording studios. Once inside, they don't feel like chapels anymore, because they've become something else. In the same way, The Valley became something else. I can't begin to imagine how or why anyone would set about turning a recording studio back into a church, but thankfully, while I still marvel at how, I know that someone set about turning The Valley back into a football ground.

In the early days, of course, it just about claimed the title of a football ground, despite looking far more like a building site with a lawn in the middle. In fact, a lawn is pretty much what it was, as Paddy Powell explains:

> When we first got back, we just got the rubbish off the terrace, stuck some topsoil on, and grew a pitch in a bit of a hurry. Pitches have a limited lifespan anyway, because you're doing all the wrong things to them, in order to keep them very flat with short grass. I treat it a bit like a lawn to be honest. I must know every blade of grass on it, the times I've walked up and down it.
>
> I look at every divot that comes out. In fact, I spend half the match looking at the pitch and wincing.

So, having spent his playing career wincing as tackles came flying in at him, he now spends his 'second career' wincing when tackles miss wingers and players skid, taking chunks out of his pitch.

Events elsewhere around the ground in the early days made life on the pitch appear relatively calm. Tony Fewell has worked for the club for more years than he cares to remember, both stewarding and supervising teams of stewards. For him, the excitement of getting back to the ground was tempered with a sizeable dose of reality:

> I can remember getting down here to the little Portakabin where all the stewards' coats had been stored. It had been perched in the middle of a load of rubble when I put them all in there, but someone had sorted that out by the time I got back. It had been tarmaced – a nice, big black strip of fresh tarmac, about three or four yards wide, still smoking a bit and obviously having been there for about half an hour at the most.
>
> I couldn't get into my storeroom, because I'd have left great big footprints across it on my way up to the door, so I had to leave it until later. I ended up setting the alarm and getting down here at two in the morning, just to make sure that everything was all right and I could get the coats without a hitch. When I got down here, I think everyone else had the same idea. Nobody could sleep anyway – it was one of those days you never forget.
>
> I look around now sometimes, and it still doesn't seem real. When you walk along the touchline, towards the north stand,

and instead of the covered end that was there for years, there's a huge big two-tiered stand wrapping round to meet up at either corner. It just doesn't seem real, it really doesn't. There's been some bloody miracles worked at this place, there really have.

From those early, well-documented and affectionately remembered days, the story of Charlton has been one of a club refusing to sit back on their laurels and always looking for the next step forwards. There are 8,337 people with legitimate claims to having been in The Valley for the first game back, and about ten times that number who claim to have been there subsequently. As with most football stories, if everyone who said they were there actually had been, the game would have been too large for Wembley to stage, let alone the original venue.

A friend of mine, Charlie, is the only person I know who makes no claim to have been there, preferring to honestly admit that he couldn't get a ticket, but stood up on Charlton Heights, a sloping access road overlooking the south end of the ground. The irony, as any football fan will predict with a suitably unimpressed expression on his or her face, is that later in the season getting a ticket was not nearly so difficult, as performances failed to pick up particularly; a mid-table finish was eventually achieved.

I know of someone else who purchased his first season ticket about five or six years ago. On asking where he could sit, he was met with a blank stare, which basically invited him to occupy a seat anywhere, as long as it wasn't in the dug out. Now, as I have said, we have well-publicised and attended 'swap days' before the start of the season, so that people can shift about the ground a little. Times have certainly changed.

Having concluded that life could not continue with 'three sides' – not least because of the confusion Curbishley was unleashing on the press every week – the decision was made to build a stand on the site of the old east terrace. Seating 6,000, while it was a vast improvement on the crumbling and largely ignored concrete slope which towered over one side of the ground, it was a far cry from the glory days of years before, when tens of thousands would cram onto the terrace.

I grew up, as did many other football-loving men of my age, with tales of how my father had been passed down over the tops of heads to sit on the cinder track at the base of the terrace. I'd stood on it a few times, but the numbers were sparse, and it was almost impossible to imagine how it must have been to have been crammed shoulder to shoulder, swaying and surging with the ebb and flow of the crowd.

By the time I reached my teens, and stood there by myself, a passing movement worthy of the Harlem Globetrotters would have been required to get a small child from the top of the terrace to the bottom. At least one lob of 20 yards or more would have been involved, as the gaps between people grew occasionally more pronounced. Football was never going to be the same again, and after the disasters of Hillsborough and Hysel, terraces were going to be a thing of the past.

The campaign to get crowds standing once more is a vocal one, but seems unable to grab more than partial support among today's followers of the game. I recall sitting in the press box at a pre-season game one year, and watching as a couple of thousand Charlton fans were crammed into a pen on a terrace capable of holding far more.

Finally, after tempers had become very heated indeed, common-sense prevailed, and, after a door was unlocked, they were allowed to disperse into the wider expanses of terrace. It told its own tale though. Even in conditions far from life-threatening, the anger was all too apparent – the fans remembered what had and could happen, and they weren't going to put up with it. When faced with the reality of suddenly being thrown back to the 'good old days' of terracing, many of them decided, swiftly and loudly, that it wasn't quite so good back then after all.

The campaign these days may be based around alternative ways of setting out terracing, and it does accept that the old safety standards were obviously insufficient, but that is plainly not good enough for the fans. The memories of those terrible sights remain, and regardless of how modern and well designed the terracing is, there are many who, having grown used to sitting down, won't consider standing again.

The vast terrace, therefore, was replaced by a 6,000-seat stand, eventually opened in April 1994. In keeping with the way the club tends to do things, the ribbon was cut by a fan specially selected for the task by way of a draw, looking more than a little incongruous on the video tapes of the occasion, dressed in his suit in front of a crowd of red and white replica shirts.

The game which followed was also a typical Charlton effort. Having lost the previous five league matches, just as with our return to the ground the previous season, we didn't expect to see the occasion greeted with anything too spectacular. A dour and goal-free first half seemed to confirm these fears, and offered no hint of what was to come. During a second period in which the home side went three goals ahead against Southend, only to be pegged back to level terms, a late Alan Pardew strike claimed a memorable, if not entirely comfortable, 4–3 win.

A very young Chris Powell threw himself around the Southend

defence and trudged off looking understandably disconsolate at the end, little knowing the significance the opposition was to have on the rest of his career. Just in case we were getting a little carried away with our development, four consecutive defeats followed, and 11 defeats in our last 15 league games ensured a mid-table finish. With Crystal Palace running away with the title, it was a good job matters off the pitch were going so well, because on it these were still far from glorious times for the club.

Remarkably, despite this background of mundane footballing fare, the following season saw the supporters' club's 'Target 10,000' initiative bear spectacular fruit, as the average attendance crept into five figures. David Whyte scored 19 goals in the league and a couple in the Coca-Cola Cup, to become the first Charlton player for 14 years to notch up 20 in a season, but an ever-obliging defence leaked goals at a majestic rate, condemning us to another mid-table finish.

Whyte never really received the praise other strikers were to attract subsequently, but with only two sides in the whole division conceding more than Charlton managed that year, without him it's highly possible that the redevelopment of the club could have gone spectacularly off the rails. We might have been edging slowly away from chaos, but we were still doing it by means of a tightrope – and not a very secure one either.

And so it remained, at least for one more season, as the need to balance the books came ahead of the need to secure the big-name signings, which we assumed were obligatory if further progress were to be made. Thankfully, Curbishley had a longer-term plan that was about to pay off.

Lee Bowyer was sold to Leeds for £2.8 million, and with a necessarily, yet indecently small portion of the proceeds, Curbishley secured, among others, Mark Kinsella and Mark Bright. The remainder of the money was set aside for possible further developments to the ground, as the progress made on the pitch brought that requirement ever nearer.

A new main stand was constructed, with the potential to be improved and extended to a second tier if matters continued to progress. Kinsella proved to be one of the shrewdest signings the manager ever made, and set about repaying his £250,000 price-tag by imposing a sense of leadership on the side which belied his slight stature. The season which followed was again reasonably forgettable, yet with attendances remaining safely into five figures, the foundations for progress were there.

The 1997–98 season culminated in that most famous of Wembley play-offs, and suddenly the Premiership was coming to The Valley, accompanied by another tier on the west stand. The late end to the previous season meant that it was always destined to be something of a rush to finish the building in time, and as such the fans had to wait until mid-September to see the upper tier populated.

It was something of an irony in that first season in the top-flight that only 16,000 were able to cram in for the opening home win of the season, when Southampton were dispatched 5–0, yet 19,516 were able to endure a 2–1 defeat at the hands of Derby. The year remained truly memorable, however, despite eventual relegation on the last day of the campaign, with the highlight undoubtedly the 1–0 home win over Liverpool.

The crowds had plainly enjoyed what they had seen, and despite gloomy predictions to the contrary, the average attendance for the following year was only 300 down on the figure attracted by the Premiership. While Curbishley plotted a return to the top flight, the board were involved in planning the next extension to the stadium – an extension which would arguably have the biggest visual impact on the ground since it was first cleared and reclaimed for football.

If The Valley was the spiritual home of the club, the north stand, or 'covered end' as it was known to generations of supporters, was where the true fanatics gathered. Ramshackle and blessed with little in the way of facilities, the covered end was where the noise came from, where the real passion existed and where the players went to celebrate on their way off the pitch. It was no accident that Kinsella chose 'F' block, at the end of the north stand, to give his clenched-fist salute after a home win – he knew his audience.

Over the course of the championship-winning season, the board put together the finance, and Varney worked endlessly with architects and engineers to produce a design for the extension of the covered end. Although the rumours of a new development were circulating fairly wildly around the club at the time, it would be fair to say that there was an amazed silence when fans first saw the plans. All over the place, as the plans were unveiled on the club website at the same time as the press conference to announce the development was going on, the thudding sound of chins hitting desks could be heard.

There was no doubting the fact that the new stand would be, by some considerable distance, the most ambitious and noticeable development ever undertaken by the club, bringing the ground closer than ever before to the standards set elsewhere in the Premiership. The existing structure was retained, but improved and utterly dwarfed by the framework constructed around it. The new upper tier would be flanked on either side by two 'quadrants', which wrapped around the stadium, totally enclosing the north end of the ground.

The architect's drawings were greeted with lots of wide-eyed staring and silent grins. We were never told that our ground was going to end up looking anything like this. It looked like a proper Premiership ground, but the pictures had loads of Charlton players – our players – running around on the pitch. It was going to take a bit of getting used to, as the board freely admitted. Richard Murray said:

> It's a nice way to mark my tenth anniversary on the board, and I think when the development is done, the stadium will look very special.
>
> When we came back here we only had two sides, and now we've got four and we're about to extend one and fill in the corners. I must admit I have a personal preference for these rounded stadiums, and the artist's impression looked wonderful.
>
> The north stand is very much the people's stand. I think that anybody who knows me well knows that I'm a people's champion. I'm a working-class man myself, and I just think that it's very, very important, and I made this commitment when I first got to Charlton, that we will always have a price which is suitable for our working-class fans. There are 9,000 seats in that area, so it's nice to know that the largest part of the ground is the cheapest.

As well as the impact of the building, however, and despite the celebratory atmosphere which surrounded the announcement, Murray was, as ever, also keeping his eyes set very firmly forwards, and anticipating what the new development would actually mean to the day-to-day future running of the club:

> We'll be adding an extra 3,000 in November and the same in December. Alan and the players have done an awful lot to improve our credibility on the pitch, but we really needed a bigger stadium than 20,000 to ensure the same thing happened off it. If we want to attract players of a certain standard, then we need to have a stadium that really impresses them.
>
> You have to remember that Southampton have got a 30,000 capacity, Fulham with their new ground, will be around that mark, and Blackburn are around the same size. If we stuck at 20,000, we'd be by far the smallest club in the Premier League, and that's not where we want to be.

The increase in television money maybe lessens the impact of gate money on our finances, but I think the larger crowd that we've got here makes a vast difference to the atmosphere, and I'd say that was the main reason for looking to develop further. I think the atmosphere can get better yet, and I think with the pricing policy we've got, which is very reasonable, we'll ensure that our noisiest supporters will be there in that north stand.

I think another point to consider is the impact which television has on the game, and the new stand is going to have a huge impact in front of the cameras, especially when you think what it is replacing. Hopefully we'll get the cameras here a little bit more often now, because we make a lot of money when they're here.

I personally think that a London club with over 30,000 capacity could probably be competitive – but that still doesn't mean with Manchester United. I think, though, what people have to remember is that the income from 30,000 people in London is equivalent to 40,000 in Middlesbrough or somewhere like that, simply because you can charge more for your VIP packages and your hospitality areas.

Martin Simons, meanwhile, who strolled around the crowds at the announcement of the launch with an even bigger and more thoroughly deserved grin that ever, chose to look backwards in order to make a point about how the club had gone forwards:

Things were desperately run down during the '50s, '60s and '70s, and I honestly think we probably just about caught it in time when we got back and started rebuilding. I genuinely believe that we can be a giant again, because you have to remember that this club once averaged over 40,000 fans for an entire season, and there's only been 14 clubs that have ever done that.

We certainly were a very large club, and we've got to try and get back to that level. Take the noise for example. We've got to look at the acoustics in that new stand, and make sure the drummers and the noisy lads sit in the right places. With the wraparound, it's got to be noisier than ever before, certainly than it was when the corners were open, so we're looking forward to those drums getting a right banging.

I can remember standing in the San Siro when we were doing the deal with Inter Milan, and we were a First Division club then.

Now we're in the Premiership, we've been pushing towards Europe, and if we can get there, we'll need a stadium much larger than 26,000. The ten years I've been involved have been tremendous times, and I look forward to trying to push it forwards that little bit more.

Now completed, the stand lived up to everyone's expectations. Well, almost everyone's. I well recall the first time I heard fans complaining because the chips were cold, or their burger wasn't quite right or their beer was flat. It's times like that, I think we could do with running a video of what the place used to look like on the concourses at half-time, rather than letting Rodney Marsh drone on to himself on a television with the sound muted. Once you've looked back on that, it's hard to feel that anything matters too much, at least as something as trivial as the half-time catering is concerned.

From roots that were not so much humble as they were recovering from having been replanted, the development of The Valley is perhaps the most immediately obvious sign of how far Charlton Athletic have come in the last ten years. More people were coming to see the side than at any time for the last half a century.

Back in post-war Britain, good, solid post-war British names, such as Sam Bartram, Harold Phipps and Bill Robinson, were the heroes of the day, their every syllable today summoning up images of lace-up footballs and heavy, high-cut leather football boots. By the turn of the next century, a more cosmopolitan group of players were ensuring that the good times were returning to SE7.

4

HEARTS ON THEIR SLEEVES, NAMES ON THEIR BACKS

Football clubs, no matter how well run they are, or how magnificently the board and the fans have combined to ensure their survival, are about football players. There's no getting away from it, despite the fact these young men earn more money than most of us will ever come close to. We feel the need to shower them with additional glory and protracted bouts of hero worship. It's what being a fan is all about.

You might occasionally hear the off-the-field business sung about from the stands, but as it will consist of little more than chants of 'sack the board, sack the board, bo-aaaaa-rrrrd', it's probably recognition most people could do without. Similarly, apart from the occasional affirmations that 'We are so and so's red and white army', unless the fans want to see the back of him, the manager tends to keep a pretty low profile in the songs department.

It must get confusing for managers, what with the colour of their armies changing all the time. David Moyes had a black and white army at Preston, only to transfer to a blue and white one at Everton. Kevin Keegan has had so many different-coloured armies, he needs an interior designer to keep track of them. From red and white with England, to black and white with Newcastle and Fulham, round to blue and white with Manchester City. He's traversed the country, while his theme song has leapt around the spectrum.

Alan Curbishley has only ever had a red and white army, albeit that it's occasionally turned up in blue, green, yellow, black and ecru. I was never quite sure about ecru, which, to tell the truth, and although we all talked about it as if it were a perfectly ordinary colour, made me think the yellow and black shirts had been washed together. But, in the spirit of football fans everywhere, we took to it as if it were the most natural kit in the world, and even bought the shirts in their thousands, despite the fact that they were, quite honestly, horrible.

The reason we bought them, of course, was an absurd desire to forge a connection with the team that played in them, and an attempt to emulate, or at least associate ourselves with, the players who wore them. We haven't had, as you might have guessed by now, millions to spend on household names, and in the early days at least we had some players who weren't even that well known in their own households. However, that's never stopped fans from having heroes and we were just the same.

It's very difficult, when looking back at the last decade, to pick a handful of players who stand out without ending up with half a dozen from the current side and a couple from the teams which preceded it. As the fortunes of the club have grown, so the quality of players has increased. We raise our eyes to the heavens and complain about players in the current side who would have been considered footballing giants in some of the sides who played at The Valley shortly after our return.

It is strangely in keeping with the club, though, that the real affection has usually been for the players who have seen the whole journey through, and who can remember life at Charlton when it was far less glamorous. While foreign imports such as Jonatan Johansson and Claus Jensen have had days when they have undoubtedly been heroes, there has always been a genuine affection for the Steve Browns and John Robinsons of this world. Probably because, as far as the fans are concerned, they understand the nature of the club and can view the wider perspective more closely than any of the other players.

This is not to say that the newcomers are greeted with anything approaching a grudge, but rather that the old stagers are the people with whom we find it easiest to relate. Then, of course, there's the exception which proves the rule.

It's quite fitting in a way, if we turn things on their head and look at the most recent hero to arrive at the club, albeit that his stay was as brief as it was motivated initially by reasons other than the progress of the club. Jorge Costa was playing his football very happily in Portugal, captaining Porto to a handful of Portuguese titles, shoring up the centre of the defence for both club and country, and never taking any prisoners.

Then, in the way of these things, a chain of events kicked into action, which culminated in his arrival at The Valley. He had a row with the Porto coach, who, with a combination of bravery and lunacy, decided Costa had played his last game for the club. In terms of Portuguese football, if you imagine Tony Adams being told by Arsène Wenger about two or three seasons ago that he didn't want him anymore, you're probably halfway to understanding the uproar it caused among the Porto fans.

Costa had a World Cup on the horizon and knew that he needed to be playing first-team football if he was to make the trip to the Far East. With the benefit of hindsight, he might have been better not going, given Portugal's dismal showing, but thankfully for Charlton, while he was blessed with an exceptional ability to read the game, it didn't stretch quite as far as reading the future.

He turned up at the airport, and travelled through south London with Peter Varney, while his management team discussed figures with him in the back of the car. Amazingly, at the end of the negotiations, the figures suggested as 'just about acceptable' by Costa's advisors, were matched almost exactly by Charlton. Some cynics would suggest that the fact Varney spent three years working in Portugal as a young man helped him to have a better idea of exactly what they were about to demand. Some spoilsports may go as far as to suggest that Varney might not have been 'playing the game' when he failed to disclose to them that he could understand every word they were saying.

It matters not – all negotiations need something of the uncertain about them anyway, don't they? Costa signed a contract to play for the club for the rest of the season, and Jorge mania had begun. His first outing was at Stamford Bridge, where he would face Jimmy Floyd Hasselbaink and Eidur Gudjohnsen, who were fast becoming the most lethal strike-force in the country. At his press conference, Costa grudgingly disclosed that Hasselbaink had never scored against him and we all laughed appreciatively.

We shouldn't have laughed. It didn't take us long to learn that Jorge didn't really do too many jokes, possibly because they distracted him from tackling, manhandling and bullying strikers. He only got on the pitch for the last ten minutes, but even then we got a taste of what was to come. Mark Fish signalled to the bench that he had a sore knee, and Mervyn Day told Jorge to warm up. Jorge bent down, touched his toes, stood up, took his tracksuit top off and pronounced himself ready.

Fish then indicated that his knee was easing up a bit and, given another five minutes, he might be able to continue. Mervyn told Jorge to keep warm and hang on for a bit, and was greeted with a blank stare.

Jorge was standing there, on the touchline, ready to go and not about to delay his entrance for anyone. In the end, they had to put him on, lest he grabbed hold of either Fish or the fourth official and made the substitution himself.

Within five minutes, Mikael Forssell had been sent flying, Hasselbaink had been pole-axed, Charlton grabbed a winner and Jorge had become a hero. It went on from there really. Every week he'd live up to his nickname of 'The Tank', in between showing a few of the touches which allowed him to prosper at the very highest level.

It was a wonderful five months and Jorge plainly grew to feel a real affection for the club – a club he freely admitted he hadn't heard much about before he got here. The night before he signed the deal, Curbishley took him for a meal and tried to explain something about us to Jorge. Through an interpreter, the manager sought some common ground, asking Jorge if he played golf. There was a moment of contemplation from the interpreter, before he explained that Jorge had a club, but he didn't really play.

'You should get some lessons, pick up a set and have a round with a few of the boys,' Curbishley explained.

The interpreter stepped back in. He was sorry if there had been any confusion. Jorge didn't own a golf club – as in the metal stick with which you hit the ball. He owned a golf club. With its own course and clubhouse. He didn't play himself, but his advisors had told him it was a good investment, so he'd got one. We were in a different league to anything we'd come across before.

He made his last appearance for the club at Old Trafford, where he ensured we ended the season with a goal-free stalemate. He was magnificent and at the end of the game was pushed off in the direction of the fans. Not predisposed to public displays of affection, even Costa seemed shocked at the reception he got. They had created for him his own, expletive-ridden song, based around him coming from Portugal and not liking Millwall, and the fans sang it over and over again.

Costa waved, pointed at the badge, gave the thumbs up and jogged back to Portugal. It was all wonderfully moving and at least one Charlton player, who sadly must remain unidentified, admitted to being in tears at that moment. It may have originally been a marriage of convenience, but we grew to love Jorge Costa, and he wasn't slow to admit the same.

I only ever had one conversation with him, although as it went on, it became clear that he maybe spoke a little bit more English than he was letting on. He talked of Charlton being a place with 'good people' who had 'heart and passion'. He went on to draw a distinction with some of the big clubs we faced and how their players 'should feel shame, because they had not played with passion'.

He was certainly intense, and dressed in his black Armani suit and shirt with his black shades on, he looked more like a Bond villain or a hired assassin than a footballer. He wasn't being deliberately standoffish, though, and it wasn't an attempt to bolster his reputation, because he certainly didn't need to do that. He just took football very seriously and expected everyone else to do the same. For my part, I just nodded a lot. It seemed safer.

It's probably fair to say that Jorge was our only really foreboding hero. Usually we've been perfectly happy to chant the names of far more approachable men, to the extent where, certainly in a few cases, we've made heroes out of people on the grounds that they look like they might be good company over a couple of pints. It doesn't really matter that modern footballers, or at least not our modern footballers, hardly drink anything anymore, the rule of thumb that says 'he'd be a nice bloke to have a drink with' still operates.

Harking back, yet again, to our roots, and the tale of how we came to be where we are today, it might well be that search for normality which has affected our choice of heroes. As I have said, it's the fact that they've been there through the bad times which has led people to make such a fuss over men like Steve Brown and John Robinson.

Brown has never played his football anywhere other than at Charlton, and has spent much of his career here playing second fiddle to a variety of other centre-halfs. The only player in the current squad to have experienced life at Selhurst Park, Brown has seen every single development of the last ten years from the very closest of viewpoints:

> I'm part of the furniture, as they say, and I think that as the years have gone past, that's one of the factors that's made me stay each time my contract has come up for renewal. It's very difficult to up and leave your roots, and although I've been made some very attractive offers to go elsewhere, especially over the last couple of years, it's going to be very hard for anyone to leave here at the moment.
>
> We're moving upwards all the time, there are some great players here, and the way the club's run means that it's not the sort of place that you're going to want to walk away from. You might not get, and in fact you probably won't get, the same sort of treatment and especially the atmosphere at many other places.

It's never been too hard a decision to make to stay here. I love playing my football here, and I feel, as I say, part of the furniture. I've been here so long, and seen so much happen at the place, that it would be very difficult to make a commitment anywhere else. You're not meant to get too involved with the emotions of the whole thing if you're a footballer, because you've got a job to do, but I can't ignore the fact that Charlton means an awful lot to me.

It would be easy to conclude that Brown was just spinning a line, and one he knows will go down very nicely with the fans, but the evidence doesn't really support the theory. He's already had a testimonial season, so it's not the money, and as he admits himself, his first-team appearances are growing rarer with each passing season. It's certainly not a campaign to become a fans' favourite and keep himself in the side. The truth is, after all this time, he plainly, and sometimes you suspect almost to his own annoyance, loves the place.

It's not hard to work out why. Most people rely on a huge transfer deal or a desire to cling on in the game for an extra year or two in order to see the game from its two extremes. Brown has managed the feat without ever having to move clubs:

I was here in the really hard times, harder than anyone else in the squad has seen, and I can remember when it was all very different to the way it is today. If you ask some of the side, especially the ones who maybe only started to take notice of us when we got into the Premiership, they couldn't start to believe, let alone tell you, what things used to be like here.

Going back ten years, there really was no money whatsoever, and we were really scratching around. People joining the club now and seeing what's going on, they couldn't comprehend the journey we've been on. That's not their fault either, because I think sometimes we just expect everyone to appreciate our history, and until recently, in terms of a slightly bigger stage, we just weren't the sort of side that anyone noticed.

I've seen the good times as well, and that's probably got a lot to do with why I don't want to leave now. Why should you go through all the bad times, make sure that the club gets through all of those, and then leave just as things really start to sort themselves out and the team really starts to get properly strengthened? Even if it does mean I'm not in it as much as I'd like!

Brown is an interesting person to interview, not least because he still seems to retain the belief that he has to end every statement with a piece of self-mockery, almost as a defence mechanism in case the interviewer thinks he's taking himself too seriously. He also tends to not only answer the question, but offer a few other thoughts along the way. This is a rare thing indeed among the professional footballers of today, who surrender extraneous opinions in the way sharks surrender their lunch.

Answers are currency, as are opinions. It matters not that there is hardly ever anything which could reasonably be described as an opinion offered, in among the host of qualifying statements and caveats. Dissect the average Premiership footballer's interview, and by the time you've discarded the meaningless conversational padding included with each response, there's precious little left, and certainly nothing that will tell you anything you didn't know already.

It's very refreshing to interview a player who doesn't just say slightly more interesting things, but even shows some sign of appreciating that there is a life outside football. He hasn't got any reason to rely on the self-mockery, because much as he might get too embarrassed to say it, he's actually got something intelligent to say.

> I know what my job here is going to be now, and it doesn't involve playing nearly as much first-team football as I'd like, but it doesn't do anyone any good if you just sit around and have a good moan about it. If people had taken that attitude a dozen or so years ago, we wouldn't have a club to play for and the fans wouldn't have a club to watch, so that's not really the way people do things around here.
>
> I'll give everything I've got whenever I'm asked, because that's the least you can do, and if you're a professional, that's what you get paid to do. I've got friends who aren't in football at all, and they have to work hard all the time – they can't have a slow day just because they're feeling pissed off. One of my best friends works cleaning offices, and he gets up at ludicrous hours in the morning, works all day, and then goes home, says hello to the kids and does it all over again. If he can do that without moaning, then what right have I got to start complaining with what I got dished out?

There are some players who could tell you that tale and you wouldn't even come close to believing them, but Brown makes it sound so normal that it never crosses your mind that it's not true. Besides, he's only recently taken the big plunge and bought a BMW – for the last six years he had been turning up at the training ground each day in an Escort estate. He explained that there was plenty of room in it for the kids, and besides, it hadn't broken down on him yet. It says something about him that we still mock him for stepping out of the BMW each morning far more than we ever did for getting out of the Escort.

The game has turned full circle it seems. If you phoned up the editor of the *News of the World* and told her you had pictures of a Premiership footballer and an escort, she wouldn't blink an eyelid, putting it down to just another Gary Flitcroft moment. If you told her you had a picture of a Premiership footballer and a Ford Escort, suddenly you've given her an angle – she's got a story. It's a mad world sometimes, and football does very little to buck the trend.

Brown is fully aware of both how far the club has come, and where it could yet end up. He appears to confirm it with a cheerful shake of the head, as if to accept that it could easily be a story straight out of *Roy of the Rovers*, as a real-life achievement in which he had played a considerable part:

> We're going onwards and upwards now, and having seen the bad times, it means that I probably want to see the good ones even more, just to know that I was part of the story all the way from start to finish – if this is the finish. There's a lot of ambition here, and I think one of the reasons so much has been achieved is that people were never happy to sit back, take their foot off the pedal and boast about what they'd done. There are people in charge who have planned this out each step of the way, and they're probably working out how to take the next leap forwards as we speak.

During Charlton's abortive first attempt to stay in the Premiership, on the penultimate Saturday of the season, they found themselves locked in a 3–3 draw at Villa Park. As the other results that day went against us, only a win would be good enough to ensure our continued Premiership safety. Andy Petterson, the Charlton keeper, got himself sent off, and without a reserve keeper on the bench, Brown stepped into the role. Tucking his shirt into his shorts and pulling on a pair of gloves, his first action of the day was to leap across the area to palm a freekick to safety. Two minutes later, he cleared up field, we won a freekick, and 30 seconds later had made it 4–3; we remained safe for a further week.

It's not even talked about with any real regularity now, such are the wealth of tales surrounding the club over the last ten years, but as a true *Roy of the Rovers* escapade, it stands up there with the best of them. Charlton's third goal that day, and undoubtedly the most demented celebration of the season, was claimed by another long-term figure at The Valley: John Robinson.

Since arriving from Brighton in 1992, Robinson has berated referees and infuriated the opposition more frequently than anyone cares to remember. Along with Brown, who can trace his time at the club back even further, Robinson was at Charlton while they were based at Upton Park, and played in the first game back at The Valley against Portsmouth.

He's also our very own little enigma. You see, Charlton fans, by and large, love him. They see someone who never stops trying, who runs for as long as his legs will carry him and who really can't be bothered with being overly pleasant to the opposition. If he played for anyone else, I'd hate him, and there's no point trying to disguise the fact. That fact alone, though, brings us to an interesting truth about the nature of being a football fan – namely, that we all retain an extraordinary ability to view our side from only the most flattering of angles, all the time.

Robinson gives us plenty of opportunities to perfect this slightly skewed view of the world. Whichever side we're playing against, he wants to be the thorn in it. Combative, argumentative and fiery, he makes no apology:

> I play with my heart on my sleeve and I can't play any other way. If I tried to do it another way, I'd lose a bit, so that's a non-starter. If I don't get myself going like that, I don't feel like I'm properly involved in the game. I have curbed it quite a bit, but just because I know how far to take it, doesn't mean I feel it any less, I'm just getting slightly better at controlling it. I'll never change though. That's the way I am and I think it's the way I'm meant to be.
>
> Sometimes it gets me into trouble with referees and it damages me both professionally and financially, but, as I say, that's the way I am. Professionally I hate it because if I collect five bookings, I miss a game and I don't ever want to miss a game. Financially I hate it because Curbs fines me every time, without fail.

As fans, whoever we support, we always tend to complain that others don't see the whole picture when they talk about our players. Take someone like Robbie Savage, for example. Many people think him a player of hugely limited ability, with a penchant for diving and writhing around on the floor at the slightest provocation. If you travelled to Leicester, though, and doubtless it will happen in Birmingham soon as well, there could be little doubt that there was real and genuine affection felt for him. Their fans plainly saw something that the rest of us did not; he's not the only example, either. Alan Smith is a hero to Leeds fans, but a villain to the rest of us, as is Alan Shearer to Newcastle, as was Eric Cantona to Manchester United and as will be any number of players in the years to come.

Maybe, despite all the talk about loving him because he's been here forever, Robinson is a fine example of just that one-eyed way of viewing things. If I'm trying to be dispassionate, I can see that there might be something in that. If I'm speaking as a fan though, I don't care whether he's being viewed from an odd perspective or not. He never stops running and he never stops trying – and that will do for me.

> We've turned the expectations through 180 degrees from where they used to be. Charlton fans have always loved their team, but they used to be waiting for the kick in the teeth that arrived when the team failed. Now they expect us to succeed and that's a huge turnaround.
>
> Don't get me wrong, I haven't got any problem with people having high expectations. That's how it should be. We're proud of what we've achieved and there are a lot of teams who would love to be a bit more like Charlton.

If, and it's a fairly big 'if', the world can be viewed like a Warner Brothers cartoon, there can be little doubt that Robinson is the devil sitting on your shoulder, complete with trident and red robe, whispering ungodly suggestions into your ear. Chris Powell, by total contrast, would undoubtedly be the angel, exhorting us to ignore everything the mischief maker on the opposite shoulder was telling us. Powell is undoubtedly a hero at The Valley, despite being more radically different from Robinson, at least in terms of his demeanour on the pitch, as it is possible to be.

It's always a good idea to compare him to an angel as well, because he gets embarrassed about it, and when he gets embarrassed, he breaks into one of his grins. A Chris Powell grin isn't like anything else you've ever seen, containing enough brightness to light up a small power-cut-struck city.

He was already a fans' favourite before the extraordinary events of last year, which brought him to national prominence. The national sporting media was waiting keenly for the announcement of Sven-Goran Eriksson's first England squad, for the friendly against Spain. They needed an 'angle' to work on – someone who wasn't expected to be there, or someone whose selection would cause something of a stir. Powell's inclusion supplied them with both.

Powell selection deservedly drained the superlative reserves as people tried to describe what it meant for our club. *Roget's Thesaurus* sadly fails to include a category for 'nice bloke', but if it did, after the years of coverage Powell received in the press, he would certainly find himself listed.

The selection of the club's left-back by Eriksson not only lifted diplomatic relations between Charlton and Sweden to previously unprecedented levels, but became one of the stories of the year, at least as far as the football press were concerned. A ninth-place finish in the Premiership the previous year had attracted a smattering of headlines, some patronising and some not, but it would be hard to argue that the Addicks had captured the imagination of the national media. Powell, however, was a story that had everything the media could possibly have wanted.

For a start, it wasn't any old England squad he joined, but Eriksson's first squad as manager. The press attention surrounding its naming was intense, and when the gaffer (as none of his players have yet got round to calling him) had the decency to include someone rarely featured on the back pages, the stories started writing themselves. Having assumed that his chance at an international career had long since passed, the man who started at Southend had been selected by the man from Sweden. If you can't make a headline out of that, you're really not cut out to be a sports journalist.

Much of it was the cause of embarrassment to Powell, but it was handled with dignity and intelligence. I spoke to him the morning after his first game and despite the fact that a calf injury had forced him off at half-time, there was still a very evident sense of stunned delight about him. He had celebrated his international debut by, among other things, knocking the ball through the legs of Gaizka Mendieta, and collecting it on the other side. There are no prizes for guessing which bit of the videotape of the game is going to wear out first in the Powell household.

> I said to Andy Jones [Charlton's physio] this morning, 'That's something I'm never going to forget'. I've pulled off a few nutmegs for Charlton before, but doing it for England. That's got to be one of those that you remember for a very long time. And

the fact that we were playing against Spain was special, because they are a very good side.

It's not every day that you get to play players of that calibre and I think everyone sits up and watches the game a bit more closely when it's against a side of genuine international quality. They started the game very well, but we concentrated hard . . . it's so strange saying 'we' when I'm talking about the England side. This one's going to take a bit of getting used to!

I'm the sort of player who doesn't get injured too often, and I felt my calf just before half-time, so I made them aware that it was a bit sore. I told them that I thought I'd be all right, but they weren't taking any chances with anyone getting hurt, so off I went. To be honest, I was half thinking of the look on Curbs' face if he found out that I'd told them that my leg was sore and then I went on to hurt it properly.

I was deeply disappointed at the time, but I've got 45 minutes under my belt and I know what to expect if there's a next time. Now it's all gone past in a flash, and I'm just trying to get back to earth again, I just want to wander down the road and do a few normal things like pop out for a loaf of bread. I went to the corner shop this morning, and the bloke behind the counter recognised me. That's something I'm going to have to get my head around a little bit.

He got a few more chances to get his head around it and in the process became our most-capped England international. Maybe, as the season slipped onwards and the next one rolled in, we suspected that he wouldn't make the World Cup squad, but after the initial delight, it scarcely seemed to matter. Powell had brought us more media attention than virtually anything else we'd managed over the last couple of years and the 'little-club' tag was slowly slipping further away all the time.

Of course, not all of our international call-ups have enjoyed the fanfare that accompanied Powell's. Some of them have passed the wider world of football right by, causing ripples only in the countries directly involved. By the end of the qualifying period, however, no fewer than 13 Charlton players had participated, representing 11 different countries. Their squad had fed more teams around the globe than Manchester United, Arsenal or Liverpool. In fact, Charlton Athletic were providing players to more nations than any other club in English football.

For reasons I can't begin to explain, this fact produces a smile and chuckle every time I think of it or have to write it down. Thankfully, the vast majority of Charlton fans won't need me to explain why. In a period of time too brief to be properly absorbed by most supporters, footballing tentacles were stretching out from SE7 and reaching to the furthest-flung corners of the globe. Whether it be in Zimbabwe or Iran, Denmark or South Africa, Charlton were involved in the tournament around which the footballing world revolves.

Not all of them made the trip all the way to the Far East, obviously, but there were a few faces sprinkled about on the coverage that looked a little bit familiar. I think it's fair to say, especially with England already 3–0 up against Denmark, that, late on in the game, most Charlton fans were cheering for Claus Jensen's chip to duck beneath the bar. Unfortunately, that was a trick Mr Seaman was saving for another day, and Claus ended his World Cup without a goal.

Had the ball crept under the bar, it would have been a goal with the stamp of Jensen all over it. Never one to fire through a crowd of players if he can curl it around them or loft it over them, the Dane adds a cultured touch to the Charlton midfield, the like of which we may not have seen before. And yet, it would be wrong, despite all the positives, to place him in the category of 'hero', just because there are still those who demand more than he offers.

For every ten people salivating over his passing, his ball control and his extraordinary vision, there is one who moans that he 'doesn't tackle'. Personally, I've always taken the view that, admittedly, Jensen's not a great tackler, but then Michelangelo didn't paint many fences either. In the current climate, with players worshipped for little more than the ability to keep churning up and down the pitch, where a 'good engine' is more important than a decent first touch, anything which places the artistic over the mundane has to be celebrated. For this reason alone, Jensen, with his permanent grin and balding pate, remains something of an icon for many down at The Valley.

However, despite all his remarkable talents, the Dane failed to pick up the crown as even Charlton's most influential midfielder at the World Cup. With a week until the tournament began, Mark Kinsella looked set to be left on the bench, with Matt Holland and Roy Keane patrolling the Republic of Ireland's central midfield. One argument, a bit of posturing, an ill-considered public outburst, and the announcement that his manager was a . . . well, not someone who met with his approval, and Keane was logging up the air-miles and flying back home.

Well, he was flying back to England, where he lives, earns an extraordinary sum of money each year and seemingly never stops taking the dog for a walk. The Irish captain was going back home to the leafy and affluent suburbs of Manchester, largely, if his outburst is to be taken at face value, in protest at the fact that his coach was English. There's an inconsistency there somewhere, I'm sure of it . . .

Kinsella was the natural replacement – fiercely and proudly Irish, yet married to an English woman and living in Essex. If Keane saw things as intolerable, and the politics surrounding the continued employment of Mick McCarthy as offensive, Kinsella chose not to comment. All we saw of our club captain was him gratefully accepting the honour of representing his country, presenting a united front with the rest of the Irish squad and pledging to do his very best every time he was sent onto the pitch. Within the space of four games, which stretched the emotions every way possible, we could safely say that we had never felt prouder of him.

Except, of course, that Kinsella has frequently led us to mutter about having never felt prouder, with our opinions changed on virtually a season-by-season basis. Collecting the play-off trophy probably tops the list, but every time we win at home and he charges at the north stand, plants his left leg and swings a short, stabbing celebratory uppercut, opinions have to be revised. Some players seem to go out of their way to receive the acclaim of the crowd, whether it be through extravagant gestures on the pitch or inflammatory statements off it. Others just set about their business and attract the passion of the crowd through their actions. It's not difficult, especially after the events of the past five years, to know how to categorise Kinsella.

When I first came here it was 1996 and everything was still made up of Portakabins all over the place. Slowly people start to tell you a little bit about the history of the club, and you go to things like the Back to The Valley dinner and you start to realise exactly what getting back to the ground means to everyone.

I think getting back to this place was the starting point for most of what we've achieved over the last few years, because it wouldn't have happened if we'd been playing our football somewhere else. We've got 27,000 fans in here every week, and every bit of the club is on the way up.

I spent seven years with Colchester and I watched the World Cup and the Ireland team, and I knew that I couldn't make my way into that side playing where I was. They knew that as well, to be fair, and tried to help me get somewhere bigger. That was my apprenticeship and I don't forget those days. In fact, I think

it's more important to remember them when you've got to the top
than ever before, because it helps to keep you on your toes.

At the end of the 2002 season, having shone in the World Cup, and
become the very pulse of the club, Kinsella, in a move which shocked
many, left Charlton and joined Aston Villa. There were huge emotions
stirred by the transfer, of which more later, but nobody, even those who
backed the decision to sell, could underestimate what the man had done
for the club. For a lot of people, things would never quite be the same
again.

Alongside Kinsella in the Far East and his last line of defence when
playing for Charlton, Dean Kiely is another who has claimed a place in
the affections of the fans. Toothless and fearless, he has trodden a
familiar route to his captaincy, making his way through a lower-league
career with York and Bury, before getting the chance to move to
Charlton in the season after our relegation from the Premiership.

A record equalling 19 clean sheets in his first year, coupled with a
formidable presence on the pitch, have brought him to the attention of
a wider audience than ever before. For a man who once spent the
summer laying cables on motorways for extra money, it's maybe no
surprise that he approaches the game with an almost fanatical zeal.

> I've stripped my life bare to do what I do. I've basically got my
> wife, my kids and my football, and all I want is to be Charlton's
> goalkeeper. I don't want to be their keeper because it gets me into
> a club, or a restaurant or a golf course, I want to be their keeper
> because that's what I do. I'm not interested in the trappings of
> being a footballer, because they're just other things that would
> take me away from my game and I don't need that. There's time
> for that when I pack up.
>
> I'm quite quiet off the pitch and I like to get my head down
> and do my training, but sometimes I admit, I look at a film of
> myself or I see myself on television, and I'm thinking 'Bloody
> hell! Is that me?' I'm bawling and shouting, ranting and raving,
> but it's just that it's the 90-minutes release a week when you get
> to do your thing and you've got to do whatever you need to do
> to get that win.
>
> You've got to be right and you've got to be up for it, otherwise
> what's the point? After the game I'm alright though – I come
> down and I'm just normal old me again.

Kiely's progress through the goalkeeping hierarchy has been slow but steady, but with hard work, determination and a frightening degree of sheer bloody-mindedness, he's pulled himself to the top. When he reflects on the merits of making the journey via the route he has chosen, it's easy to see why he's taken to life at Charlton so well. It's hard not to conclude that there's a certain similarity between them.

> If you're honest and genuine when you train and play, and you do things properly and give 100 per cent, then if things go wrong you'll get the benefit of the doubt and you'll be better prepared to bounce back from it. If you get cocky and you spend your time getting in people's faces, then maybe it won't be so easy for you.

I'm a bit wary of using phrases which hint that 'people are our biggest asset' simply because it sounds like the sort of motto Arthur Anderson and Enron took a liking to. Come to think of it, people were Enron's biggest asset, or at least their pension funds were . . . but I digress. When you look through the nature of our heroes though, and reflect on the characters of the people we deluge with praise and glory on a weekly basis, you have to conclude we've not done too badly over the years.

We might not have too many who have caused the world to sit up and take notice, although a few have played on the biggest stage in the game, but we've had virtually none who have let us down. Whether that's because of the nature of the players we bring in, or because the nature of the club helps to shape them, is a moot point.

Whatever the reasons, our heroes have generally lived up to their billing, on and off the pitch. In a modern game awash with money, excesses and temptation, that's a long way from being the smallest of our achievements.

5

'BORING, BORING CHARLTON?'

At first glance, you wouldn't have thought there were likely to be too many thrilling games associated with Charlton Athletic. After all, as a result of what went before, there's an air of cautious reticence running throughout the club. What with the way things are run at board level, the instinctive reluctance of Alan Curbishley to play overly expansive football and the lack of money around over the last decade with which to buy star players, most of the facts seem to be on your side.

And yet, without even troubling to include the triumph at Wembley in this particular list, the roll call of famous games is far from brief. We seem to have developed an ability to create drama from events still far from crisis point, eschewing the simple route home for the most perilous path available. Leads of two and three goals have often been surrendered and then regained, and we've frequently watched the last ten minutes of a dramatic fight-back, only to curse and question what would have happened if we'd discovered such battling qualities half an hour earlier.

There's nothing unusual about that – all fans do it – it's just that we seem to do it with a greater and more monotonous regularity than anyone else. The first few times it was fantastic, and we loved every second of it, and then the next few times we were enthralled, but had started to mutter about the benefits of doing it the easy way. By about the fifth close escape, though, we were complaining, loud enough for everyone to hear, about our habit of continually flirting with disaster. It was like going on a particularly vicious fairground ride. The first stomach-churning circuit was cheerful enough, the second was OK, by the third we were feeling a bit queasy and after that we threw up with gusto whenever we thought about it.

Ever since that early experience of being ushered from the ground five minutes from the end, hearing the cheers of an appreciative crowd watching an engaging punch-up, I've always had a dread of leaving the game early. There have been times, admittedly, when it's struck me as a particularly ridiculous habit, but thankfully, sitting in the press box, I can always claim that it's not really my decision – I'm being paid to be there until the end.

The truth is, that were I just sitting in the stand, I would find it equally impossible to leave early, albeit that my continued presence at some of the more complete demolitions would have doubtless marked me down as a weirdo of the first order. Watching the games for a living at least frees you from the choice of whether to escape or not. I remember sitting there at Bradford on Good Friday, as we slumped neatly to a two-goal deficit with a combination of terrible defending, appalling passing and goalkeeping the like of which is rarely seen outside of the big top. The laptop in front of me didn't quite act as a ball and chain, but it might as well have done. Without it, I would have been tramping down the steps and out of the ground as soon as Sasa Ilic went on a walkabout and Benito Carbone put the game beyond us.

Looking back, it had all the ingredients of a great Charlton away defeat. We had been on a decent run, with our last dozen Premiership contests having seen only Manchester United and Leeds defeat us. Bradford hadn't won since just before the last ice age and seemed to have accepted relegation with a resigned grimace. It felt too good to be true and so it proved.

It was a similar tale at Upton Park, three months earlier, when I celebrated Boxing Day by watching my side get battered. It was bitterly cold, we were three down at half-time and five down when the referee finally brought matters to a close. Had it been a boxing match, it wouldn't have got past the first half, as a sympathetic ref would have wrapped an arm around our weary shoulders and muttered something along the lines of 'You've taken enough for one night, son. Time to call it a day.'

Sadly, there was no such option, and we trudged through the 90 minutes staring bleakly as fate laughed in our faces. There are many marketing ruses used by football clubs, some reasonable, the vast majority a form of legalised deception, but I've never seen the West Ham experiment tried. Somehow they couldn't quite get the chirpy phrase right.

Battle through the Blackwall Tunnel to spend the day after Christmas away from your loved ones, watching your side disgrace themselves, in sub-freezing temperatures, with one loo per thousand people, no hot drinks and the scorn of everyone else in the ground directed at you. Yours, for just £27 that you really can't afford after everything else you've had to spend money on over the course of this supposedly festive season.

I think you see their problem.

There is, of course, an upside to all this, and it comes in the form of not missing the tail end of some of the great revivals of the last few years. I watched in disbelief last year, as one Charlton fan walked out of Stamford Bridge with the scores level and five minutes remaining. Quite apart from the fact that, at Chelsea's prices, he was turning up his nose at about £3.50 worth of football, he also missed Kevin Lisbie rising in the penalty area to nod us to our third consecutive victory over them.

It wasn't a classic game by any standards, but, having shown early signs of cracking, we forced our way into the match and then struck when it was too late for Claudio Ranieri's men to do anything about it. There's also something about beating Chelsea which leaves Charlton fans beaming from ear to ear. They're just so different to us, run so differently and with different expectations all over the place.

The players expect to be paid a fortune, the chairman expects them to win everything in sight, the manager expects to get pressurised constantly by the chairman and the fans just expect to be treated like dirt. Three of those four tend to happen, with the latter two guaranteed, and thanks partly to our habit of turning them over twice a season, the second one is always just out of their grasp.

As far as classics are concerned, we rarely manage them, either when they come to The Valley or we go to Stamford Bridge, but it doesn't seem to matter. Singing songs about how they're going to go bust, getting the result and then strolling out into the Kings Road with three points and a load of disgruntled Chelsea fans is very hard to beat. When I said that we didn't do jokes about bankruptcy at Charlton any more, I have to admit I lied – or at least I forgot about Chelsea.

Some sides can't help but try to pat you on the head and hint at the fact that you must be delighted just to be at their ground. They talk to us the way Londoners talk to tourists when they want to fleece them for a few quid. The feeling of doing things the 'right way', supporting a club who behave 'decently' and revelling in the contrast just adds to the enjoyment. It's amazing how worthy and pious you can become after a victory at that place . . .

Ben Hayes, a lifelong fan and chairman of the Bromley branch of the supporters' club, understands exactly:

> There are teams you take a dislike to, and some of them not the ones you'd expect. I can't stand Chelsea, because they've just got such a high opinion of themselves, yet they never win anything that matters, or produce the performances right the way through the season. They remind me of the Harlem Globetrotters – they're not a proper team – and when we beat them it's fantastic.
>
> Another thing about them that people ignore, is that none of their fans come from Chelsea. I get particularly annoyed when I hear people like David Mellor moaning that Manchester United fans don't come from Manchester. That'll be the same David Mellor who comes from Weymouth and supports Chelsea, having previously supported Fulham, then?

It's a particularly good point, not least because it means that Hayes becomes the first person in the book to point a less than flattering finger in the direction of David Mellor. Mellor writes a column each week in the *Evening Standard*, which frequently offers a gleaming and cheery view of both the latest football club in his life and the chairman of that organisation, Mr Ken Bates.

It would have been nice to speak to Mellor. That's probably not true actually – it would have been instructive to speak to Mellor. Unfortunately, I noticed with some concern on a slick, corporate website that his fee for an after-dinner speech was between £2,500 and £5,000, which probably put an interview slightly over budget as far as I was concerned. Instead I opted to have a look at some of his pronouncements made in the *Evening Standard* over the last few years to see if Charlton fans were being a bit hard on him.

One of the more recent articles was headlined 'Football's Greed Means Fans Always Foot the Bill'. Bearing in mind the price of season tickets at Chelsea, the vast expanse of unsold £1 million-per-year corporate boxes at Stamford Bridge, and his own request for up to five grand for a doubtless well-rehearsed recital after dinner, I feared I'd stumbled across an inconsistency. After all, one of his earlier pieces was titled: 'The Stats Do Not Lie'.

It's probably things like this that left Ben Hayes, myself and many thousands of others cheering so loudly on each of the four consecutive occasions when we claimed all three points from the west London club. Whether it was Martin Pringle's mad, David Pleat-like galloping skip across the Valley turf after he scored to make safe the first of our series of wins, or Kinsella's wild gesticulating to the travelling fans as we completed the double at Stamford Bridge later in the year, it was the nature of the opposition, rather than the quality of the games, which made the moment precious.

A year later and it was Kevin Lisbie's goal in the last minute which made it two in a row on Chelsea's own ground, and then Jason Euell's neat lob over Carlo Cudicini wrapped up the win at The Valley. As I have already happily confessed, I can get quite pious about the whole thing and I like to look back on each of the four games as an individual morality play. Did I say quite pious? All right, very.

With the exception of a few, truly outstanding games though, it tends to be the ones with a wider meaning which stay burned into the memory. There's something about putting things right on a football pitch that satisfies an urge so deep, that quiet reflection afterwards leaves us feeling almost uncomfortable. There's an easy way to check this, involving walking up to the average Charlton fan (and most of us are extremely average) and whispering the name 'Nicky Weaver' in the fan's ear. Oh, and if you get easily offended, take a step backwards as soon as you've said it.

Until the afternoon of 20 November 1999, Weaver really didn't mean all that much to Charlton fans. He had a reasonably favourable press, looked to be pushing himself into the England squad and caused us no more upset than any other opposition goalkeeper. Admittedly, it was a big game, with Weaver's Manchester City side pushing us hard at the top of the table, but there wasn't any real history of bad blood between the two teams.

And there probably wouldn't have been to this day had Weaver not started acting like he'd just finished a course at the Bruce Grobbellar school of footballing humour. We could have lived with the defeat – just about – but the sight of the opposition keeper walking up and down in front of the covered end, waving and joking at the home fans and asking to be reminded of the score, was a bit too much to take. I can't stand all that hooligan-based posturing, when red-faced, thick-necked men pretend to take huge offence at some perceived affront to their 'territory', but, in Weaver's case, I probably came closer than ever before to understanding why those people feel the way they do.

When we were both promoted, the fixture list decided, with exquisite timing, that the opening day of the season would be a decent moment to send City to The Valley for the first Premiership meeting between the two sides. There was, to put it mildly, a degree of anticipation among Charlton fans as to quite what reception Weaver might get. As it turned out, it was to be only the first half of the fun and games we were to have with Manchester's less successful half.

Inside the first half, we were two up, with Andy Hunt claiming the first, and John Robinson the second, after Weaver had inexplicably tried to volley clear a decently struck drive and sliced it into the corner of his own net. As far as the Charlton fans were concerned, he couldn't have come up with a finer comedy moment if he'd donned a red nose and big shoes, as the wheels of his car had blown off and a bunch of flowers had popped out of the exhaust.

People were fighting hard not to hug themselves, and indeed anyone else who came into range, at half-time. The reason we stayed reasonably calm was because we knew it couldn't get any better than this – 2–0 up at half-time on the opening day of the season, and Nicky Weaver had already made a berk of himself. How wrong we were. Kinsella's third was flicked away off the outside of his right boot with a combination of calmness and contempt, while he even had time, on his way through the centre of the City midfield for the fourth, to wave at the linesman to show just how far onside he was. Weaver tripped him up and we got a penalty.

He wasn't allowed the mercy of an early bath, so we all got to give him even more stick as Graham Stuart sent him the wrong way for the penalty. The keeper dived towards Woolwich, the ball went upmarket, towards Greenwich, and nestled happily in the back of the net. We were euphoric. Never had one player's piece of posing come back to haunt him so thoroughly.

It left us, however, feeling a bit wary about the return journey, in late December. We had celebrated Christmas by giving ourselves to West Ham as a present, in that Boxing Day massacre, and I could easily see us coming a terrible cropper at Maine Road. Extraordinarily, my concerns were groundless.

Within half an hour or so, Jonatan Johansson had given us the lead, and then, just before half-time, Weaver mis-kicked, straight to Radostin Kishishev, who hurtled down the pitch before cheerfully slipping the ball to Johansson for him to score his second. With ten minutes to go, Stuart sent Weaver the wrong way from the spot for the second time in four months, and in the last minute of the game, Claus Jensen made his first block tackle of the season, being rewarded by the sight of the ball rebounding over Weaver's head from at least 45 yards out.

It didn't matter that we let in a late penalty. There was hardly anyone left in Maine Road to see it happen, anyway. Looking back, we might have been a bit harsh on Weaver. He didn't kick anyone, or try and maim anyone, he didn't really cheat or try to kid the ref, he just did what Robbo had been doing for us to opposition fans for years and years. Then again, looking back at my looking back, he deserved it. He came to our ground and he tried to take the mickey. Better players than him have come and beaten us on their own, and they haven't stopped and mocked along the way. No, eight goals was about a fair sentence, and if he ever gets back into their first team, we'll officially call a truce.

Dean Kiely was about as far as it was possible to be from Weaver when the incidents happened, as much in terms of mental approach as geographical location, I'd imagine. If about a hundred yards separated the two on the pitch, about a hundred miles stood between their respective approaches to the game:

> I honestly think that now he's had time to look back at that, and to reflect on things, because I know if I were him sitting here now, I'd want to say that there were things I would have done differently.
>
> Obviously the Charlton fans remember the incidents and they shouldn't have happened. If you try and make yourself into some kind of a pantomime villain, you need to realise that there isn't going to be a lot of sympathy floating around when it all goes wrong.
>
> Maybe he should be thinking about keeping his head tucked in a little bit more, and not trying to be in people's faces the whole time. Maybe some of his non-goalkeeping choices and decisions will be a bit better made in future.

If the joy of beating Chelsea was all bound up with the sort of people who support them, and the delight at City's defeat was largely because of the nature of their goalkeeper, there was one victory which went deeper still. When we went to Selhurst Park at the end of March 2000, we were already, barring an outbreak of plague, going to win the First Division title. The ground had represented the bleakest times the club had known in its history and the legacy of paying rent to a side we had always detested was still at the forefront of many minds.

Having defeated them on Boxing Day, which on reflection was the high that had to be countered by the following year's Upton Park low, victory meant more different things on more different levels, than many of us were prepared to start trying to come to terms with. If there was one ground in the entire division at which we wanted to win, Selhurst, or Sell-out Park, as it became un-affectionately known, was the one.

It was a dreadful game, on a rain-drenched quagmire of a surface which had already been cut to ribbons throughout the course of the year by both Palace and Wimbledon, who were the latest lodgers. Impoverished Palace had already agreed that Charlton could have as many tickets as they wanted for the game, which left us with the Arthur Waite stand full of red Charlton shirts, with the Palace crowd relocated to various other bits of the ground. The whole thing felt far more like a home game than an away one, albeit that the home was scruffier than the one we were used to.

We'd started the day 13 points clear at the top of the table, and to be honest, as it came around to the last quarter of an hour, I think most people were prepared to take the draw and see the lead reduced to a 'mere' 11 points. We were more than a bit blasé about things at the time, but there wasn't really any sign as to where the goal was going to come from. Earlier in the week we'd scored four against Grimsby and seen the debut of Paul Kitson, who we had on loan from West Ham. Kitson was a decent striker, but on that surface, nobody could claim that it was easy for any of the players to show what they could do, least of all a light and nimble front-man.

With 15 minutes remaining, Curbishley replaced Andy Hunt with Kitson, and just five minutes later, chaos erupted. Chris Powell sent the ball bobbling along across the face of the six-yard box and everybody seemed to ignore it. It really was as if the whole episode were played out in slow motion. Somehow, in a crowded penalty area, the ball was sent neither into the net nor into the safety of touch, until Kitson aquaplaned in from about ten yards out and diverted it into the back of the Palace net.

We hadn't won at Palace for about 65 years and a bloke who had joined us earlier in the week, and had still only played 40 minutes of football for us, had ensured that a small footnote in the record books would require updating. It was one of those moments when you saw the emotion of the game really take over. Grown men were standing there, trying to pick each other up in their delight. Realising this was impossible, and not really caring why, they just hopped from foot to foot, screaming at the people behind their new-found cuddling partner.

It's the sort of scene you only see at football matches, and even then, not with all that much frequency. A few years ago, people were quick to mock Alex Ferguson (as he was then) for coming up with nothing more original in the aftermath of his side's Champions League triumph than: 'Football! Bloody hell!' It might not have been the most incisive comment Ferguson has ever made about the game, but I challenge anyone who was at Selhurst Park that afternoon to prove that they can come up with anything all that much more meaningful.

I know of one fan who looks back with pride on starting up a chant of 'We'll never play you again', adding enthusiastically that 'Clinton Morrison even mentioned it in the paper, so it got to him!' It was a day for celebrating, and a day to thank a player who, quite literally, popped up in the right place at the right time.

Kitson didn't stay with us at the end of that season, returning back to West Ham, where he never really found his way back into the side. In fact, he waited two years to start a first-team game, until he was presented with his chance one night and grabbed it with both hands, claiming a hat-trick. It doesn't take a genius to work out who it was against either – but we didn't really have the heart to complain. So what if, two years down the road, Kitson had cost us a victory in a live Monday-night Premiership game? Some results live on in the memory for a very long time and the one caused by his goal on a wet Saturday at Selhurst Park will stay there for longer than most.

The common thread between the games against Palace, Manchester City and Chelsea was our really deeply held desire to put one over on the opposition, not just because they were the ones standing between us and three points, but because we really didn't like them. Sometimes, however, we went on to get results and play in games which would never be forgotten, yet involved far less needle between the sides.

Possibly our first experience of that, at least during the ten-year period covered by these scribblings, came right at the beginning when I can't really imagine that we had very much reason to hold a grudge against Portsmouth. As the mafia used to say, they were just in the wrong place at the wrong time – it was nothing personal, just business. In this case, rather emotional business. Colin Walsh's strike and Brian Moore's perfectly pitched commentary, as I've already said, will stay with us forever, but I must confess that until I began writing this book, I hadn't appreciated what the defeat meant for Portsmouth. Ben Hayes, on the other hand, knew only too well:

> They must have been gutted, because they missed out on promotion on goal difference that year, and let's be honest, they were destined not to get anything that day, despite the fact that our form going into the match had been so dreadful. If it had

been anyone else we were playing that day, Portsmouth would probably have gone up, and you can't say what a difference that might have made to them in the long run.

That, I suppose, is the ultimate example of, well, call it what you will: the fates conspiring, or your luck being in (or out), a perfect illustration of one side's win being the other's loss. Throughout the course of the season, Portsmouth will have dropped a silly point somewhere, a back pass will have been hit too softly, a chance will have been seized upon too meekly. At whichever end of the pitch, there will be some reason why they didn't go up other than that defeat at The Valley.

The fans won't view it like that though, and to be honest, neither would I. Football decided that Portsmouth weren't going up, and it did so via the cruel trick of making them play against a side who were physically and emotionally incapable of losing that day. That's about as much sense as I can make of the whole situation – the more I think about it, the more insightful and meaningful that quote from Sir Alex was. Football! Bloody hell!

In the years which followed, there were decent games among the hundreds of draws which seemed to come our way, but with the benefit of hindsight, it's difficult to look back at them and put them in the same category as our more recent triumphs. For example, 4–3 over Southend and 2–0 over Millwall at The Valley, or 4–2 over Arsenal at Highbury. I think you get the point, which is not to decry the nature of the performances or the determination of the side during the mid-'90s but just to acknowledge how much more thrilling the Premiership can be.

The game at Highbury was, for me personally at least, the one that required the greatest number of pinches to be administered before I could fully take on board what I was watching. For the opening half an hour, we got battered, absolutely murdered, by a side that would go on to wrap up the title by beating United at Old Trafford. Thierry Henry was lethal – fast, intelligent and brave – but could only convert one of the half a dozen or so chances he was handed throughout the opening exchanges. I say exchanges out of habit, and because it's a nice 'football report' sort of phrase, but now I think of it, it doesn't fit at all. 'Exchanges' hints that we were offering something back in return and that just wasn't the case.

Within the first six minutes, Arsenal had hit the post, had one cleared off the line, and then finally taken the lead, as Henry slotted home inside the far post. For the next 25 minutes, the ball did everything except go into either the Charlton net, or anywhere near the Arsenal half. That same boxing referee we had prayed for at West Ham would have certainly stopped this contest – and he wouldn't have heard a mutter of protest from either the Charlton players or fans. 'We were getting battered, absolutely battered,' Steve Brown admitted to me afterwards, adding with the charming turn of phrase which marks out professional footballers, 'I was breathing out of my arse after 20 minutes.'

And then, over the course of 20 incredible minutes either side of half-time, the game stood on its head and refused to follow logic or momentum any further. Just before the break, Brown, possibly with the assistance of a particularly big breath, rose above the Arsenal central defence to meet Paul Konchesky's freekick, and we were level.

I can vividly recall, and it's now on thousands of videotapes forever more, that as Brown met the ball, a yell went up from the Arsenal area. It was as if everyone else was stunned and only the bloke who scored the goal knew for sure what was going to happen, as soon as the ball left his head. Admittedly, his celebration was typically apologetic and embarrassed, but if you were having those kind of respiratory problems in front of a crowd that big, you'd look embarrassed too.

A couple of minutes later and Richard Wright managed to punch another Konchesky freekick into his own net, to send us 2–1 up before half-time arrived, like a breath of cold air and a strong coffee after a few too many lunchtime pints. Within ten minutes of the restart, we were off the wagon again, as Claus Jensen produced a moment of pure genius.

Having pick-pocketed Patrick Vieira, the Dane scuttled away to the far side of the area, before flighting the ball back over the bemused figure of Wright and into the far corner of the net, off the underside of the bar and the inside of the far post.

Again, the silence is such that you can actually hear the ball hit the inside of the post before the visiting fans explode. There's a lot of noise at the stealing of the ball from Vieira, then Jensen tried this absurd chip and the ball flies through the air in almost total silence. I know that sounds like a stage direction from a Rocky film, but that's how I remember it, and watching the tape back again shows that my memory isn't playing tricks.

It was, by a considerable margin, the best goal I have ever seen from a Charlton player. Shaun Bartlett had actually won Goal of the Season the previous year for a majestic volley against Leicester, but I couldn't see how it could compare to Jensen's. Give me a hundred attempts, and while there will be some amazing hooks, slices and complete misses along the way, I'll manage to replicate Bartlett's in the end. Ask me to replicate Jensen's and I won't need a hundred goes, I'll need a tent – because I'll be out there all night.

The goal left Highbury stunned, and when Jensen ghosted through the midfield and laid the ball off to the feet of Jason Euell, I can remember simply staring in amazement as Euell strode confidently on, before burying it beyond Wright to send us 4–1 up. The entire upper tier of the main stand at Highbury was silent, apart from a dozen Charlton directors who were going absolutely berserk. Memories like that stay burned onto your brain for a very long time.

Arsenal pulled one back, with a dodgy penalty, but it wasn't enough and we beat them 4–2. I think, outside of the play-off final, it was the most remarkable game I've ever seen Charlton play. If, one day, science discovers a way to take you back to any one moment in your life in order to relive it again, I know where I'm going. At the risk of causing huge offence to family, friends and all normal people, I think I might just end up at Highbury on that Sunday afternoon, just for the glorious combination of shock and euphoria. That's what supporting a football team does to you, I suppose.

The really great games, the ones we genuinely never forget, seem to be the ones that wring the emotions, and send us out of the ground both grinning and shaking our heads. Personally, although it ended in failure, with relegation being delayed rather than averted, I'll always prize the memory of winning at Aston Villa on the penultimate weekend of our first year in the Premiership.

We kept getting pegged back, and the lunatic, leaping screaming of John Robinson when he sent us ahead once more will always stick in my mind as a magical moment. Maybe not to the same extent, though, as the sight of Steve Brown jogging onto the pitch and pulling on the goalkeeper's gloves after Andy Petterson had been sent off for a half-nelson on Julian Joachim, when we didn't have a keeper on the bench. Brown's first touch was a leaping save from Paul Merson's freekick, and a few minutes later, Danny Mills had pinballed home the freekick which gave us a 4–3 win and temporarily ensured our perilous top-flight tenure was safe for one more game.

It didn't matter in the end though, because we crumbled on the last day and went down anyway, and Mills isn't a player who commands many warm memories when the fans look back. For sheer emotion though, I think that day takes a fair bit of beating. Others disagree, and I can see their point. Ben Hayes again adds a voice of reason:

> I can't look back on that Villa game with all that much affection.
> I mean, it was a really great game, and it was my birthday, but at
> the end of the season, we didn't stay up. Funnily enough,

although the season had another game to go, and I think there was a fortnight break just to string it out a bit more, if we had stayed up, I would probably look back on it a lot more fondly. I suppose that just shows you how much you can be affected by the emotions surrounding a game when you look back on it. As it was, we got relegated, it was all in vain, and I look back and know that it wasn't the great escape that all the commentators were describing at the time, because we didn't escape.

Which is the sort of logical response that leaves me feeling like an over-excited schoolboy, but I can't help feeling the way I do when I look back on it, and I don't suppose I'm alone. I'm not the only one who still punches the air when that last goal goes in, and I don't suppose I'm the only one who suspends reality and kids himself that we might not go down yet. If only the results go the right way on the last day of a season that ended three years ago. All right, maybe I am the only one.

I still look back, from time to time, on the draw we snatched against Manchester United, having been 3–1 down with 20 minutes to go. I watch the tape and snigger as Beckham and Keane are substituted, with the game seemingly safe. I scream at Mark Kinsella to nod the ball to Robinson on the edge of the area so that he can try an impossible cross-shot which might just beat Raimond van der Gouw and find the far corner to level matters. Football, eh, Alex? Bloody hell . . .

I tell Dean Kiely to go to his left when a nervous Nelson Vivas steps up to take a penalty for Arsenal at The Valley, then feel my hands curling into fists as I watch the ball palmed away and victory ensured. I plead with Mark Fish to find Jonatan Johansson with his backwards header, so that the Finn might try an overhead kick to save the game against West Ham, in which we were paying back our footballing dues to Paul Kitson.

And the truth of it is, I do all of it in the knowledge that it was so nearly not even there to be watched. All the fans in the world feel a similar surge of emotion when it's their club involved, but few do so against the background that Charlton have faced, and none at such a high level, having previously been so low. It's the change in fortunes, the turnabout in matters on and off the pitch, which makes us appreciate things even more.

If Manchester United or Arsenal win or lose things next year, they still won't experience the sense of achievement felt by people who go to The Valley. They might spend another £50 million or £100 million this year, but it will be in the cause of going higher still, not completing a transition from death's door to healthy competitor.

In the aftermath of the play-off final, someone asked Keith Peacock if he was worried about the number of new fans that were there, if he felt that the day was in any way 'diluted' by the presence of people who hadn't lived the journey from its earliest steps. He answered:

> I don't think so. People get out of days like this what they put in. It's proportional really, everyone's cheering the same on the outside, but deep down, and when things calm down a little bit later on, the ones who saw it through the bad times will have the memories of the journey we've made. Like I say, you get out of it what you put in, both as a player, and especially as a fan.

Having played almost 600 games for the club, Peacock was well placed to make such a judgement and took full advantage of his position to make possibly the best point about the growth of the club that any one person has made over the last decade. It's a point that expands to cover the events of the last decade just as well as that single Bank Holiday afternoon at Wembley.

You get out of it what you put in. Even if it doesn't look it on the surface, you celebrate in direct proportion to the heartbreak you've suffered. Viewed like that, as a Charlton fan it might have been easier to pick the bad games than try and select the great ones . . .

6

MYTHS AND LEGENDS

Football clubs are, ultimately, just like any other place of work. It must be true, because I heard a financial expert on the radio telling me so. Apparently they must behave like any other business, refuse to let the emotion of the 'product' allow them to get carried away, and generally conduct themselves in the same way as the Acme copper-tubing company. I came away from the radio none the wiser about footballing finance, but with the sneaking suspicion that I'd learned something of value about financial experts and especially about ones who want to be on the radio. Charlton may well be an unlikely club to suggest blind, financial indulgence, but if you remove the emotion from the game, then surely there's not much point left in playing it? It wasn't simply being financially sensible that saved Charlton, but having the ability to combine common fiscal sense with the excitement and emotion of the game.

Given football's extraordinary history of misadministration in this country, with its insular habit of pointing at the occasional European league and muttering that 'it's worse over there' and the glacier-like progress towards making the game more accessible to the ordinary fan, it hasn't got all that much to crow about. Admittedly, Manchester United, as even people who have never heard of football can explain to you, are worth millions, while several of the larger clubs in this country have large grounds, and often plans for larger ones still.

But it's hard to look at the whole picture, with half the Premiership clubs boasting debts like long-distance phone numbers and about three-quarters of the Nationwide League going financially bankrupt as a result of a morally bankrupt media company, without thinking that it looks decidedly gloomy. In a way we seem to have been lucky, not only did we survive, but we seem to have learned our lessons before the stakes became so terrifyingly high.

Back in 1982, before we had left The Valley, let alone started the journey back, Charlton had their first experiences of serious financial peril. Mark Hulyer, a rather flash new chairman, had allegedly fallen behind with repayments on a loan from Michael Gliksten, the old chairman and member of a family intertwined with the club over a period of years. A bankruptcy petition was lodged and, following their failure to complete the payments on two separate transfers, the club was placed under a transfer embargo.

There were a series of lights spotted at the end of the tunnel, with each one proving to be little more than another train heading in our direction, intent on mowing us down. By June 1983, Leeds United were attempting to gain a winding-up order against us for failing to pay the seemingly paltry fee of £35,000. Slowly but surely, the Inland Revenue, the ex-chairman and some bloke we once met down the pub, had all combined forces to add to the legal and financial pressure being applied. Actually, I might have made up the bloke down the pub, but it might be true. At the time, it certainly seemed as if everyone was against us.

The scale of our plight can be judged by the fiasco over the purchase of Ronnie Moore from Rotherham, who was obtained for £30,000, after the fans had clubbed together, got a certificate each for their troubles, and chipped in £8,000 of it. Colin Cameron remembers it only too well, which is unsurprising. As the club statistician, there simply isn't anything he doesn't know about the place.

Discussing the club with Cameron is like sitting down with a talking and smoking version of the *Rothmans Yearbook*. In the course of a career spent chronicling London football, and Charlton in particular, Cameron has seen highs and lows of huge proportions. If anyone understands the scale of Charlton's achievement in saving itself and then prospering, Cameron does. He also knows a scheme destined to end in disaster when he sees one:

> I can well remember the campaign asking the fans for a donation, and I can well remember the mess the club was in at the time. I gave a donation, because I wanted to do my bit, but I made sure that the cheque was made out to Rotherham United Football Club. You had no way of knowing what it was going to be

diverted off to otherwise – there were debts needed paying all over the place, and I wanted to make sure it ended up where I'd intended it!

A few months down the line, despite Cameron's astute move, Rotherham were on our case as well, having still received less than 50 per cent of the money. We went through more wind-ups than Jeremy Beadle's researchers and through a process so tortuous that playing football must have come as something of a light relief – well, it might have done, had we been any good.

At one stage, the kit had to be surreptitiously moved out of the ground before the Official Receiver locked the gates, as there wasn't any way we could buy any new stuff in which to play the next game if it got locked in. Games were postponed, and a rescue package was only agreed by the Football League's solicitors five minutes before the deadline set by the High Court expired.

Five minutes. Five short minutes. It seems ridiculous now, probably as ridiculous as it appeared hopeless back then. We were five minutes from being an ex-football team. When we look back on the history of our club, there should probably be a place found safe for Judge Mervyn Davies. Without his agreement to a restructuring and rescue package, there wouldn't have been a team left to get back to The Valley.

The story chills me because of the seemingly inconsequential, by modern standards, sums of money involved. Either football was run in an absurdly and artificially destitute way for many years, which I can just about believe, or the money sloshing around the modern game is evidence of total financial madness, with many Premiership clubs as huge temples of greed, built on the flimsiest of foundations. There's probably a bit of truth in the first statement, while the second seems to be what I believe is known among the racing fraternity as a 'dead cert'.

When the club was at its lowest ebb, and when oblivion seemed certain, the total debt was said to be, whisper it quietly, 'almost one million pounds'. That'll be a David Beckham hair products ad then, or ten weeks of his salary, or Rio Ferdinand's little finger. Or just about the combined total of performance bonuses that Terry Venables picked up for leaving Crystal Palace and Portsmouth in reasonably similar conditions to the one we suffered.

What would, in today's game, be viewed as a drop in the ocean, was almost enough, less than 20 years ago, to see more than 80 years of footballing heritage and history swept to one side and my club given the 2-asterisk treatment, just underneath Accrington Stanley. Things can't have got that much bigger and better, that quickly – it just isn't possible. I'm sure we were in a terrible mess back then, but I'm equally sure that there's a lot of smoke and mirrors at work now, as slick and insincere men try to convince us of the value of the football 'product'. Financial things just don't grow that big that quickly – or at least, when they do, they tend to end up going pop, rather than deflating gently.

The reason I hark back to these dark old days, despite the fact that they've been recounted previously both by people who were there at the time and who actually understood the financial detail, is because of a throwaway comment made to me while this book was being written. As with all the best throwaway lines, it was much too good to throw away.

'In real life in my proper job I'm involved in management development and organisational development.' It was an admission made by Ben Hayes in a brave, if slightly misguided moment of candour.

> There's a theory about what helps to define the character of an organisation, which talks about 'myths and legends'. You see it in all walks of life, when the senior partner harks back to the days when he worked 25 hours a day and drank for 26 hours every night, and it's gone on for so long, that it's started to be accepted as fact. I think those myths and legends exist around Charlton in much the same way they exist around other businesses.
>
> The whole 'back to The Valley' thing is riddled with legends, and to be honest, as in any other walk of life, after a while, whether they're true or not really ceases to matter too much. It's a bit like Spurs, where the fans still like to talk about how they've got a tradition of playing the Glory Game, when they haven't done that for about the last 40 years. That's the legend they'll always be after though, and they'll want flair players and everything to be done a certain way, and it's almost as if they've convinced themselves that that's the way it was in the very recent past.

It set me thinking about the nature of life at Charlton, how our close encounters with disaster had changed us, and the way in which, as a result, we viewed both our club and our game. Are we really different from other clubs, or have we just managed to hypnotise ourselves, by constant repetition of the same stories to the same, ever-willing audience?

The problem you face in trying to find an answer to the question is: who do you ask? Just about everyone connected with the club makes no bones about the fact that they think we're not just a bit different, but completely unique. Everyone does it for different reasons, but everyone does it, just the same.

The fans think we're unique, because fans always do, or at least, fans always should. Besides, if you're prepared to sing songs about your club being 'by far the greatest team the world has ever seen' every week, then the least you can do is to quietly justify and explain to people the uniqueness of your club. The players will claim one-offness, because, much like the fans, the players always do. From the moment they sign, they start saying the right things, and they carry on saying them until the day they go and get paid a fortune to play for someone else. Then they start saying it about them. That's football.

Managers tend to fall into much the same category as players, or at least they do these days, now that the cult of the manager is fully established and running happily out of control. Have you noticed the way the managers have taken over the game, to the point of owning the clubs outright. It's now Sir Alex Ferguson's Manchester United, Sir Bobby Robson's Newcastle United and insert-name-of latest-bloke-in-the-firing-line's Chelsea. Once upon a time, they just picked the team, now they rule the footballing world.

As for the staff at the club, they choose not to criticise their employers for very similar reasons to the manager, although usually on a smaller scale. Oh, and the marketing staff will tell you everything's splendid anyway, because that's what they're paid to do. Whether it be footwear, foot spray, foot baths or football, they always tell you their version's the best. If they really believe everything they say, they must be the happiest people in the whole world.

It still leaves us with the problem of who to ask about the uniqueness or otherwise of our club. Football inspires and demands passion, rather than cool detachment, thus virtually guaranteeing that all the views expressed are suitably skewed. Sometimes though, even when it's a biased view, being expressed to a biased listener, there's something within it that convinces you that it's the truth.

Glynn Snodin has seen a lot of football in his life, and he's played even more. Now Charlton's reserve-team coach, he logged up more than 600 first-team appearances in an 18-year career which took him from one side of Yorkshire to the other, taking the trip 'down south' when his playing career finally ended. Speaking to Snodin you feel that, while, just like every other coach, he's not going to upset his latest employers, he's seen enough of the game to give you an honest opinion. So, how does the outside world view the club?

They've been getting more respect with each passing year. I think there were people back then, and I can remember those days only too well, who were talking about what a pity it was that such a big club was going out of business, because that was how people of a certain generation viewed it – a big club.

Now though, it's more a case of the next generation looking at the place as a sort of plan, a blueprint for how to do things properly. There's foundations in place, and there's decent people in charge – that's not as common as you might think in football. I've seen some clubs put together on bloody promises and IOUs in my time, and it never ends up happy in the end when it's done that way.

This place got out of a right mess, and decided that, as everything was on the floor around them, they might as well start from the beginning and do things right. The fans have responded to that magnificently, and when the outside world looks at Charlton, they see a club that's been put together very solidly. If the money does drop out of the game, it's not going to be nice for anyone, but there will be a lot of sides getting into bother before this place starts seeing the bailiffs walking up the front path.

It's an interesting and informed viewpoint, but it probably doesn't take our understanding of the situation anywhere it hasn't already reached. We know the finances are good and although it's nice to know that some of the rest of the footballing world looks on at us admiringly, to be honest, it's not that we don't get any praise. It's just that what we do get is still swamped, both by the patronising press we receive and the pats on the head we put up with from other, larger clubs.

When looking to examine whether we are all just living a myth, and when seeking to discover why we prize this club so highly, we need to put our finger on something that nobody else has achieved. Something that makes us unique.

As much as I tried to uncover that one element however, the same explanations and stories kept cropping up. We are, it seems impossible to dispute, a club with a relationship between the board, management, team and fans that doesn't exist anywhere else, or at least not on the same scale. At the end of 2001, a television production company got in touch with the club and asked if we would be interested in taking part in a programme designed to highlight the differences between large and small organisations. It looked likely to be the same old story, as we were lauded as plucky little Charlton, before it became apparent that this was going to be slightly different – we were going to be the big club, the club that had achieved something.

The role of the smaller organisation was filled by Plymouth Argyle, who were enjoying a decent season in the Third Division. As it transpired, their season was set to get considerably better, with a championship title by the end of it, but at the time the programme was made, it's fair to say that they were a combination of hopes, dreams and trepidation. Their chief executive was a retired nuclear submarine commander called David Tall, and I spent a very enjoyable week with him, as we went through the motions of watching him forced to do everything eight or nine times, just to keep the camera crew happy.

A year later, and Charlton were on a pre-season tour to the West Country, allowing me the opportunity to catch up with Tall once again. We get on very well, despite being poles apart on just about every issue you could imagine. His politics branch right, mine left; he's a monarchist, I'm a republican; he devises systems and creates order, I destroy systems and exude an air of chaos. You get the picture.

He had, at the end of the year, decided to step down from his role as chief executive and instead sit on the board as an associate director, which is a far more civilised way of spending his retirement. The sense of order generated by his naval career, however, coupled with his time dealing with the difficulties of lower-league life at Plymouth, allowed him to view Charlton from a particularly well-informed position:

> What's been done at Charlton is amazing, just because it's so straightforward on the face of it, yet obviously so difficult to get right. If it were as easy as they were making it look, there wouldn't be so many clubs getting into trouble these days, and there would be more Charltons in the world.
>
> After the first night of filming, I was given a video with the story of the return to The Valley and some footage of the ground when it was deserted. I had to look twice to make sure it was actually the same site that I'd been walking around all day – the difference was quite staggering.
>
> There's an attention to detail about the way things have been done at the club and that really appeals to me. I can also see the clearest reasons for your success being the nature of the people at the top of the club, from the chairman to the chief executive to the team manager.
>
> There's a continuity there, and a refusal to panic when you've suffered a few stumbles along the way. All businesses and all

football clubs are going to have the odd stumble, but the ones that keep faith with the manager and the systems they put in place are, in my opinion, the ones who will win in the end. For no other reason than they'll spend less time adjusting to constant changes in personnel.

The combined praises of Snodin and Tall, and believe me, they're as odd a couple as you are ever likely to encounter, offer maybe the largest hint to what makes us a bit different. Throughout football, and to the game's shame, it's happening more, rather than less often; the bigger clubs, or at least the more successful clubs, are turning their backs on the smaller ones.

They don't seem to be trying to hide it either, but just muttering into their current accounts about market forces, supply and demand and other such non-sporting factors. The ITV Digital collapse and the shameful backtracking of Carlton and Granada could have seen swift and decisive action taken by the Premiership clubs. They had seen their little brothers having their dinner money stolen, and they were perfectly placed to step in and confront the bullies, but instead of behaving as they should, they mumbled something placatory and let the mugging continue.

Against this background, it's maybe surprising that any lower-league clubs want to have anything to do with the Premiership. Unless they are one of the lucky, bankrolled few, with a realistic chance of making it up to the top flight, the Premiership is simply a land of plenty, doing all it can to make sure its leftovers don't drop down to the benefit of the hungry living below.

Many Premiership clubs, of course, are seen in precisely this manner. They stand detached from the outside world and unwilling to consider the plight of anyone making their way through the footballing jungle with less success than themselves. At Charlton, and I fully accept that there's a vast element of bias about this, we're seen slightly differently. The proximity of our recent financial chaos, and the nature of our escape route back to prosperity and relative health, mean that we are not seen as having forgotten what it's like to stare bankruptcy in the face.

Many of the names associated with that period in our history can still be seen around the ground, and they, in turn, invited most of the current board to come and join them. David Tall would have been forgiven for getting thoroughly fed up with Charlton during his time there. Unless the club is being very careful indeed, it would be horribly easy for us to appear like the smug little old man so perfectly depicted by Harry

Enfield, constantly popping up on the other side of the fence, cheerily intoning that 'You don't want to do it like that . . .'

As it transpired, he didn't view us quite like that:

> It's not just the fact that you've had a troubled history, or really that you've learned from it, but more that you haven't forgotten it. I can see that you've got one eye fixed firmly on the future, but I can also see how well you make sure that everyone remembers the past. If you want to make progress, keeping your feet on the ground is very important, because it gives you something to push off from.
>
> There's nobody I've met around here who hasn't got their feet on the ground, and that's the one thing I think I'd take away with me – apart from the squad, the stadium and the 20,000 season ticket holders, of course!

I pondered this response, and the reflections of others, as I looked back on Hayes' 'myths and legends' theory, before trudging to an uncertain conclusion. Of course we're guilty of some of the things he observes, but, then again, which club isn't? Part of what we are as a club, or at least part of what we think we are, is doubtless the result of such a process. We view things in the past with rose-tinted spectacles, we rely on romantic recollection to dull the painful memories, and we think we're unique in the same way that every set of first-time parents thinks that their little infant is unique.

What makes us different is that we get these thoughts echoed back at us from a variety of different sources, whether it's lines dropped in to football commentaries, or glowing references inserted in the occasional newspaper feature. The rest of the world agrees that we've come a long way and we've made the journey by doing things properly, carefully and decently.

We've retained an eye for self-criticism, which is far stricter and harsher than the one the outside world keeps on us, and while it's occasionally a destructive process, it almost certainly remains the reason why, as Tall pointed out, our feet stay so firmly on the ground. It's not always been easy to be a Charlton fan, and we'd braced ourselves against disappointment and prepared for failure for such a long time that when success finally arrived, our history of heartbreak proved to be a fairly good way of not getting carried away with it.

It's strange to think that we take our good press for granted when it's something that dozens of other clubs – and certainly most other

Premiership clubs – would gladly pay for. After all, they've shown every sign of gladly paying for everything else you can think of. Many of them get bigger, more frequent headlines than Charlton and their television appearances are far lengthier, but it arrives at a price, and the price is criticism.

We don't get criticised all that much and although this might be because we're generally too busy getting patted on the head to be slapped in the face, I suspect that after such a long period of media acceptance, the shock of fierce and intrusive criticism would hurt. Indeed, one of the myths that remains to this day is that we get a terrible press. As fans, we tend to be obsessed with the fact and the mildest of dismissive statements directed towards us produces a wholly inappropriate level of indignation.

With a ground capacity that puts us firmly in the lower quarter of the Premiership and with away support that has been as impassioned, but never as large, as at some other clubs, we remain, by Premiership standards, and for the time being, 'little' Charlton – at least in as much as the media defines 'little'. Although, as Alan Curbishley reflected last year, 'Maybe we're not quite so little any more?'

In reality, though, and taking on board all the myths, legends, fishermen's tales and shaggy-dog stories that seem to go along with supporting a football team, I think I can live with being called 'little' Charlton for the time being. Compared to 'bankrupt' Charlton, 'skint' Charlton, 'have-to-sell-half-their-squad' Charlton and 'in-danger-of-losing-their-ground' Charlton, it's not so bad. Many of the sides considered 'big' look likely to face demoralising and demeaning downsizing exercises over the next couple of years, as they are faced with the prospect of trying to repay vast debts.

We may not be going into debt to get to where the 'big' clubs are now, but through the process of balancing their books, they might end up returning to our level a lot more swiftly than they planned. On balance, I'd rather meet going up, then going down. I think Hayes was right: a lot of the folk tales surrounding a football club are exaggerated, but I also think that they're largely based in truth, and just blown up for the sake of being more entertaining when told over a few pints. The problem is, that when you look at the bald statistics and the bare facts, ours look like they've already been blown out of all proportion.

When you've got a recent history like Charlton Athletic, you don't need to create far-fetched stories, there's no need to over-egg the pudding or gild the lily. At The Valley, our truth is stranger than everyone else's fiction.

7

'MANY GAMES HAVE I SEEN'

On Saturday, 10 August 2002, Wimbledon Football Club opened their First Division season with a game against Gillingham at Selhurst Park. Just over 2,000 people were reported to have turned up to watch the game and many of the occupants of the press box openly expressed their amazement at the attendance, suggesting that the true figure might be about half that number. This was no ordinary opening-day crowd, but the circumstances surrounding Wimbledon were equally odd. A rival, non-league side, also bearing the Wimbledon name, had been formed and was attracting far larger gates than the supposedly larger and 'original' side.

Wimbledon sold slightly less than 100 season tickets for the 2002–03 season and are seeming to wither away before our gaze. Their chairman, Charles Koppel, had announced his intention to take the club to Milton Keynes, either unaware or unconcerned (or both) that there could possibly be any reason to leave a side called Wimbledon playing anywhere near the place of their name. The arguments against are obvious and compelling to any football fan, and are only marginally complicated by the fact that Wimbledon Football Club already play away from home every week, as they are forced to share a ground with Crystal Palace. Indeed, that alone is likely to evoke gasps of sympathy from most Charlton fans.

The leap from Wimbledon to Selhurst Park is not an unimaginable one, though, and the fans could still make the journey with a modicum of inconvenience. To up sticks and move almost a hundred miles to

Milton Keynes is plainly to surrender all rights and to express no further desire to actually be Wimbledon Football Club. Will they continue to play under the name of Wimbledon FC once Koppel has had his new office carpeted and they've settled in at their new home? If the name does change, to better reflect their location, will a new club have been born, operating far beyond the starting position for other new clubs? Can it be right to purchase a footballing identity and with it the favourable league position to which your acquisition would appear to entitle you?

Koppel was entering the world of the footballing franchise and was receiving the sort of media attention that makes the average football club chairman – and he is certainly no better than an average football club chairman – wince. As he has shown, he doesn't appear to care about the fans – proper football fans, who remember the game when it wasn't a craze, fans who made up their minds about the merits of the game without the assistance of someone from an advertising agency hurling gleaming new television campaigns at them.

He may yet carve himself the place in football history he plainly desires so badly, with his plans to, temporarily at least, retain Wimbledon's name, yet change its home. Aware that the current location of the club, sharing Selhurst Park, is seeing it lose money, he wants to uproot the whole venture and give it a new home. On the face of it, there's nothing wrong with that – it's little more than Charlton did in the early 1990s surely?

The difference, of course, is as vast as could be imagined, and underpins the entire debate. When Charlton left Selhurst Park, they moved under the momentum of the combined might of fans and directors. They also, and this is the crucial and obvious point, righted a wrong, and went home. They didn't sneak off to a location of convenience, but they looked at their history, pondered their name and went to where it demanded. Koppel seeks to move Wimbledon with no mandate from the fans, plainly precious little support, and to a destination determined by convenience, not conviction.

To start a new side in Milton Keynes, the concrete-cast suburb where he wants to build a new stadium, would require the inconvenience of starting at the bottom and working up, just like every other new team has had to do. Koppel, who appears to be unable to differentiate between the moral responsibilities of running a football club and a fast-food franchise, can't be doing with that sort of inconvenience. Like a man who loves his house but hates the location, he wants to pick things up brick by brick and put them down again where he wants – and he wonders why his approach is generating a degree of protest.

It is the first step down the road to a franchise system being launched, and brings no credit to anyone involved. Koppel maybe couldn't be expected to understand the offence and upset he was causing, as the occasions where finance and sympathy for the beautiful game run smoothly, hand-in-hand through the fields, are few and far between. The Football Association has adopted its finest head-in-the-sand position, aided and abetted by a chief executive who shows a fondness for the camera in times of triumph and a crippling shyness in adversity. He may treat those two impostors the same, but he only opts to have one of those meetings publicised.

Carrying the name of Wimbledon Football Club like a passport of convenience, Koppel will take his acquisition to a new home, and try, for a while at least, to persuade people that the club is the same entity as when they lived back in south London. Obviously, even then Wimbledon didn't have a home of their own, but having seen Plough Lane fall into disrepair, Selhurst Park was at least vaguely in the same part of the world. Milton Keynes represents the breaking of the link, almost certainly to a terminal extent, and an attempt to persuade the supporters that they are the ones being unreasonable.

I make the point not just to attempt to expose the gaping holes in Koppel's logic, although God knows he deserves it, but because the situation highlights the two most important things about football clubs: fans and grounds. The papers may sometimes have you believe that the truly essential components of the game are the chairmen, the agents or the players, probably in that order, but the true order of importance tends to become clear only in times of crisis.

At Wimbledon things have gone too far. The fans have broken away and formed their own side – AFC Wimbledon – which currently attracts support in far greater numbers than the former 'parent club' currently manages. You can almost see them appearing on one of those ghastly mid-morning coffee and trauma television shows – 'My parents deserted me, but I'm doing fine on my own.'

It doesn't have to be like that, though, and much as people may disagree, there have been examples of the board and fans working together to sort out a solution to a seemingly impossible problem. I bet you can't work out which club gets mentioned next?

Football clubs, as we have already established, are about fans. Everything relies on them, and if they hold their nerve, and retain their self-belief, they hold the collective power of veto over practically anything the board of directors choose to do. As Charlton has witnessed over the years, they can achieve just about anything they want when they get sufficiently riled and agitated.

They also find themselves routinely ignored, insulted, taken for granted and defrauded by many of the clubs they choose to follow. There may be hobbies which see more scorn directed at the paying customer from the proprietors of one's heroes, but few that you'd be happy boasting about publicly. For years, fans have been crammed into conditions that would cause protests from the animal-rights lobby and should have seen greater intervention from civil-rights groups.

Football fans are a club's greatest asset and yet have historically been treated as their greatest liability. Principally this is because the fans that bring shame and disgrace to their clubs and themselves will always attract bigger headlines than the ones who campaign quietly and determinedly, accepting that not everyone is going to agree with them. Indeed, the hooligans appear to relish the publicity. When you used to see England fans gathering abroad, preparing to turn a quiet market square into a battlefield, you could almost sense them waiting for the moment when the cameras arrived, in order that none of their thuggery would be missed by their loved ones at home.

For years, this has allowed clubs to operate a kind of double standard, advertising one sort of match-day experience, and offering something quite different. The slick brochures would have you believe that it's a world of happy, smiling families, sitting in comfortable seats, enjoying the thrills and spills of the afternoon, while engaging in some friendly banter with the opposition.

The reality, in my experience, is a little different. To enter some Premiership grounds, and many more in the Nationwide league, is to experience a siege mentality of the highest order. The legroom is non-existent, the toilets have been stripped of extraneous fittings to the point where they look like Hannibal Lector's cell, and every move you make is tailed by closed-circuit cameras that make Big Brother look like a distinctly uninterested babysitter.

In the circumstances, it's odd that there's any affection left whatsoever for actually going to watch the game – if you're a visiting fan in particular, an open prison is a kibbutz compared with a football ground. Swindle a few million out of a pension fund, or tell a load of lies and win a crooked libel action, and you'll get a room to yourself, a gym and all the fresh air you can gulp down. Do nothing wrong, but pay thirty pounds to watch your football team, and you'll be treated like a bank robber, scrutinised, searched and herded up with other equally innocent people, all enjoying their afternoon of being treated like convicts.

Amazingly enough, it doesn't appear to be the nature of the facilities that causes the most offence, but the reasoning behind the treatment. At Charlton, especially just after our return to The Valley, things were not always comfortable – scaffolding boards do not create the most welcoming of stadiums. What was different, though, was that the fans rarely, if ever, felt that they were being fleeced. In any event, if they looked over to the middle of the main stand, the directors were sitting there, in exactly the same conditions. It's hard to get upset at perceived inequalities when the board is bouncing up and down on the same boards as you.

Just to complete the 'one big, happy family' image, one of the fans was sitting with the board, voted on as a 'VIP director', and there to observe and participate in the way things were being done. Nobody else in the Premiership does this, and it seems increasingly unlikely that anyone else will. The history of the relationship between club and fans is, admittedly, forged from more traumatic circumstances than most will have to experience, but it remains strong to this day.

This is perhaps the only club where, in order to explain the nature of the link, you could start with the club chairman and not be pilloried by the fans, for a shocking display of fawning and grovelling, but that's the way it is. Martin Simons sums it up neatly and succinctly:

> Any director will always say that their club is unique, but I think we are, because the board go back to a time when we weren't even at The Valley. When you've lost your ground and fought that fight, what with political parties and all that, to get back to the ground, it makes the fans feel like part of the club. The directors felt part of it as well, but it couldn't have happened without the fans.
>
> What the fans did was unique. Nobody has ever got round to forming a political party, on the sole issue of getting planning permission in order to get their club back to its home. But, they did, and as a result of what they did, there's never been an 'us and them' situation. We've only ever been holding the club alongside and along with the fans.

Switching from the club chairman to the plc chairman sees no break in the continuity of the story. When Richard Murray stands at The Valley now, he looks back on a football triumph that could so easily have not happened. When he explains his feelings, however, he does so tempered with the sort of cautious determination that makes it abundantly clear just why it succeeded so spectacularly.

I became a director of the club in 1991 and chairman of the group in 1995, and I have to say that for the whole of the '90s, our ambition was to reach the Premiership and to try and establish ourselves there. This is my tenth anniversary now, and I'm looking back and thinking to myself, 'Yeah, I think we've done it.' I think everyone knows how much of a team effort it's been, though.

We fill our ground each week, but we've still got to be careful. The really important thing for us is our fans. They've got to have realistic aspirations for our club, as the fans on the board do, and that [aspiration] is, and certainly will be for the foreseeable future, that we just want to play in the Premiership and everything else is a bit of a bonus. That's not a lack of ambition – that's being financially sensible and making sure that we don't do anything to undo all the good work which has made this club become what it has been over the last decade.

It's an approach that is appreciated by all Charlton fans, and one that stands up to the deepest and most intense scrutiny. Ben Hayes recalls his experiences in being involved in the formation of a branch of the supporters' club, and how his subsequent experiences have failed to dent his belief that the club really does have a special relationship with its fans:

The branch was set up in 1994. We just wanted to set up a Bromley branch and I ended up being asked to be social secretary or something similarly vague. In terms of running the branch, I took a year out when my son, Joe, was born, but other than that, I've been in charge of getting things sorted out there for a while now.

Hayes has evidently had cause to meet fans of other teams along the way, discovering first-hand evidence that there is a different relationship between the fans and board than that which exists elsewhere. To the eternal delight of Charlton fans, it could only really be one club that provided the contrast.

I knew a few people who were involved with the Crystal Palace Supporters' Trust when they were going through their problems, and without getting too smug about it, things were different there. They couldn't get Simon Jordan to offer them a place on the board, despite the fact that they'd showed their commitment by raising a million pounds. I can't imagine Richard Murray doing something like that.

Other supporters are always amazed that players and officials just turn up at these branch meetings and they can sit there and listen to them speak, ask them a question, and generally be in fairly close contact with them in a very relaxed and informal atmosphere.

The informal atmosphere, it would appear, leads to the occasional surprising encounter:

> I remember writing to the club in the early days and asking for a few players to come down to a meeting. A few days later I got a call from someone who asked if they were speaking to Mr Hayes. I was just about to get stuck in, thinking it was a double-glazing salesman, when he introduced himself as John Robinson, and suddenly it all became clear. We had to clear that one up a bit, I wouldn't have been too happy with Charlton players calling me 'Mr Hayes'. It makes me sound a little bit self-important. It was very relaxed though, simply a case of sending them a map and they'd turn up quite happily.

Perhaps he should have told Robinson he was a linesman. That would have soon seen to the 'Mr Hayes' problem. His experiences, though, are overwhelmingly positive, when, given the hours of work which go in to running a supporters' club branch, the opportunities to get annoyed and irritable at the slightest thing must be endless.

Ian Cartwright can testify to that. Having been a former secretary of the supporters' club and now working as club development officer, he has seen the club from both sides, as fan and employee. In fact, your perception of him probably discloses how long you've been following the club.

To some, he is the man trying to sell you a season ticket for the north stand. To others, he'll always be the eternally cheerful, permanently busy bloke with the train tickets, smiling and bounding around, while attempting to shepherd several hundred fans onto an Inter City 125, at the same time as musing about the chances of an away win, the state of the opposition's ground, and a decent pint of Guinness at the other end.

> There's people come through into this club now, and they don't

have any idea that I used to work for the supporters' club, and what I used to do there. I can remember sitting on Euston Station at 3 a.m., just so that people could get the first train out to an away game and be safely tucked up in the pub at the other end at opening time. It wasn't always the greatest job in the world and the stress of it used to get to me every now and again, but that's life.

I don't get too upset with the fact that there are people who don't know about that, though, principally because I never did it so that everyone would know me anyway. That wasn't my motivation and I don't get upset if they don't. The other reason is that without the newcomers who have come along, we wouldn't have Premiership football, because they help to finance it. They're the reason we needed a bigger ground and that attracts new players; and so the cycle continues.

Cartwright knows Charlton fans as well as anyone – he was, and still is, as fanatical as any of them, and now he makes his living studying them, understanding them, and explaining to various senior figures exactly why some of their ideas will end in triumph. More importantly, he'll also try to explain why some will end in disaster. There are only a couple of people who have travelled the route Cartwright has followed, through the ranks of the supporters' club to the club itself, and they are better qualified to explain the dynamics of the Charlton fan-base than anyone else.

I think we've got about 16,000 hardcore supporters, who will renew their season tickets no matter what because they've been bitten by the bug. Within the other 4,000, that's where the effort goes in, because they might well just decide not to bother this year and walk away.

The figures talk for themselves. Clive Mendonca made his debut for us in front of 10,000 fans, probably about 8,500 of them Charlton ones. At the end of that season, we took 35,000 fans to Wembley for the play-off final, so it doesn't take a rocket scientist to work out how much of a floating support there was out there.

As with every other facet of the club, the desire not to take anything for granted seems to underpin anything else:

There was a time when we could just look at south-east London and there was nothing else for kids to do, so they ended up drifting along to football. These days, we've got to be realistic and professional about it, if you like, and accept that there are loads of other things that they could be doing. It all comes down to this central idea that you don't, as a football club, have a divine right to expect people to come through your turnstiles, and there's a lot of clubs learning that the hard way. We sensed it was going to start to move in that direction and we've tried to plan for it and make sure that we keep one step ahead of the situation.

Things have changed with the game as well. When I started travelling to away games, the cost of travel was more than the cost of the entrance to the ground – that's reversed now. You also used to stroll around the place and know everyone – at least to nod to. Now it's a different experience completely, and that's because of progress, which is something to be welcomed, rather than shied away from.

Tony Evans is someone who would agree that things have changed, and also that the changes should be welcomed with open arms. A Charlton fan for almost half a century, he accepts with a self-depreciating air that he still approaches the game with a combination of dread and delight. Years of depression surrounding the club have left their mark, no matter how hard he tries to convince himself that the threat of extinction has been eradicated. As he looks at the past, and ponders the future, his habit of smiling and shaking his head tells you a lot about what fans of his age have had to deal with and how they've almost had to battle to come to terms with success:

You tend to look back on those days with rose-tinted glasses. You couldn't even conceive of being in the Nationwide these days, especially after seeing the Premiership, so I suppose that the club has to do everything it can to make sure that it can pay the wages to keep hold of the players that will keep them in the Premiership.

I know it's maybe not the way I'm supposed to look at things, but I can't relax until we've got to 40 points and we're past the figure where we all know it's virtually impossible to get relegated. That's not a lack of faith in the side, or a pessimistic streak, but I think there's a lot of people who approach the season in much the same way – at all clubs, not just Charlton.

Evans also retains the authentically Charlton approach to the question of where the money in football is going, and whether the whole thing is sustainable:

> I'd like to think that it can't carry on forever – that the big clubs can't just carry on running up bigger and bigger debts and ignoring the reality of the situation. If that comes to an end, then maybe we have a chance of playing on a level playing field, but I can't see it happening. Maybe I just think that everything's always conspiring against us!

Maybe he does, and maybe they are, but he's not alone in his view. Cartwright offers an alternative version, though, and it's one that possibly holds more weight with each passing day:

> I think we're well liked in football and I think people think we deserve what we've got. There's also the element of being the underdog and it's a very British thing to stick up for the underdog and want them to do well. Also, because I think we've conducted ourselves well having become successful, there aren't too many people who think we've got above ourselves, and we're not seen as preaching to people about how well we've done and how we're a bit of a blueprint for other clubs. Probably because we've been too busy just getting on with things and making them work for us.

Now it's possible, and I'd go so far as to say probable, that they're both right in slightly different ways. I've always thought that the outside world does hold a bit of a soft spot for us, but at the same time it patronises us, because it still sees us, despite the results and the progress, as no real threat. So there you have it, one of us thinks we're picked on, while the other thinks we're well liked and the author's simply paranoid that they're all being nasty about us behind our backs. And we wonder why nobody understands football fans?

To get a true perspective of the last decade, though, it seems you have to rely on people who have seen what went before and who can understand the extent of the journey which left us where we are now. Colin Cameron understands especially well, having followed the club for longer than most. He's also followed Charlton at closer quarters – and certainly with a keener eye for detail – than anyone else:

All of those battles have almost been obscured with time, but I always think that the expectation level of a lot of the newer supporters isn't realistic. They've got to remember that it's only 20 years ago when we nearly went out of business. At that time, I never thought that Charlton would get promoted to the top division. They were just a sterile club, and there wasn't the desire or the planning to get them back there – it was just impossible.

The last ten years have been the happiest I've ever known at Charlton and I've been a fan for 56 years. My favourite players might tend to come from back in the bleak old days, but in all honesty, there's never been anything, not during the time that I've been following the club anyway, to compare with this. The stability of the club, the way it's been done here, all gives me so much pride and pleasure, because I know it will all get better still, or at least the potential is there and the foundations are in place which will enable it to get bigger.

Cameron is also quick to point out not only where he believes the credit should go and where the fair share of the blame belongs. The players may be the ones who claim the goals and the glory, but the men behind the scenes and especially those in the boardroom, also play a vital role. After years of scrutiny, Cameron is well placed to make the conclusions he does:

Don't get me wrong, I don't think that we had crooks on the board, but we had amateurs – people who succeeded in other businesses and then came into football for a little bit of an ego trip. They just weren't equipped to make the thing work any better than the average man in the street, because football was a totally different business to the one they were in.

When I look around me now, this is a professional organisation from top to bottom. I honestly think these days, and people might think that I'm mad, but it's more important for us to keep hold of people like Richard Murray, Peter Varney and Alan Curbishley than it is for us to keep hold of a star striker, or a favourite player. The players, if we're all being businesslike about it, are replaceable, but the management structure that's been put into place here – that's like a framework that holds the whole thing together. It's vital that it stays in place, because it made sure we got where we have, and it will make sure that we're in a position to take the next step forwards.

It seems to be the combination of watching it all slowly unravel and the chaotic attempts to put the club back on its feet again in the 1970s and '80s that really got to him. As deeply in love with Charlton as he is, it's hard not to hear a frustration almost bordering on anger when he talks about the 'dark days':

> I go back to 1946 and, to be honest, back then I took a lot of things for granted. We were in the First Division and I just assumed that we were always going to be in the First Division, and everything was always going to be fine. It wasn't that I thought we had a divine right to stay there, but I just didn't question that it was ever going to be any other way.
>
> We spent ages just about scraping through and making do, and we were always in the bottom half of the table. There were years like that, and there was some heroics and some amazing escapes, and somehow we never actually took the plunge downwards that seemed inevitable, but it was no sort of basis for progress. We just hoped that each year someone would come along and save our bacon and then we could have the summer off and do the whole thing all over again the next year.
>
> It's important to realise the state of mind of the average Charlton fan at the time, because if they hadn't [abandoned us] already, they were right on the brink of giving up. Things were just getting no better, and there wasn't any reason to believe that they ever were [going to improve]. It wasn't so much the fact that things were so bad that got you down to be honest, but the fact that there just wasn't any light at the end of the tunnel. There wasn't any ambition, and there wasn't any drive about the place.
>
> If you look at how they perform now, it's a team effort, all the way through. We've had a couple of very good players dotted around the place and we've had a lot more who were very shrewdly purchased, but basically it's a testimony to what you can do if you're all pulling in the same direction. That's not something you necessarily see all that often in the Premiership these days, and that's what makes me proud to be a fan here at the moment.

Speaking to Cameron was fascinating, not least because for Charlton fans of a certain age, he has become known largely as the man who does the statistics and his opinions are not sought nearly as often as they might be. He has a column in the programme, but naturally and reasonably enough, it's largely statistical and offers him little opportunity to express, or at least to expand upon, his thoughts on the game. Given a few hours and the opportunity to fully explain his opinions, Cameron proved to be as fascinating as anyone I spoke to in my search for the heart of the club. As with Tony Evans, though, the scars of what happened plainly run deep:

> When Richard Murray and co. took over, I have to be perfectly honest, my first thought was 'What's in it for them?' because we had such a history of opportunistic chairmen and boards. They all had these great plans that always ended up crumbling to nothing, but I'm delighted to say that my fears were totally unfounded. That's their real achievement, on one view. Not just what they've done to the ground, but what they've done to the perception of the fans about the nature of the people who run our club, because they've given everyone their faith back again, and that was no easy task.
>
> It took me about a year, maybe two, to say these are good people, they care about the club. The people in the past cared, but they had no idea how to run things at a football club, and, most importantly, they were part time and they couldn't spend the time they needed to make it work.

His memory of those 'people in the past' is razor sharp, but his interpretation of some of their actions is characteristically generous. When he was spending more time at his typewriter and less at his calculator, Cameron's eye for detail was obviously not a welcome presence, particularly when the finances were less than healthy. If you were trying to paint a rosy picture of proceedings for a group of fans back in those days, in an age when much of the financing of football was kept under a veil of secrecy, Cameron was probably the last person you needed. His constant quizzing might have been of great service to the fans, but it was not appreciated by the powers that be.

> I got banned from the social club down here for ten years at one stage, because I questioned things and I criticised and they didn't like it. They said it was to do with the breaking up of a fight, but nobody believed that – it was because I wanted to know the truth about things. I've said a number of times that it seemed a bit rich that I got a longer sentence than most murderers just for making a few observations about a football club.

They 'catted' my little phone box at the back of the stand, where I used to go and put over my copy at the end of the game. I went in there one afternoon, and there was the carcass of a dead cat in there. Looking back, they probably included it in the attendance as well.

But seriously, it's worth remembering, when people want to have a bit of a go at the current system, and when they say that it's resistant to criticism and other opinions, that compared to the things that used to go on, it's better than you can possibly imagine.

You can trust the board now and that's something that I couldn't have always said down here. They're professionals and they run it in a professional manner, but they've got the same interests as every Charlton supporter at heart, because they are Charlton supporters themselves.

His interpretation of the development of the club is supported by Ben Hayes, who has watched the latter part of the period in question from a slightly different viewpoint, yet come to a strikingly similar conclusion:

There is a lot of harking back goes on, but not all of it in a positive way. Because it's now on video though, you can actually check back and show that a lot of it is nonsense. I know you get people talking about how it was better when there was only 3,000 people and we were away at Huddersfield or wherever, but once you've looked back at some of the players, you realise that they're mis-remembering it.

Because I've got a young son, he wants to watch some of the videos with me and learn about the team, and I've watched a few of the tapes of seasons gone by. I remember thinking at the time that we had one or two players who weren't quite up to it, but the truth is we had loads of players who weren't quite up to it and a couple who were just terrible.

There are a lot of the players who played for this club as recently as six or seven years ago, and they wouldn't get within a million miles of the current squad. I also think that the youth system still seems to be working, but we see fewer of its products now. I know we had a reputation for not being afraid of putting youngsters in, but to be honest that was simply making a virtue out of a necessity, because we didn't have the money to go into the transfer market.

It's maybe not something that many of us think about all that often, but the truth is that it's a lot easier to support Charlton these days, especially compared to years gone by. My nephew had a birthday party a couple of weeks ago and the magician who was providing the entertainment was asking the kids what they wanted to be when they grew up. About half of them said that they wanted to play for Charlton and I was struck by the turnabout.

When I was at school, I was the only Charlton fan and, given the way things were going, it wasn't something to boast about, because it didn't impress anyone all that much. Now there's loads of kids wanting to boast about supporting the club and the number of shirts and car stickers you see dotted around the place is out of all proportion to what it was when I was growing up.

Not everyone, as is immediately obvious, has been coming down to The Valley for as long as Hayes, Cartwright and Cameron however, and in the interests of getting a balanced picture, it seemed logical to talk to someone who had arrived rather more recently. Mike Wad has seen the very tail end of the bad times and arrived at the club with the green shoots of recovery already starting to break through. A casual Northampton Town fan by birth, he lives in London and decided to see what it was like at Charlton:

The thing that's attracted me to it is that it doesn't have the feeling of a big, faceless corporate club, or at least it didn't when I first started coming down here about six years ago. That's changed a bit now, and there's a lot more commercialisation, with the club trying to kid the fans that it's still the same as it ever was, but it's not as bad as lots of places.

If you have a look around other clubs, like Coventry and Forest and QPR, and you look at what's happened to them since they got relegated, it just reinforces why it's so important to stay up. If we slip away now, there's no guarantee that we'll ever get back again because of the way it's gone.

As I say, I got a season ticket down here for the first time six years ago, and I've seen an amazing turnaround. They were still running out of Portakabins when I first started coming down to The Valley and now you only have to have a look around the place to see what's happened. It doesn't matter to me that I haven't got the dozens of years as a supporter under my belt, because I can see a huge improvement during the time I've been coming here. Some people might say I'm a Johnny-come-lately, or that I've jumped on the bandwagon, but that's their opinion. Anyway, it still didn't feel like that much of a bandwagon when I first got on it.

His point about it not being the same as it always was is an interesting one and possibly arises as a result of not having seen things when they were at their worst. He's certainly not one of the most recent arrivals, though, and it's interesting to see how he echoes many of the points made by people who have been following the club far longer than him. Maybe the idea that we're a 'little family club' is unsustainable in the Premiership of 2002, but that shouldn't mean that we don't still remember what it was like when we were.

I don't think people have forgotten, actually, but I think we've just got more pragmatic about the business of running a football club. Once upon a time we were dreamers, dreaming our way to extinction. Now we study the past to learn lessons for the future. It used to be considered perfectly reasonable to send children up chimneys, but I'm not sure that anyone's suggesting that we've lost touch with our roots because we've dispensed with the practice.

Alan Honey is a contemporary, give or take a few years, of Cameron's. A familiar duo at the ground, they have, between them, seen more of the fall and rise of Charlton Athletic than almost anyone else. To sit them down together over a few pints, and invite them to offer their opinions of life at The Valley over the last ten years, is to invite a sudden price hike in the shares of cassette-tape manufacturers. They churn out stories about every conceivable angle of the club, and recall things that have long since passed into the flotsam of history.

The records show, however, that when they criticise someone now, they are doing exactly as they were back then. Saying one thing to someone's face, and another behind that person's back, is not a trait with which they identify. Honey's recollections of the recovery of the club are, as with Cameron's, based on understanding the full extent of Charlton's slide into obscurity, a point he makes with characteristic good humour:

They were desperate times we went through then. Hulyer was involved in the commodities market, and there was one occasion when there was this bloody boat laden down with rubber and it was supposed to be arriving in a port in some far-flung place. The money came through, so we were told, when the boat landed, and we didn't have any other source of income. For a while Charlton's salvation depended on this boat making it safely to port, which made life a bit interesting for a while. We all prayed there weren't any big storms. Bouncing cheques and rubber boats – that's what they'll call it when they make the film!

It's easy to forget how bleak it got. When we had to postpone the game against Blackburn because we were waiting to see if we were going to get wound up or not, they tried to charge us for the cost of the pies that they'd bought for the game and then had to throw away! Talk about kicking you when you're down . . .

Michael Gliksten went on record as saying that his major source of pride was that we always managed to pay the milkman. We were going out of business with debts all over the place, but the chairman said not to worry because we'd always managed to pay the milkman – and people wondered why we worried?

Now we've got players like Jorge Costa coming over here and that's raised the profile of the club, both here and abroad, and it's all part of that process that raises our profile. When Allan Simonsen turned up, he was the best player by a mile, and it was almost embarrassing at times – when Costa got here, he fitted in, and wasn't always the best player. That's how far we've come in the last 20 years or so.

Reassuringly enough, though, and just when you think he's recovered from the upset of all those years of chaos and disappointment, he leaves you with one last blast, just to remind you of the frustrations of that time:

Back in the dark old days, it wasn't just that we were mediocre, but that we celebrated being mediocre for so bloody long. It was as if the people who ran the club didn't believe we could ever do anything all that special. Well, if they didn't, then why should anyone else think we could? Now, we believe that just about anything is possible, but only if you prepare for it properly. Trying to do it with no foundations and no preparation is just asking to fall flat on your face, but not trying to prepare to do it is accepting that it's beyond you. That's something we used to do here and it drove me up the wall. It doesn't happen any more.

I've been coming down here for donkey's years, so there's nobody going to suggest that I've jumped on a bandwagon. Well, they might, but it would be a pretty daft suggestion – it wasn't a bandwagon that was going anywhere very quickly!

Thankfully, it doesn't. Foundations have been set down at The Valley for the last few years, which should support the club long into the future and ensure that the dark days of the past are not revisited. With a group of fans who have achieved the amount they have, and with the price they had to pay over the last two decades, it's hard not to conclude that it's just about all we deserve.

Ironically enough, in a chapter dedicated to the fans, and to their perception and opinion of the club, it's worth ending with the views of the players on the fans. John Robinson and Steve Brown have been there through it all and are uniquely placed to tell the story from the perspective of the players. During the course of the preparation of this book, someone said to me, in slightly exasperated tones: 'Nobody wants to know what Steve Brown and John bloody Robinson think about things.' With respect, I think they do. They might not be household names outside of SE7, but to Charlton fans they represent something very important. Anyway, as Robinson proves, they say all the right things:

> When he signed me, Curbs said, fans like that will be around for a lot longer than the two of us will ever be. That's the first sign that the club is going in the right direction. Having a good relationship with them [the fans] is a big part of my game. There isn't another set of supporters like this in the country, so I'd never want to play anywhere else.

Brown, of course, hasn't played anywhere else. If it was bad for us, just having to wait and wonder what was going to happen to our team, wondering if we'd ever get home, how much worse was it for him?

As a 19 year old, recovering from a cruciate-ligament operation, the future of his career looked as tenuous as the future of his club. About 20 footballers were on the brink of having to go out and look for a new club. He was one of them, and he could hardly walk, let alone kick a ball or make a tackle. It's no wonder he always looks so laid-back now – he used up just about all the nervous tension he had before he turned 20. He's honest enough to admit that it wasn't always comfortable back then though. If he ever wore the rose-tinted spectacles, he took them off a long time ago, and they haven't gone back on since.

> Back during the bad old days, you could have told me what was

going to happen here, and I would have just laughed because there was no way that I could see that it would even have been possible. At that stage, I'd be lying if I said that I never thought that there might not even be a future because there were a lot of times when it looked really more likely than not that we just weren't going to be around anymore. When things have got like that, you don't start to hope what might happen in the future, you just hope there's going to be one.

I think the play-off final, and winning that, with all the extra revenue it brought in, started a bit of a snowball rolling and we've managed to keep that momentum going with a push here and a push there, and grow into a really successful club. Obviously there's the right people in the club from the chairman down and it's starting to pay real dividends now, but that's not come without a hell of a lot of hard work from a lot of different people.

It was a 'hell of a lot of hard work', and it did come from a lot of people. It was also being cheered on by an ever-growing band of supporters, who felt an affinity with their club possibly not matched anywhere else. If it really was destined to follow a Hollywood movie script, and it seemed to have done for most of the last five or six years, it needed a big emotional set-piece ending.

Not for the first time, Charlton didn't disappoint. What was to follow was just about the perfect antidote to 'being mediocre for so bloody long'. It didn't involve going to Milton Keynes, either.

8

JUST ANOTHER MONDAY AFTERNOON

Whisper it quietly, lest the Sportswriters Association hears you and puts out a contract, but some games really can't be all that difficult to report on. That's not to say that anyone can do it, because the best will still do even the most mundane of games better than everyone else, but sometimes it just doesn't seem all that hard.

Dour draws, when papers only want a couple of hundred words and the managers are kind enough to spew out line after line of quotable, good-humoured nonsense, could surely be done, on most of the available evidence, without even going to the game. As long as you get the names of the goalscorers and the quotes from the manager, putting the whole lot together can hardly be a Joycean feat.

For a start, as we've already been shown, you won't have to even mention Charlton, and even if you've got one of those little 'factfile' boxes to fill out by the side of the report, you can try and be really clever. You could focus on something like David Beckham signing his new contract before the game and make it the 'key moment' of the afternoon. All right, so it's a tired old gag, and it screams at the reader to notice the writer, rather than the writing, but so what? It'll upset Charlton fans, but, hey, they're only visiting the Premiership, and they're just glad to be playing these big clubs in the first place, aren't they?

Even if they've done something ridiculous like had their left-back picked for England, you can try and use the next 90 minutes as an objective way of deciding whether or not he's up to the job. After all, you've never seen him before and you're clinging onto one fact about him having once been on loan to a very small club somewhere, so you can hardly write anything fair or informed. You can then do a quick scribbled note about the fortunes of the other side, cram the goals, or lack of them, into two paragraphs at the bottom and be away in time to get the early train back to London. There is a rumour that we, as Charlton fans, can get a little bit touchy about journalists doing stuff like that, but speaking personally, I've never suffered from it, thankfully . . .

But it's fair to say that there are certainly games like that and it's a toss up whether it's better to write about them or just watch them. On the plus side, if you're watching, you can always have a beer beforehand and you can leave early if it gets really bad. You won't – leave early – of course, because we've already discovered that rational behaviour like that is confiscated at the turnstiles, but the option is at least open to you. On the minus side, you've had to pay for a ticket, and it's your team out there, the side holding your hopes and dreams, that are underperforming so woefully. The journalist, on the other hand, is getting paid for it. On balance, you'd have to be a very narrow-minded scribe to claim that you've really got it worse than the fans.

Usually.

There are games where you feel so involved, so wrapped up in them that the idea of sitting there quietly, trying to describe calmly and concisely what has been happening, would be more than you could bear. Mostly, I can imagine that keeping control wouldn't be too hard, as the nerves kept you naturally subdued for most of the game. Not responding overtly to a goal going in would take a bit of getting used to, but surely it couldn't be worse than sitting in the away end and trying to look upset when your side grab a late winner?

Occasionally, though, it just wouldn't be possible. Say, for example, you came from behind three times to find yourself drawing 4–4 at the end of normal time, with your hero scoring a hat-trick, and your centre-half scoring his first goal ever – four minutes from time. You then watched both sides score all five of their penalties, sending the shoot out into sudden death. After that, your side score two more before the opposition finally missed one, and you win. Three hours after it all started, you finally win.

Oh, and the game was at Wembley, in front of a full house. And the prize was a place in the Premiership. Who on Earth could keep their head during a game like that? Then again, what are the odds on a game like that happening? The staff at *Roy of the Rovers* had a game like that, it's rumoured, but they kept it locked in a glass cabinet, marked 'use only in emergency'. They never encountered a storyline requiring a contest of such ridiculous drama, so it never got used.

At this point, Charlton fans may, not for the first time I suspect, look a little smug, stare off into mid-space, transport themselves back a few years and start to become misty-eyed. If you look carefully, you might be able to see them mouthing the words 'Super Clive', but stay alert, because sooner or later they'll try and demonstrate a neat little flick and turn of a trap and volley. If they've had a drink, a dive to their left and a deranged run, head tipped back and ball held out in front of them, has been known. It doesn't last long though, as a load of blokes in cream suits come along and jump on top of them.

Other fans argue about their favourite moment, their most glorious win, or their greatest day. We don't. We just argue about our favourite moment of our most glorious win on our greatest day, because everything happened all at the same time. Even with all the achievements and plaudits gathered by the club over the last decade, there isn't a shadow of a doubt from anyone as to what was top of the list.

If life is a series of peaks and troughs, for many Charlton fans, Monday, 25 May 1998, at about 6 p.m., marks the highest point. There are fond memories aplenty of marriages, births and special occasions, but there is probably only one event which still makes the hairs rise on the back of the neck. Looking back now, it was a game we'd been growing towards gently, for about two or three months beforehand, edging our way more and more firmly into the top six, but never quite managing to break into the top two.

Nottingham Forest and Middlesbrough had claimed an automatic Premiership place, finishing first and second, and when we disposed of Ipswich in the semi-final, and Sunderland beat Sheffield United, a red and white day at Wembley was guaranteed. Well, it would have been, had Sunderland not lost the toss and opted to play in the worst away kit of all time.

What started as gold and navy blue, transformed itself into something muddier and darker by the time the players started to sweat. Unfortunately for Peter Reid's men, given the stifling heat of the day, this was shortly after they emerged from the dressing-rooms. By the time Allan Johnston stepped forward to take a penalty, hours later, he looked as if he'd had a really good night out and had been sick down the front of his shirt.

We, by contrast, had signed a new kit deal in the days running up to the final, leaving most of our fans asking what the name was on the front of the shirt? It was a tale of two computer companies: Viglen had got us to the final and Mesh, so we hoped, were going to get us through it.

The game itself has been so widely chronicled, that it's almost superfluous to go over it in too much detail. Even if you weren't there, or didn't support either of the two teams, you'll have seen it re-run when Sky do their best-ever matches compilation each year – and the penalties get a mention whenever a game gets to a shoot out.

Clive Mendonca started the game with 26 goals for the season and ended with 29 and a penalty shoot-out strike, as well as a place in the Premiership, Charlton history and a song of his own, to be sung whenever the fans felt like it. Kevin Phillips started the day with 34 goals for the season, playing for a side who had finished a point ahead of us in the normal season. He ended on 35 goals and the heartbreak of contesting the next year back in the same division where he'd played this one. Even through the delirium, it was impossible not to feel sorry for Sunderland, whose depths must have sunk every bit as low as our highs had soared upwards.

Mendonca put us ahead, taking the ball from Mark Bright's flick-on and spinning between two defenders who ended up hugging each other, wondering where the striker had gone. Eyes pointing towards one corner, he let Lionel Perez follow his gaze, before slotting the ball in the opposite direction to make it 1–0. We'd come into the game on the back of nine successive clean sheets. This was the end of May and the last goal Sasa Ilic had picked out of the back of his net had been against Nottingham Forest, two months earlier. We all understood what was needed – all we had to do was score, and we were up.

A great theory that turned out to be, as Niall Quinn swooped onto Nicky Summerbee's near-post corner to draw Sunderland level, before Phillips latched onto a header from Michael Gray and did what he'd been doing all season to put them ahead.

That really should have been it, Sunderland should have closed the door and denied us a route back, but somehow, they just couldn't. Midway through the second half, Keith Jones picked up the ball just inside Charlton territory, saw Mendonca lurking, and gave him something to chase. Mendonca set off after his target, kangarooing across the turf, skipping past the challenge of Darren Williams, controlling the ball with the sole of his boot and eventually sliding it past Perez to draw us level.

Euphoria! We were back in it, and those two goals weren't going to be fatal. We were back level and busy trying to convince ourselves that the momentum was going our way. It would take a monumental effort, we half-reasoned and half-prayed, for Sunderland to get back in front now. One monumental effort later and they were.

After failing to concede a goal for a couple of months, Sasa was making up for lost time, like a drunk falling off the wagon in the most public way possible. Michael Ball and Summerbee combined neatly down the right flank, before Lee Clark sent over a cross for Quinn that eluded everyone. The Irishman brought down the ball with a delicacy that mocked those who said he was only good for winning headers and smacked it past Ilic, inches inside the near post.

I was sitting there watching it with my dad. We don't often get to watch games together, certainly not if watching them on television doesn't really count, which, of course, it shouldn't. Despite being in my late 20s at the time, I still didn't, and still don't, tend to swear in front of him and vice versa. Looking back, Wembley represented a triumph of attempted restraint on both our parts, as we sought to continue a profanity-free discussion in the face of the fiercest provocation available.

I seem to remember a calm and detached 'That's buggered that up then' coming from him as Quinn scored, followed by that biting of the lip and the long gaze into the far distance he does when he's trying to come to terms with sudden bad news. I was suddenly consumed by a desire to scratch the back of my head, exhale, and pretend nothing had happened, as if my calmness might transmit itself down to the pitch and lead us to another equaliser. It didn't look promising though.

Finally, with five minutes remaining, Perez pulled off a piece of reflex magic to deny Bright and as the ball screeched the wrong side of the post, it looked to be all over. John Robinson swung a corner over, Perez made a mess of claiming the cross and Richard Rufus, acting as if he did this sort of thing every week, nodded the ball home. Gray stood on the goal line, but couldn't do anything about it, as the ball looped and dived into the other corner of the net, sending it to 3–3.

It was Rufus' first goal in 165 games and he landed amidst total chaos, as red shirts from all over the place descended on him. I think, at this point, the non-swearing thing might have been undergoing a temporary truce. Rufus stood there, trying to comprehend what he'd done, with this silly big smile on his face, while 35,000 Charlton fans beamed similar expressions straight back at him.

Rufus is a very engaging character. Modest almost to the point of being shy, he always says hello to people, bears none of the arrogant trappings of young players at some other clubs and generally conducts himself with a quiet dignity. I asked him once about the goal, and what he remembered of it.

'I was just waiting my time. When you don't score many, you've got to make sure that the first one happens in the right place!'

It was said with a grin as large as the one he wore when he scored it and was followed up with an explanation that he was only joking, and an attempt to explain how pleased and delighted he was, lest he thought he was appearing a bit full of himself. At that precise moment in time, for all I cared, he could have declared himself King. Having equalised in a play-off final with five minutes remaining, especially under those circumstances, he could have been just about as full of himself as he liked. It's even better that he's not, though . . .

Suddenly, we were back in the world of the ever-optimistic fan, hanging onto the belief that Sunderland's morale must once again have plunged through the floor – they were five minutes from the Premiership, how could they possibly come to terms with that? It took us about ten minutes of extra time to find out. Summerbee collected the ball from Gray's toe, eluded the lunges of Robinson and Eddie Youds, and steered it beyond Ilic and into the back of a net that was going to start looking worn out if this carried on for much longer. More biting of the lip and about four more minutes of staring into space, searching for an answer. We couldn't lose this now, it just wouldn't be fair.

When people ask me why we all call him 'Super' Clive Mendonca, it's the moment four minutes after Sunderland went 4–3 ahead that I think back to. Steve Brown cut someone in half looking to regain possession, Mark Kinsella slipped the ball to Steve Jones, who galloped to the dead-ball line before pulling the ball back across the face of the six-yard box. Mendonca reached backwards, killed it with a touch and whiplashed himself around, to bury a right-footed volley beyond Perez and level it once more. Suddenly, there seemed a general consensus to forget about the no-swearing thing until afterwards.

Amazingly, Sunderland couldn't find it in themselves to take the lead once more and the game staggered on towards penalties, dragging emotionally exhausted fans from either end of the country with it. If the game had been tough on the nerves, penalties were going to be a bloody nightmare.

Clive went first, crashing the ball home as he had done all afternoon, while Summerbee returned fire for Sunderland. And on it went, and on and on. Brown for us, Johnston for them. Jones for us, Ball for them. Kinsella for us, Makin for them.

Alan Curbishley and Peter Reid sat there passively, chewing hard and staring out onto the scene which decided their fate. Their ties had come undone and they had that fatigued look around the eyes that undermined their attempts to pervade calmness. They looked like two men waiting for the jury to come back and pronounce its verdict, which isn't actually that far from the truth. Back in the real world, it carried on. Bowen for us, Rae for them, until we got to sudden death.

At this point, I just felt that the whole thing had gone far enough. We'd played a whole season, and now, almost ten months after it started, we were trying to sort it out based on one person's mistake at the end of more than two hours of football. It was like stopping the two leaders in the Mall and explaining to them that the London Marathon would now be decided by the toss of a coin on Westminster Bridge, so if one of them would like to call?

I half expected that big, booming Monty Python voice to come over the Tannoy. The one that orders, 'Stop it now, that's quite enough. Stop it now, this is silly.' You may or may not be amazed to hear that no such announcement was forthcoming, so on we plunged, somehow managing to feel more numb and more nervous, all at the same time.

At home, my wife was trying to put our daughter, Honor, down for a sleep, coping with the hair-trigger crying reflex that all parents recognise as coming as standard at three months of age. Any noise or sudden jerk would be fatal, causing Honor to snap noisily back to life, despite only seconds earlier having seemed certain to sleep peacefully for the next few hours. In terms of the need for smooth movement and precise touch, it's a bit like trying to defuse a bomb, only the results if unsuccessful can be a lot louder. It was, with hindsight, the wrong game to attempt such a manoeuvre. At least I can claim that my daughter ended up watching the game, although I can't guarantee she always shouted in exactly the right places.

As the agony continued, Robinson scored for us and Quinn promptly strode forwards and scored for them. It was amazing stuff, with the goal seeming huge every time a yellow shirt walked up, before shrinking to the size of a shoebox as a red and white one replaced it. Newton ambled up for us and caused me the worst moment of the day, when he opted to take the kick after just a three-stride run-up. It was too calm and laid-back, and I knew he was going to regret his attempt to appear unbothered, right up until the time when he scored, when I reverted to never doubting him. It was to be the last time I had to worry about a Charlton penalty that day. Michael Gray took his turn, and the rest is history, as Alan Curbishley recalls:

> I'd watched all of them up to then, but then Keith [Peacock] starts telling me not to watch this one, because Gray's left-footed, and we haven't had a left-footer so far in the shoot-out and he's got a good feeling about it. To be honest, I didn't have the energy

left to argue by that stage, because it was a hot day and it had been a long afternoon. I sort of stared at my feet and next thing I knew all sorts of chaos had broken out. Keith was screaming something in my ear, but I already knew, because the cheering had come from the other direction. You got into a sort of rhythm, with the cheering coming from either your left or your right, depending on which side had gone up to take the kick.

I think Sasa got quite close to their fourth one and there was a bit of a noise from the Charlton end, but as the ball sneaked by him and over the line, the noise was swamped by the Sunderland fans. When Gray took that kick, the loudest noise of the afternoon suddenly hit me and it was coming from our fans. One minute there were loads of people sitting on our set of benches and the next they were all gone, running off across the pitch. I bet they regretted buying us cream suits once the lads starting jumping on top of each other and skidding around all over the place.

I needed to say well done to a few people, but I needed to speak to Peter Reid as well, because we've known each other for a long time and I could imagine how he felt. I think everyone was a little bit numb in the moments after it ended, because it had been such a great game, and there was that feeling that you couldn't leave it with nothing to show, because it had been such an occasion.

Our fans looked stunned, despite the fact that they were all delirious. You don't expect to see a game like that on an occasion like that; it's meant to be a tight 1–0 or 2–1 job, but that had everything. It was a privilege to be a part of it, and after everything we'd suffered as a club, it was right that when we made it into the Premiership we did it with a bit of style. I don't think anyone could dispute that we did.

I don't think anyone tried actually, not that we'd have cared at the time. Looking back, it's a good thing that we couldn't really make out Curbishley from the stands, because it wouldn't have done much for our nerves. Sitting there, with his head in his hands, his new suit and a huge flower in his lapel, he looked like the jury had just come back – and it wasn't good news. In fact, he looked worse than that, with the flower ensuring he ended up looking like a groom who'd just been jilted. Keith Peacock may have been onto something with his theory about Gray being left-footed, but at the time it didn't make the manager look any more confident.

In a game of the highest drama and quality, the highest of all the dramas was created by a moment of the lowest quality. Gray scuffed the ball, left-footed into the arms of Ilic. It travelled so slowly, it's almost safe to call him the waiting Ilic, arms outstretched, welcoming the ball to him and the Premiership to Charlton. Gray collapsed in a disbelieving heap and much as I'd love to say how sorry I felt for him, and how much I hoped it wasn't going to haunt him, that wouldn't have been true. I didn't care, I was just trying to come to terms with what had just happened. The whole thing had been much too much to take in.

It hadn't been much easier for the players. Steve Brown remembers the effort of trying to seal everything else out, at least until his part in the action was finally over.

> I didn't think of any of the wider things surrounding the game and especially not when it got to penalties. I just tried to cut out everything around the stadium, which wasn't easy because I can't pretend that I'd ever played in anything like that before. I was fine until the shoot-out and suddenly it's more difficult to stay focused because you've got to do that bloody walk, all the way from the centre circle to the other end, and it was towards the Sunderland fans as well.
>
> I can remember talking to myself, telling myself not to change my mind, to pick a spot and keep a clear head and put the ball where I'd decided it was going to go. I was telling myself that if I stuck to the plan, the ball was going in and there was nothing Perez could do about it. There's a lot of bluffing goes on in a situation like that and mostly it's people trying to bluff themselves, rather than the keeper or the other side.

It comes as no surprise at all to learn that one man kept his nerve with more nonchalance than anyone else could muster:

> Everyone who walks up to take a kick is trying to convince themselves that they're not nervous, when they're absolutely terrified. Everyone except Clive, that is. He's set up differently to normal people, I swear he is. He never looked nervous once and the Sunderland lot knew he wasn't as well, which made him a perfect person to start things going. Apart from anything else, he hadn't come close to missing all day, so he wasn't going to cock it up from 12 yards out.

Mendonca may have been keeping his composure, but not everyone could make the same claim, as Mike Wad remembers, with a degree of amusement you feel he may or may not have enjoyed at the time:

> I'd only just got back from holiday and I couldn't get a ticket for the game, so I had to watch it in a pub close to where I live. Things were getting worse and worse and then better and better with each passing minute and the beer was starting to disappear at a bit of a frightening rate.
>
> I can remember burying my head in my hands each time Sunderland scored, and really genuinely thinking that it was all over, and we'd never pull back from it, but we just kept grabbing our way back into the game. When Mendonca scored to make it 4–4 I was just yelling at the television screen, beer going everywhere, and looking like some kind of wild man.
>
> When Sasa went gently down to his left and saved that penalty, I've got to be honest, I can't quite remember what happened next. All I do know is that when the excitement had subsided a little bit, I was able to piece together what had happened over the last few seconds. I'd leapt to my feet, with my arms outstretched, so that my pint was somewhere over my head, tipping back down on top of me with every fresh jump up into the air – and there were a lot of them.
>
> That would have made me feel fairly silly normally, but it seemed like nothing to worry about, partly because we'd just got promoted and partly because of what else had happened. I'm a fairly big and heavy bloke and after an afternoon of excitement, that final leap to my feet was just too much for my belt, which must have snapped.
>
> As a result, I stood there, at the front of a large crowd of people, just in front of the television. I'd had a decent drink, I was virtually crying with delight, my pint was busy splashing over my head and my trousers were around my ankles. I knew I was happy and I was aware I might cry and I suppose I also had it in my mind that I was getting wet. Unfortunately, I didn't notice my trousers for a good 30 seconds, as I jumped up and down and screamed and cheered, while the rest of the pub collapsed with laugher, pointing at me.
>
> My mates, who I go to the game with every week, were pointing and howling with the rest of them and loving the fact that I hadn't noticed that everyone in the pub was either cheering

Sasa or laughing at my underpants. It's funny, the memories you have of moments like that . . .

Locating heroes from a day like that isn't all that tricky an assignment. Usually there are all the standard clichés about there being '11 heroes', but such was the stranglehold he exerted upon proceedings, Mendonca seems to have swept the board. Ian Cartwright doesn't disagree, and goes on to explain why he knows he's bestowed hero status on the right man:

I went through every emotion in life during the course of that game, from feeling drained to being utterly euphoric. People try and come up with games that were better than that now, just because they want to come up with a different angle. You can't though, in all honesty, look back at our history and find anything that combined such a great game and such a great achievement all in the one afternoon.

I didn't have any energy left after that match. I went back to The Oak, it was fairly busy and I was thinking that if everyone else was up for it, it might turn into a great big night, but everyone was knackered. The atmosphere was stultified and everyone was just staring straight ahead with these daft smiles on their faces, trying desperately to take in what had happened.

I've never been unquestioning of players when it comes to hero status, because I don't think that's all that healthy, but there are some who come a lot closer to it than others. Clive Mendonca, during the course of that afternoon, elevated himself to God-like status as far as I was concerned. He had a whole stadium in his hands and when he stood there screaming at the crowd after his second goal, we found ourselves screaming back.

He just turned up, got on with things and did the job. There was never anyone who had such an impact in such a short period of time down here and he never took it for granted, got above himself, or expected any special treatment. Just before the start of this season, we had Porto down at The Valley for John Robinson's testimonial. I was walking around the ground before the start and I saw Clive and his son queuing up at the ticket office.

I asked him what he was doing, and started to tell him not to be daft and that we'd get him in somewhere nice. It seemed ridiculous that he was having to stand in a queue for a ticket, but he wouldn't have it. It was a testimonial for one of his mates and he wanted to buy a ticket for it. Buy a ticket for a ground that was at least partly built as a result of what he managed to do at Wembley that afternoon! That'll do for me, when it comes to heroes – he grew even bigger in my estimation when he wasn't even able to kick a ball any more!

That, of course, is the note of sadness hanging over the day. Mendonca was able to play only a partial role in the seasons that followed and ultimately had to retire from the game with a recurrent hip injury which refused to allow him to play without pain. Had he continued, there was the possibility that he'd require a hip replacement and that was a risk too far for a man who had a young family and still wanted to be able to run about with his children.

It's almost impossible not to look back on that game and feel that we were somehow cheated out of the best of Mendonca, regardless of the fact that he came so close to perfection on the biggest stage of them all. He refuses to fall prey to self-pity, though, and when I spoke to him just before he was forced to call it a day, he showed the determination that made him such a fine striker. All the time the dream of playing was still alive, he wasn't inclined to wallow in the past:

I can honestly say that I must have seen that game at Wembley two times and that's honest to God. Obviously it was a great occasion for me and the club, but you've got to be mentally strong as well; it's been in my mind all the time that I'll get back and play football and I'll start looking back when I haven't got anything left to look forward to.

I've been asked what the best goal of the three was hundreds of times and I can honestly say I change my mind every time I think back at it! From my point of view, as a striker, it was the first one, though. I took the flick on, pulled off a nice little turn to mug off the two centre-halfs, and then gave the keeper the eyes. He went one way and the ball went the other and he never had a chance in a million of saving it, so that had all the little bits and pieces in it that strikers like to look back on.

All I want to do is play football and because of that I'd have to look back over the last few years and say that there's been more downs than ups. Obviously, Wembley was a massive, massive up and I'll never ever get a better day in my career than that and that's for sure. Since then, though, I've suffered a lot with injuries and it's been more frustrating than I can say. Unfortunately for me, it's just not carried on the way I would have wanted and that makes me sad.

Wembley was a wonderful experience and it's not lost on me that I missed out on most of what followed it. I had been quite lucky through my career with injuries and it's only been since I came to Charlton that I started to suffer with them. The first season I played over 40 games and we did really well and got promoted. The next year it was 19 games in the Premiership and a few goals, the same story the next, with both of them cut really short because of injuries.

I don't want to get stuck into talking about what I did in the past, because that would be like giving up the future, and I'm not going to do that. Not until someone tells me that I've got no option and it's time to call it a day. It was a great day though, I'll give you that, a bloody great day.

Mark Kinsella has good reason to remember it as a 'bloody great day', simply because he ended it lifting a trophy at Wembley. As he recalls the agonies gone through on that afternoon, he echoes the sentiments of Brown when looking around for somewhere to place the lion's share of the credit. It's also strangely reassuring to know that there were people out there on the pitch going through the same turmoil as we were in the stands.

I'd never scored a penalty before and I don't think Curbs knew that when he came marching up and told me I was taking one. I started to argue, but he had a list in his head and he wasn't going to start changing it around just because I was losing my nerve. It's moments like that I'll look back on, because it was Clive and the way he set about it that made you think you were going to be all right. A little bit of calmness, as long as it's genuine, goes a long way in a situation like that.

Clive was something else that day. He knew that was his stage. He was playing against the place where he grew up and he put on a show. Some of his finishing was amazing and he was so cool in the middle of that atmosphere that it sort of caught on among the rest of us. Normally you have someone geeing everyone else up, but that day we had a bloke who was convincing us that it was all going to be all right, and that he had all the answers. He did as well . . .

If the return to The Valley had been the start of the journey back to full health, Wembley provided Charlton with another huge shot in the arm. Just six years on from being homeless, they were in the Premiership and had reached it courtesy of one of the most amazing games ever seen at the stadium, and surely, the most dramatic domestic final ever staged there.

Their progress, which had already, up to now, been hugely impressive, was about to take a quantum leap forwards, propelling the club to a position and a status few felt it would ever hold again. It seems fitting, if we're trying to place it in some kind of historical context, to let Colin Cameron have the last word on the day. Was it really as good as I remember? I'm delighted to say that Cameron seems to agree wholeheartedly:

> It was just an unforgettable game and I don't think we overdo it at all when we look back on it because it really was that good. It was certainly the best game we ever had. I mean, you've got the 7–6 game with Huddersfield way back when, and, of course, the 250,000 people who claim to have seen it. I wasn't one of them, I was in the army at the time. I wasn't lucky enough to have got to the 1946 Cup final either, because we could only get one ticket in the house and that went to my dad. I'll always admit the ones I couldn't get to, unlike some people!
>
> I can't honestly imagine that there was ever a better game than that, though, because of all the drama and the pressure attaching itself to the game. It had everything that you could ever have wanted from a football match and that was before you even started to think what was resting on the result. I'd been to Highbury and seen us win before last season, and that was a break of a few years, but although it was worthy of note, it wasn't as historic as this. That day at Wembley had everything. That was as good as it gets.

9

A SMALL FISH IN A BIG POND

It's a strange experience, winning a play-off final, especially when it gains you entry to the Premiership. You get promoted, you celebrate for a couple of weeks and then you slowly put your hungover head back above the barricades, only to discover that everyone's got you down as their sure-fire automatic relegation candidate. In terms of real life cutting across the euphoria, it's as hard to beat as it is to live with.

Reality sets in at an indecent rate and you're forced to deal with the fact that this year is going to be just a little bit different to the last one. If you follow a club determined to stick to its long-term plan, this is probably the time you're going to feel the most frustration with them, as an unwillingness to play financial Russian roulette is all too easily interpreted as a lack of ambition.

The appearance of the fixture list confirms that it is indeed all happening and that you really are going to play against the sides you used only to watch on the television. After that, however, it's a crash course in getting back down from cloud nine. It's a memory that Richard Murray can recall only too vividly:

> Going back to that wonderful day at Wembley, there were a number of emotions. Initially, of course, there were huge celebrations and joy, but looking back on it, if we hadn't made it, we might have been in a little bit of trouble, because I think we might have had a bit of difficulty keeping hold of one or two of our star players.

By getting to the Premiership, it meant we could keep everybody, but, and with hindsight we were right, we weren't going to spend more than we could afford, because I think we felt that we weren't quite ready for the Premiership. That doesn't mean that you don't take a chance when you get it, but we didn't have a strong enough squad, we didn't have a big enough ground and we didn't have the hospitality you need to gain the full financial benefits all worked out.

In many way, we had to say to Alan, 'You do your best, we'll try desperately to stay up, but if we can't we're not going to chase it financially. We're not going to put ourselves in any danger.' We went down, but lo and behold we came straight back, we won the championship the following year, and with hindsight I think we got things just about spot on.

It's hard to disagree with Murray, just as it's hard to imagine how frustrating it must have been, sticking to the budgets and watching the year slide to a conclusion that left us resenting pundits all over the place for being right. Then again, Murray is an immensely intelligent and accomplished businessman, while I, as we have sadly worked out, have no financial acumen whatsoever. Maybe it wasn't quite as hard as I'd imagined. Some people are just better at following the laws of finance than others, even all too few of them seem to end up as chairman of a football club.

One of the things that appears to have been firmly on our side is the lack of division between board, management and players about the way the season was approached. Whether there were disagreements that aren't being publicised is anyone's guess, but even now, and even if there were, four years down the line, nobody is breaking ranks to say so. Given that the life span of the average football secret is about two and a half hours, it seems reasonable to conclude that it was a fairly united club. John Robinson seems to support the chairman's version of events fairly comprehensively:

Looking back, the feeling was that we were all going to enjoy the year and if we stayed up, then it was a real bonus. We'd got there in the most amazing way you could ever hope to see and we were still at a fairly early stage of our recovery. People outside the club tend to forget, but we were without a ground six or seven seasons before we won at Wembley, and to go from there to the Premiership is an incredible thing to do.

Curbs was able to make a couple of signings, but we didn't really spend big money, because we still weren't in a position to do that. It just meant that most of the people who had got the club to the Premiership had to show that they were good enough to keep it there, or at least that they were prepared to give it everything they had to keep it there.

We could have done what loads of clubs have done and blown our cash all over the place, mucked it up and never had another chance to play at that level, but we were a bit more clued up than that. We played it sensibly, and waited for a time when we were in a position to collect our rewards. That's the sort of forward planning that doesn't get many headlines, but it's the reason this club has pulled itself up from the depths and put itself right up there in the top rank.

In any one season, there might be a side that looks as if it's doing things quicker than us, or getting there ahead of us, but you can't just look at one year, you've got to look at four or five in a row. When you stand back a little bit, you see that each of those clubs might have put a spurt on for a while, but then they fell away again and suffered as a result of over-reaching themselves. We just kept making steady progress and that's why we are where we are today, and that's really, looking back on it, what that first Premiership season was – a bit of steady progress, and a chance to learn a lot.

If there's one thing which becomes clear while discussing that first season in the Premiership, it's that hindsight alters your perception of things more than largest hall of mirrors could ever hope to. Looking back now, we were wide-eyed and gasping at the mere fact we were even playing against some of these sides. Every other week gave us the chance to visit a ground we either hadn't been to before, or which had changed out of all recognition since the last time we had been there.

We weren't entirely sure that we were meant to be at the party and snuck around like meek gatecrashers. On the pitch there were the occasional triumphs and we managed to dish out a couple of bloody noses, but only before security arrived and we were thrown out, back into the Nationwide. Compared to the way we now know we can approach the Premiership, it was very watered-down stuff.

The record books show that we had to wait until the very last match of the season to have our relegation confirmed, but anyone who tries to convince you that it was touch and go to the last minute wasn't there.

Even though, to this day, I remain excited about the penultimate game, when we looked to have thrown ourselves a lifeline (can you throw yourself a lifeline?), the truth was rather different. A mid-season collapse of biblical proportions had sealed our fate, long before the end of January, let alone the end of the season.

Between late November, when we went to Elland Road and got battered 4–1, and the second week of January, when we were beaten by Arsenal, we lost everything – literally. We went out of the FA Cup at the first time of asking, we didn't pick up a single point in the League and clocked up eight successive Premiership defeats, with the 2–0 brush off in the Cup from Blackburn making it nine on the trot.

If we'd appeared on *Ready, Steady, Cook* our omelette would have stuck to the pan and if we'd sat there opposite Chris Tarrant, seeking a million-pound prize, we'd have phoned a friend and been told the wrong answer. We couldn't win anything. I certainly wouldn't have got in a lift or aeroplane with the team at the time – they were the unluckiest bunch of people on the face of the planet.

Even when we did manage to grab a point, when Martin Pringle scored in the dying seconds against Newcastle, we should have had more, as the cameras showed Mark Bright's header having crossed the line, while the referee cheerfully waved play on. Why do referees always seem to get so theatrical about it when it's live on television? I wonder . . .

Having recovered from that, and the sound of Martin Tyler roaring 'Justice is done at The Valley' just to remind us that we should have been given the earlier goal, we then faced Manchester United – oh, good. The performance was laden with heroes, as bodies hurtled in front of everything United could throw at us and it genuinely appeared that the Newcastle game had been a turning point.

Some chance. A last-minute Dwight Yorke goal saw us fall to a heartbreaking 1–0 defeat and while we were falling out of the Premiership, I was falling out of love with it. Sod being brave and battling and losing 1–0 every week, deep down I was aching for a second-rate performance against a Crewe or a Bury, which still saw us pick up three points. All this progress and building for the future was a lot harder than we first thought.

Just in case there's anyone reading this who has recovered from the upset, I'd like to send you back to the depths of despair, from where you've only recently emerged. That last-minute Manchester United goal, hard as it was to take anyway, won them the title. Had it gone six inches higher and hit the bar, United would have finished a point behind

Arsenal, rather than a point in front. I trust that's done very little to improve your feelings about the season.

There are large chunks of that nine-game run of depressing defeats that my brain has thankfully managed to erase, but there are still a few scars lurking there. I remember the game at home against Aston Villa particularly well, sadly. I was working for a business magazine at the time, laden with advertising people I couldn't stand and a publisher who made up for his lack of stature with a strutting walk and a string of absurd phrases. It really was *The Office* ahead of its time, only with none of the likeable people.

In fact, there was one decent bloke working there, who didn't talk too much, but understood his football and sympathised with my plight, as my side spent the year sliding down the table. Nobody else really understood what it was like and the publisher actually asked why I didn't start supporting someone else, a bit higher up the league. Just as Peter Cook listed his greatest regret in life as saving David Frost from drowning, in the wake of that remark, mine remains not landing one on the publisher and strolling out of the door for the last time.

Their Christmas 'night out' was planned for 21 December, which, as luck would have it, coincided with our game against Villa. Spurred on by some mysterious force, I proceeded to make up the most extraordinary story in the world about why I couldn't come out for the evening and how upset I was about it. I knew I couldn't say that I was going to football instead, because that just wouldn't have registered in their brains, and I couldn't face a year of the silent treatment and comments about 'our company not being good enough, obviously'. I'd have killed someone.

Finally released from attending the meal, I set off for the game. They never suspected a thing – I mean, everyone has a friend who comes over from New York to do some Christmas shopping on 21 December, don't they? And they never stay for more than one night, so you have to drop everything and meet up with them. I told you it was extraordinary.

It was bitterly cold and within three minutes, Richard Rufus diverted the ball into his own net, thus ensuring the temperature dropped by at least another 15 degrees. We had a bundle of chances, couldn't score any of them and despite being the better side for about 87 minutes, lost 1–0 to that early own goal. I can remember walking out of the place, frozen to the bone and numb with disappointment. It was our fifth loss in a row and we were sinking fast.

The next morning, I sat with a fixed smile as they told me of their evening and how the bloke from accounts sloped off with the girl from personnel, and all the other sort of office gossip that makes you lose the will to live. I think I might have invented a few pubs I'd been to the night before with my non-existent friend and possibly even rounded the night off with an imaginary curry. Nobody suspected me, apart from my mate, who, as I say, knew his football. As it transpired, he knew it better than I gave him credit for.

'You weren't out with a mate last night,' he said, as we stood outside and assassinated the characters of half the office. 'You were at The Valley.'

I was still too numb to panic about being rumbled, but I was intrigued. 'What makes you say that?' I asked, not quite giving the game away, but ready to concede at any moment.

'Your eyes. Every time you think nobody's looking, you're staring into the air, trying to understand how you lost. We've all been there mate . . .'

It was a look that must have gone across the face of every single Charlton fan at some stage during the course of that season. Of 18 league defeats, 10 were by a single goal. We got a couple of 4–1 pastings (all right, four, if you want to be precise), but other than that, we weren't getting whacked every week. We just didn't have enough savvy about us to claim that extra goal, we weren't streetwise enough and spent week after week getting mugged. It was made worse by the fact that we'd started so well. Why did they insist on giving us hope if they weren't going to see it through? No wonder I was staring into the air a lot.

It's at times like this when your faith and patience in a long-term policy are stretched and tried more vigorously than ever before. We had a few players who we all knew weren't quite up to it and each week we were seeing the proof to back up our suspicion played out in front of our eyes. Despite that, though, and through the depths of despair, we were still thrilled to be there, even though the initial novelty had not so much worn off, as been battered out of us on a frequent basis.

There were some major highs and the sight of Keith Jones staring in disbelief at a ball bouncing around the Liverpool goal area before sweeping it home to give us a 1–0 win at The Valley was right up there with the best of them. Although it was an experience to play against some of these sides, what we really needed, lest it was to be more of a sightseeing tour than a football season, was to beat one.

We'd completed the first half of what was to be a double over West Ham, which was a fantastic feeling, with Julian Dicks effectively being retired by the pace and movement of Danny Mills and John Robinson. We'd also claimed three points from Southampton in emphatic style, Forest in a less-than-footballing feast, and Wimbledon, but we needed a big-name triumph to talk about for a few years to come. The Liverpool victory arrived in the middle of February, providing us with only our fifth league win of the season – looking back on it, I don't know how we stayed as positive and cheerful as we did. It meant we'd taken four points off Liverpool in the course of the season, though, and was probably the most significant achievement of the year.

It wasn't my abiding memory, however. Without trying to be one of those people who always recalls the seemingly insignificant and then instils it with paragraphs of false worth, in a bid to appear interesting and different, I'll always look back on the game before Liverpool, when we played Wimbledon.

People were saying, even then, that Wimbledon were trying to shed their long-ball image and play the ball around on the floor a little bit, but I couldn't see much sign of that. We'd lost eight Premiership games in a row, we looked like we might never win anything ever again and Wimbledon had already beaten us. On Boxing Day. At Selhurst Park. Which, with the benefit of hindsight, made the West Ham Yuletide experience we were to endure a few years later, seem only mildly disappointing.

Wimbledon came to The Valley looking to send us to an eleventh defeat in 12 games, which was probably a record, except that I'd long since stopped watching television for fear we'd be mentioned. Spending two months losing football matches does that to a man . . .

It was a freezing night and as we failed to make much of an impression in the opening half an hour, the memories of the Aston Villa game were starting to flood back. Nothing had gone right for us for what felt like, and indeed was, months, yet the football gods were about to send us a sign that we hadn't been totally forgotten.

Martin Pringle had made the, at the time, unlikely journey from Benfica to The Valley, and carried an indecent weight of expectation, as we waited to see if our continental 'star' could do something to change our fortunes. Just before half-time, he claimed what under normal circumstances would have been the strangest goal of the season and gave us a deliriously greeted lead.

Collecting the ball just inside the Wimbledon half, Pringle set off on a gallop goalwards, somehow prodding the ball around or in front of each fresh challenge. Even at the best of times, Pringle would not claim to look like the most compact of players, but on an icy surface, and with his extraordinarily long and spindly legs slipping and sliding in all directions, he just kept going.

Perhaps disconcerted by this madly flailing figure hurtling towards them, the Wimbledon defence set about falling over each other and generally taking all manner of inelegant avoiding actions. History may try to report it as a surging run forwards, but although I suppose that's ultimately what it was, anyone who has seen the goal remembers it differently. Looking like Frank Spencer in the episode of *Some Mothers Do 'ave 'em* where he was unleashed onto the world on roller skates, the Swede just kept on going, into the area and beyond.

Neil Sullivan in the Wimbledon goal ran into a couple of handily placed centre-halfs, probably for his own protection, and Pringle half shot and half slithered the ball into the back of the net. Indeed, it was probably only the presence of the net that stopped him careering straight into the covered end, screaming for someone to help him slow down. Such was the flurry of arms and legs thrown out by him, half in the interests of forward progress, half to retain balance, that it had been almost impossible to get near to the ball. Had he hidden it up his shirt and charged for the goal, it wouldn't have been any harder to stop him. It remains the only goal I have ever seen scored by a man impersonating a speed skater and it gave us hope that our ordeal might be reaching an end.

Only faint hope, obviously, because we had been kicked in the teeth so many times in the previous games, that we had virtually lost the ability to express any form of genuine optimism. Only when the gods intervened once more did we dare believe that things might be changing for the better.

We survived a couple of scares early in the second half, before the ghost of Frank Spencer struck again. Chris Powell played the ball into the Wimbledon area, and Sullivan, doubtless worried that the skater would reappear, managed to misjudge it and prod it forward with his knees. It hit Dean Blackwell firmly on the backside, who in turning around to enquire as to whether his keeper had a problem, managed to back heel it over his own line. It didn't go straight in either, but rolled agonisingly slowly, edging over the line but never seeming to quite reach the back of the net. Compared to that, Pringle's goal looked like it had been sculpted by a Brazilian side of 30 years earlier.

As the night grew colder, and snow started to fall, I can vividly remember being struck by the groundless fear that the game was going to be postponed. It should have been a baseless concern, with only 20 minutes remaining and the game being shown live on Sky. But, it was snowing quite heavily, nothing had gone right for us for ages, and David Elleray was the referee, so anything that produced a headline was a definite possibility, in my mind at least.

That's the sort of thing the prospect of relegation does to a person and

I've never been able to be quite as scornful of conspiracy theorists since. It wasn't called off, of course, and we had finally won another game. In fact, with the Liverpool game following it, and then a win up at Pride Park, we picked up three results on the trot, which was just enough to raise our hopes, even though we suspected deep down that they were about to be dashed again.

The second half of our double over West Ham looked to have given us a glimmer of hope, but two points from the next five games effectively sealed our fate. That extraordinary afternoon at Villa Park, with Brown in goal and Mills firing home a freekick at the death, proved to be little more than a stay of execution – an opportunity for the away fans to have one last celebration. By the time the final week of the season had come around, we were clinging onto hopes that Southampton would slip up and we would cling onto safety with a home win. It wasn't to be.

Defeat by Sheffield Wednesday sent us back to the Nationwide league. Even now, I can remember the look on the face of the bloke sitting next to me, when he took out the earpiece of the little radio he had in his inside pocket, turned to me and delivered the bad news.

'Southampton have scored. Bollocks.'

As far as last words and departing sentiments go, it might not go down as one of the more poetic, but it summed things up fairly well. There were about 15 minutes left, as far as I remember it, when Danny Sonner scored to put us out of our misery. Danny bloody Sonner. In the previous months, we'd faced up to executioners like Bergkamp, Giggs and Yorke, and now, here we were, with the fatal blow being dealt by Danny Sonner. After the death sentences and reprieves we'd been through, it was like finally getting beheaded by a bloke with a blunt butter knife.

I would have been more precise about the timing of Sonner's goal, but for two factors. Firstly, it's not something that I'd revisit by choice and I suspect I'm not alone in feeling like that. Secondly, I was strangely amused and pleased to discover that the club appears to have felt the same way. A quick surf through the Internet would, I hoped, enable me to clarify the details of that gloomy day, so I delved into the archives and looked up the match report.

The message was brief, to the point, and told its own story: 'Match report will appear here. Pictures are available.'

Three years on, and the pictures have now gone and I don't suppose the match report is ever actually going to get written. Then again, I don't suppose there was huge demand.

For the first time since their return, Charlton had taken a backward step – on the playing side at least. It was now that we were going to discover whether the financial prudence and careful approach of the club to their year in the top flight were going to pay off. History was littered with sides that had slipped out of the Premiership and just carried on slipping – sides with far less troubled recent histories than Charlton's.

I walked out of the ground that day, depressed at the result, both of the game and the season, and worried about the future. I trudged up Floyd Road, wondering if I had seen the good times and whether they had just come to an end. I suspect I wasn't alone.

10

DEALING WITH THE DROP

There was a time, not nearly as long ago as we sometimes like to believe, where the pattern of a football club's year-by-year existence could be dramatically different to the way it appears today. Up until the formulation and formation of the Premiership, and especially up to the point where television companies began injecting cash and distorting the shape of the game, promotion and relegation represented either a bonus or a setback.

You sometimes had the good fortune to follow a team who were said to be 'established' and occasionally ended up with a side who just sat in the middle of the lower leagues, finishing mid-table, neither threatening or being threatened by anyone or anything. The injection of money into the game, however, and particularly the way in which that money had been distributed, had changed matters considerably.

The remaining category belongs to the clubs who historically found themselves slightly too good for one league, yet not quite good enough to consolidate their position in the league above. They were affectionately known as 'yo-yo clubs' and, much as the name suggests, seemed to spend their time bobbing up and down on a string of successive seasons of triumph and disaster.

Each promotion season saw them being tipped as finally having broken the mould, of making the next step forwards and preparing for new challenges ahead. The following year would end in recrimination and gloomy acceptance that the players who had brought them up, weren't, on reflection, good enough to play at the higher level.

Sometimes it was because they were too old, occasionally too young and inexperienced, and depending on who you spoke to, because the luck just didn't go their way.

At the time people spoke of relegation as a disaster, but with the benefit of what we now know, it wasn't anything so serious. They were rarely in any sort of real financial peril, and they just picked themselves up, brushed themselves off, and got on with it again. Relegation was something that meant that you hadn't been good enough for that particular division – nothing more and nothing less.

Suddenly, however, things had changed. The stakes had become far higher, and as well as looking at a fixture list bereft of the glamorous opponents of the previous year, phrases like 'loss of revenue' and 'cutbacks' became part of footballing parlance. Once upon a time, football was like a game of snakes and ladders, where you hopped up and slid down a level, before rolling the dice and carrying on. With the advent of television money being poured into the upper echelons of the game, however, the ladders were getting taller and less frequent and the snakes were getting venomous. One bite from them and you were soon getting dizzy and losing consciousness. Dusting yourself off and starting again was becoming a far trickier business.

It only takes a brief glance through the back of the newspapers to find the latest story of a club plunged into hard times and, with increasing frequency, you find yourself reflecting on just how recently it was that their fortunes and futures were so much brighter. As clubs were stretching themselves to reach the next rung of the ladder, many of them were starting to do themselves terrible injuries. The snakes were getting nastier all right, and they were collecting some major casualties along the way.

The league tables tell their own story, as names that were once tipped to be the side of the next decade start to slide further down the league, or deeper into financial trouble. A High Court Judge, the *Blackadder*-ishly named Mr Justice Darling, once argued that the law courts of England were open to all men, like the doors of the Ritz Hotel, the question of money seemingly unimportant. You hoped that there was a sense of irony at play, but given his profession, you feared the worst.

As far as football is concerned, the Premiership's accessibility stands on a very similar footing to the old Darling's view of the Ritz. Theoretically open to everyone, the cost of staying there is prohibitive to all but a very few. It only takes a brief look through the Premiership tables over the last few years to identify the clubs who have landed on a snake and suffered the consequences. Six years ago, Queens Park

Rangers were in the top flight; since then they have drifted into huge financial problems and ended up in the Second Division, having had to sell players at a multitude of stops along the way.

In the mid-'90s, Nottingham Forest occupied a mid-table spot one year before coming bottom the next. They bobbed back to the surface two years later, only to finish bottom again and never recover. They now face similar financial problems to QPR and, as the pictures of their former European glories start to fade, they reflect on where it all went wrong, chasing a dream. Crystal Palace, as Charlton fans know only too well, have suffered huge financial problems since falling out of the top flight, while Barnsley now line up in the Second Division, having failed to put the brakes on after first landing out of the Premiership and dropping down yet further.

Wimbledon, as we all know, now trade on the breadline under a name of convenience, while Sheffield Wednesday, who ultimately dealt us that fatal blow, sit in the lower reaches of the First Division. Once one of the biggest sides in the land, their fans are still coming to terms with the fact that there is no money available for a realistic promotion bid, and the next few years will be bleak ones. It gets even more ridiculous when you look at the recent departures, as clubs seem prepared to throw more and more money around in a desperate bid to avoid the drop.

Leicester kicked off their new season in the First Division playing in a new stadium, paid for by mortgaging their gate receipts for the next quarter of a century. It may be a lovely place to play, but such is their financial plight that, while some remain on reported £30,000-per-week contracts, two of their players are being paid expenses only, agreeing to the terms simply because it allowed them to remain 'in the shop window'. It's almost gone beyond ridicule.

The irony is that the cash is being spent in a bid to catch the uncatchable – the 'big six' at the Premiership summit, who are moving slowly away from everyone else, fuelled by huge amounts of money, some borrowed and some not. Admittedly Leeds and Newcastle have taken slightly longer to get there than Manchester United, Liverpool, Chelsea and Arsenal, but when you consider their spending over the last two years, the words of Mr Justice Darling come floating back into the ears. The top of the Premiership is indeed open to anyone – at the right price.

It was against this background that we awoke, depressed and bleary-eyed, to deal with the realities of life back in the First Division. We had been continually reassured that the club had not been put at risk in order to fight the battle to stay in the Premiership and we believed the board when they said it. This in itself, I suppose, marks Charlton out as a little bit different from most other places. The standard football fan's response to being told that there was no money was to shout a bit louder so that you knew it was hidden there somewhere, like a mugger angered at discovering he had picked on a skint victim. We just shrugged and accepted the statement at face value – we hadn't been turned over yet, quite the opposite, so there seemed little point in protesting, especially when there wasn't anyone obvious to shout at.

In a world where everyone was a hare and nobody wanted to be the tortoise, we seemed unafraid to accept that everything came at a price and everything happened at its own pace. Occasionally we might have stopped and complained that things were going slowly, but given the progress of the last five or six years, that just wasn't a justifiable observation. What troubled us now though, was that we had no idea if the plans put in place to ensure our safety, even if we were relegated, would actually work.

Blackburn and Forest had gone down with us that year and it didn't take a genius to work out that they were going to set about dealing with things in different ways. One of them had a multi-millionaire pumping money in and nobody was under any illusion about what Jack Walker was going to do now. They might not have been offered the huge riches that they had been given before but Walker was not going to see Blackburn dwindle away for lack of funding. Forest were in a different boat, with the warning signs present long before they finally went down.

We were somewhere in between the two of them and we knew our situation wasn't comparable with either. We didn't have an absurdly wealthy benefactor, at least not in the way Blackburn did, but neither did we have a board who had let us chase the dream of survival with reckless profligacy. It was going to be a nervous summer, if only because we looked set to find out quite a lot about the extent to which our club had recovered from its last financial crisis.

In addition to this, there was a situation developing with regard to the Millennium Dome site, located just a couple of miles from The Valley, which was causing distinct unease among some of the fans. Peter Varney had confirmed that the club had registered an interest in the site, but said repeatedly during the early part of the summer that nothing could or would happen in relation to a possible new stadium there, without the full support of the fans. The purpose of registering an interest was simply in order that the club retained the right to make any future application relating to the site.

Registering, he explained, left the options open, while not registering limited them. Predictably enough, given the history of our club, some people interpreted this as having received first-hand evidence that a fleet of Pickford's lorries had been sighted leaving The Valley under cover of darkness. The arguments against leaving The Valley were always going to be passionate, given the battle to regain it, although even now, with the benefit of hindsight, it's hard to find any evidence of anything being done 'under cover' as far as progressing the chances of the move were concerned.

Indeed, looking back over events, it's hard not to reach the conclusion that the entire episode ended up confirming to the casual observer just why we were different from other clubs. The communications manager, Rick Everitt, who had previously been so active in the Valley Party, even stated publicly that if the move was ever put forward for public consultation, as was promised if it progressed sufficiently, then he would actively campaign against it.

The board respected his view, and far from trying to quieten him, appeared to accept that it was an opinion they knew he would hold, and a stance they knew he would take. I remember standing in a pub after a Christmas party and listening to him put the case against a move quite forcefully to Martin Simons. Simons spoke utterly openly, agreed with some points and disagreed with others, and kept ordering pints of bitter, so as to ensure the smooth flow of conversation. Even though my perception of things was becoming alcoholically dulled, I remember thinking that this wasn't a scene that was likely to be replicated at many other football clubs.

In 1985 we learned of a move as a result of a pamphlet, hastily shoved into the programme – rather like a piece of 'any other business' tacked onto the end of a meeting. Now, we were being kept in the picture and promised a vote on the issue. In the circumstances, any criticisms of the way it was being handled were going to have to be brilliantly presented, so as to avoid looking completely absurd.

Some of the peripheral goings on were worthy of an Ealing comedy. One fan, who may or may not bear a striking resemblance to Ben Hayes, wrote a column under the pseudonym 'Henry Irving' in the club fanzine *Voice of the Valley*, edited by Everitt. The article hinted deeply at a move to Brands Hatch, should the Dome deal not come to fruition. Within weeks a website run by one of the fans was boasting of an interview with the boss of Brands Hatch, in which he denied that Charlton were going to move there.

The fact that it was an amusing piece of mischief by Hayes, meaning that it was almost certainly the first time the man had ever heard of the proposed alteration of his motor-racing circuit into a football ground, didn't seem to matter. The denial was plastered about all over the place, with the insinuations that something had been 'uncovered', missing utterly the point that more had already been revealed than would have happened anywhere else.

I did ponder at the time constructing a story that we were planning to move to Mars, complete with a quote from a NASA employee explaining that he didn't think we were. It would have been vaguely analogous, but it didn't seem worth the effort. Deep down, I could see no way that the club would make the move, to the Dome – rather than Brands Hatch or Mars – simply because the fans wouldn't have it. It's strange how easy it gets to take things for granted at Charlton – at other clubs, the wishes of the fans would have counted for next to nothing. Why do I keep thinking of Wimbledon's current plight when I look back at this period at Charlton?

The chronology of the Dome episode ultimately did little more than to highlight the fact that the board were being completely honest with the fans throughout the process. Having confirmed their interests, or at least the reasons behind their initial application, they went on to announce in September that they had been short-listed as part of the 'Sports Dome 2001' consortium. Fifty-eight proposals had been submitted in all, and twelve reached the shortlist. How strange that the winner would appear to be the one who suggested leaving it to decay and stand empty for two years, but maybe that's getting away from the point.

At the end of July 1999, with all manner of rumours flying about, Richard Murray made his position quite clear:

> It would be absolutely irresponsible for us not to at least put our hat in the ring to see what is available. If we could get a 40,000-seater stadium on the right terms with the sort of transport infrastructure they have got at the Dome, we would have to seriously consider it.
>
> However, I think I can make a vow that before making any decision we would hold a referendum with our fans. We are a community club and we would ask the supporters. If the majority said no, I don't think we would move. We would have to put the case for and against. If we did move then we could sell the ground for property development and give the money to Alan Curbishley for new players.

It would be a chance to become a top London club like Chelsea and Arsenal, while if we stay at 20–24,000 the best we could be is a Coventry. But we would still be in our old Valley. I run this club on behalf of the fans and do it for love. That's why I do what the fans want to do.

Discussions had obviously continued behind the scenes, however, and while the promise to have a full consultation exercise was still alive, it proved not to be needed. In December 1999, Greenwich Council granted planning permission to extend the existing ground by building a second tier on the north stand – at the end of January 2000. Undoubtedly in part influenced by the decision, the club announced it was withdrawing from the consortium, and would be pushing ahead with plans to extend the capacity of The Valley to 26,000.

As far as the 'stitch-up' a few of the fans were suggesting, it appeared to be a strangely beneficial one. We were staying put, everyone had been kept in the picture about the developments as they happened, and we were getting a huge new stand. Murray's final announcement regarding the proposal was just about everything we could have hoped for, both in terms of the decision not to move and the statement about our future.

It was entirely right that we entered the Millennium Dome competition.

The board has fully evaluated the financial aspects of building a new stadium on the Greenwich Peninsula. The projected cost of £42 million and the absence of significant grant aid made the project financially unattractive.

We are very ambitious for the future of the club, but we believe that we can realise all our immediate ambitions here. After all the club has gone through we simply cannot envisage life other than at The Valley.

We will continue to build the club in a responsible and financially prudent manner and will concentrate all our efforts in returning this great club to the FA Premier League, where it belongs.

Strangely, he never mentioned Brands Hatch. Somewhere, doubtless, the conspiracy theorists continue to mutter onwards . . .

Harking back to that pre-season period, the signs that we were not going to fall to some terrible financial fate following relegation, were starting to become apparent. In the space of a month, Danny Mills had joined Leeds for a club record fee of £4.375 million, having joined us just 15 months earlier for £350,000 from Norwich. With the East Anglian side claiming 20 per cent of the fee as a result of the original contract, it wasn't a bad sale from their point of view either.

Within a week it was announced that Paul Konchesky, and crucially Mark Kinsella and Alan Curbishley, had all signed new contracts, with Scott Parker also signing up for a further five years the following month. In addition to this, Neil Redfearn was joining Bradford, which seemed to fail to cause too much by way of wailing and gnashing of teeth. He headed up the M1 to start his third successive season with a newly promoted club. We'd gone down, he'd underperformed to a quite extraordinary level, and now he was scooting back off up north in a bid to squeeze another season in the Premiership out of another side, presumably paying Premiership-sized wages. I'm just glad nobody suggested he was only in it for the money . . .

Against this background, the fans were showing that, while Redfearn may be jumping ship, they were staying right where they were, continuing to buy season tickets in remarkable numbers. Of all the clubs in the First Division, only Manchester City would start the new season having sold more season tickets than Charlton. More than 15,000 fans pledged their support for the entire season, further ensuring the financial safety of the club. Prices had been cut, meaning that people were paying less money for more games in a bid to avert the post-Premiership slide experienced by so many other clubs.

The operating profit for the first half of the Premiership season just gone was £8.1 million, compared to £2.5 million for the same period the previous year. It didn't take a mathematician to tell you that our club was continuing to make a very healthy recovery indeed, better run and looking in better financial shape, arguably, than at any time in its history. If Colin Cameron had previously been frustrated at the part-time nature of previous boards of directors, the current incumbents were running the show with an impressively professional attitude and the results confirmed the fact.

A final piece of the pre-season jigsaw was ready to be dropped into place, when the club was advised that it could take legal action following the poaching of Jermaine Defoe by West Ham. The young striker had come up through the Charlton academy system and had shown considerable promise at all stages of his development. In hindsight, maybe too much promise, as he came to the attention of West Ham scouts and was enticed to Upton Park.

The case culminated early the following season, when the FA Premier

League appeals tribunal awarded Charlton compensation of up to £1.65 million for Defoe. If he goes on to achieve half the things of which he looks capable, that figure will probably represent about 10 per cent of his eventual worth – a fact not lost on Charlton fans. Having been with the club since he was ten years of age, and graduating through the FA National School at Lilleshall, he signed for the Hammers a month before his 17th birthday, when he had been widely expected to become a professional at Charlton.

Peter Varney was forced to accept the ruling, although even with a payment of that magnitude it was clearly far short of being sufficient to discourage other clubs from committing similar 'swoops'. With the cost of staffing and running an academy, cases, and more particularly penalties such as the Defoe one, surely bring the whole system into question.

Three years later, Defoe appeared for his new club at The Valley and scored a goal that helped to earn West Ham a 4–4 draw, as well as the goal which beat Manchester United at Old Trafford. Indeed, throughout the course of his first major Premiership season, his goals were directly responsible for six points to his club. Having ultimately finished in seventh place, without Defoe's goals it's arguable that West Ham would have ended up two places lower, in ninth. With the prize money for Premiership places being dispensed at the rate of £440,000 per position, that would have left them £880,000 worse off, which is more than half of what they may one day have to pay out for poaching him. Suddenly the fine seems even more inadequate.

The continuing references from commentators about Defoe being just another product of the 'wonderful West Ham youth system' have, to the outsider, been known to get Charlton fans irrationally upset. When you look back at the case, it's not really all that irrational at all.

We looked forward to the new season, though, and in far greater numbers than some had predicted we might. Of the three teams who landed in the Nationwide at the end of the last season, it maybe wasn't the most difficult of tasks to predict how two of them would fare. Blackburn were bankrolled and Forest were left counting the cost of the drop with no financial saviour in sight, so it was fairly easy to make an educated guess at which way they were going to go. We were, as I've said, slightly different.

Some people had said that we'd be all right, while an awful lot more had expressed a desire that we survive, just because they felt that we should. The affection and good wishes were nice, but they wouldn't have been enough had the structure not been in place and the planning not been precise and careful. Not for the first time, Charlton were exceeding expectations without even kicking a ball.

We spent hours discussing it with each other, musing over whether the relegation and squad changes that followed would weaken or strengthen the side. Would we be galvanised and ready to bounce back, or would we appear shell-shocked and demoralised? Relegation had seen off clubs that were supposedly bigger than us, and some of them seemed unlikely ever to recover.

Despite the encouraging signs off the pitch, we all waited and wondered whether we could recapture our form on it. We'd suffered so many defeats the previous year that there were people quite seriously expressing the view that we'd forgotten how to win matches. Admittedly, nobody was taking them all that seriously, but they were saying it anyway. Even with what appeared to be a genuine solidity about the place, could we rediscover the momentum we needed to force ourselves back into the top flight?

Looking back, the questions were answered more quickly than even the most optimistic fan had dreamed possible.

11

PUTTING SOMETHING BACK

At just after half past ten on the evening of 22 April 1993, a group of six white murderers launched an unprovoked, cowardly and fatal attack on a young black man, who was standing at a bus stop in Well Hall Road, Eltham, less than two miles from The Valley. His crime was to have called out to his friend, Duwayne Brooks, who was waiting to see if their bus was approaching, and witnesses reported hearing the group of white men shouting 'What, what, nigger?' before they launched their assault.

Having twice been brutally stabbed in the chest, the unarmed teenager managed to stagger 130 yards, towards Shooters Hill, where the road starts to drop back down towards the River Thames and the Woolwich Ferry. A friend of the family, Joseph Shepherd, saw the attack, and ran to the teenager's home to tell his parents what had happened. By the time he got there, their son had died.

He bled to death, in the street, with the clothing he was wearing absorbing his own blood as it pumped out. The police reaction to the killing, at least in its immediate aftermath, was the subject of harsh and detailed criticism from Mr Justice Macpherson, as the case became famous throughout the country, if not the world.

It might have been an anonymous, black teenager who the ambulance crew collected from a bleak stretch of pavement that night, but his legacy was set to live on after him. Nine years after that racist scar was inflicted on the community, the Stephen Lawrence murder, while remaining a vivid injustice and affront, has become an enduring benchmark in the social history of this country.

Having only just returned to the area, Charlton Athletic were confronted with an evil in the middle of their community. To refuse to commit to the fight against racism was to either accept that nothing could be done about the situation, or to turn our back on the community and shrug that it wasn't our problem. In the wake of the fight to return to the ground, the Valley Party had produced a series of brilliant posters, designed by Richard Hunt, a Charlton fan and advertising-industry 'insider'. One of them showed a group of Charlton players holding the FA Cup aloft back in 1947, with the slogan: 'Do you remember when you were proud to come from Charlton?'

If we really were all the things we had claimed during the course of that journey back to SE7, the club couldn't ignore what was happening on its doorstep. If we weren't prepared to do something to register our disgust at what had happened, and to try and improve the situation, then we weren't going to be in a position to talk about our 'pride' for the area again. Plans had already been made, but the events in Eltham gave them new urgency and importance.

After the light-hearted footballing tales and the string of glorious memories which have filled these pages up until now, all this stops the momentum in its tracks, as it should, and brings real life back to the fore. The grim flip side of our everyday existence never sits easily alongside the euphoric escapism that makes up the majority of our sporting memories, and surely that's as it should be.

There are many voices in the current climate, telling us that sport, and football in particular, is desperately important. They want us to believe that those few hours on a Saturday afternoon should dominate our entire week, and while it sometimes feels as if they do, is that really a healthy development? Shouldn't there be more important things in life than the success with which a bunch of men wearing a familiar shirt kick a ball around a pitch? This is perhaps a question we often forget to ask ourselves.

As the legendary John Arlott once observed, with a view of the wider world that is all too often missing in modern sport: 'We take life too lightly and sport too seriously.' The reminder that people were prone to get things out of proportion was reinforced a few years ago, during a conversation with another famous sporting scribe. 'If it's a disaster when someone misses a penalty,' he queried, 'what is it when a ship sinks or a plane crashes?'

I can't pretend that the death of Stephen Lawrence is an event relived with any great frequency at Charlton, simply because it isn't. I don't even know if he ever came to the ground, but that equally isn't all that important. At the same time as he was killed, the anti-racist scheme Charlton were launching would seek to take the club to the people and try and use football as a tool to encourage change. As a football fan, that afternoon at Wembley probably represents the proudest I ever felt about my club. As a person, the continuing commitment to anti-racism, and the lack of racist chanting at The Valley, stands right up there alongside it.

Just a few weeks ago, more than nine years after the murder took place, a woman wrote a letter to the local newspaper. Why, she demanded, did everyone have to keep going on about racism all the time? People were getting obsessed with it, and, anyway, she knew that Stephen Lawrence and he wasn't quite the angel people were making out.

It came as some consolation that the following week a stream of people had letters published, condemning her stupidity and bigotry, but it was also instructive that she felt happy to express those views with her name and address attached. She wasn't making a one-woman stand, nor was she at the end of her tether about a subject, and left convinced that something must be said. She was, without much doubt, making a statement that she'd make quite happily most days to like-minded friends and acquaintances living in the area.

It tells its own story. Eltham, located in the Borough of Greenwich, just a short bus ride from Charlton, has a serious and threatening race-hate problem. An overwhelmingly white suburb, it was becoming an area where black people were choosing not to go, especially after the hours of darkness. As the group who killed Stephen Lawrence sneered and mocked the attempts to bring them to justice, so the problem continued, and the wounds refused to heal. How could they heal, there was nothing in place to help them get better?

In any other circumstances, the local football ground may well find itself as an ideal place for racial hatred to bubble away, just under the surface, without too much fear of interruption. Just a few miles from The Valley, Millwall's ground, The New Den, has become a virtual haven for such bigotry to exist. When an *Observer* columnist wrote a scathing account of a night spent watching them play Manchester City last year, the details of the racist chanting were quite sickening.

In response, Millwall's chairman, Theo Paphitis pointed out that he couldn't believe that the writer was reporting what he honestly saw. Millwall, Paphitis argued, had more fans prosecuted for racist offences than anyone else last year, which must, in his own curious version of logic, show that they are trying harder than anyone else to stamp out the problem. The same approach, of course, also leads you to the conclusion that his football club is more vehemently opposed to violence than the Women's Institute jam-making club, as a result of all the arrests which occur whenever they lose a play-off game and riot in the streets. And the lack of old grannies remanded in custody. If it wasn't so sad and serious, it would be laughable.

Against this background of rising racial tension, however, with Eltham to the south and Millwall to the west, Charlton have not only avoided becoming embroiled, but have made a positive decision to take a stand on the matter. Along with schemes run in Newcastle and Sheffield, Charlton Athletic are part of one of only three anti-racist campaigns in the country that have run all the way through the season. It is a valuable cause for which to fight and the area surrounding the ground is an important battlefield.

The problem of racism at football grounds has been fairly obvious to all for much of the last 30 years. It doesn't happen at every ground, and it doesn't happen every week, but there are instances too numerous, both recorded and reported anecdotally, to be ignored as the work of people 'looking for racism where it doesn't exist'. It was a view, sadly, that history suggests was, at least partly, shared by the Football Association and the objectionable local paper letter writer. It took pressure from the Commission for Racial Equality and the Professional Footballers' Association to lead to the creation of the 'Kick It Out' campaign, which acts as a permanent anti-racist task force. Indeed, it took the Football Association until last year to apologise to black players for acting in such a weak and indecisive way 20 years ago, when monkey chants and bananas were aimed at them with monotonous and hurtful regularity.

Where there is gloss and glamour at the Premiership grounds, who must be sanitised and made attractive for the demands of television, tighter scrutiny on fans in addition to better policing has cut the problem down considerably. Elsewhere, where the cameras and the crowds never go, into the lower leagues and beneath, the problem is still alive and unpleasantly healthy.

In 1998, the football task force, in conjunction with Kick It Out, produced a ten-point plan, aimed at ridding the game of racism, or at least reducing it to as small a problem as was humanly possible. Yet there are still many clubs openly refusing to abide by and implement the plan, with the problem threatening to return more vigorously than at any time in the last few seasons.

The answer seems, fairly obviously, to be that a long-term approach is needed. Attitudes need to be changed, people's perceptions of what is, and more importantly, isn't acceptable need to be changed, and the new fans need to learn from the existing supporters what will be tolerated. In addition to the question of not doing unacceptable things comes the issue of positively promoting diversity, and looking back and recognising the contribution made to the club throughout its history by all races and creeds.

At some stage, the boundary between what is a football-related matter and what is a society-related matter starts to blur, and through the use of projects which link the club with local schools and youth groups, a relationship is formed with benefits to both sides. Charlton have been very active in this area since the year after they returned to The Valley – no sooner had they found their feet than they were looking at ways to forge greater links with a community they had once deserted.

It's almost a decade since that appalling night in Well Hall Road and I'm seeing at first-hand just how some of those links are being made. In about five hours' time, Charlton will kick off their Premiership campaign for the current season against Chelsea at The Valley. Almost 27,000 people will pack into the stadium to watch the Addicks try and hand out a fifth successive beating to their west London rivals.

For the time being, though, it means one last chance to do something useful with my Saturday mornings, before football comes along and swallows them up for another nine months – in this case, doing the shopping with the family. The car park in front of the supermarket is already emitting an unpleasant, shimmering heat haze and the tarmac seems determined to absorb every last drop of sunlight, in order to act like a huge radiator for the already sweltering locality. Drivers are starting to get irate with each other and parking spaces are being contested with as much ferocity as the car owners' uncomfortably warm bodies will allow.

In the midst of this particular vision of urban hell, a sight at the far end of the car park can't help but catch the eye. Standing about 15 ft in the air is a bright-red, inflatable goal, with what appears to be some kind of trampoline-type contraption on the bottom of it. A handful of red T-shirted figures mill about, while a mobile disco pumps out the chorus of Abba's 'Dancing Queen' to the unsuspecting shoppers. Splattered all over the framework of the goal, as well as on the T-shirts, are Charlton Athletic badges, in addition to a host of logos belonging to sponsors and other affiliated organisations. An already hot-and-bothered figure hurtles around, trying to organise the crowds of children who are converging on the unlikely sideshow.

Ben Tegg is Charlton Athletic's community liaison officer, and if everyone else is gently coming to terms with the day, and turning their thoughts to the afternoon's game over a cup of tea and an early morning bacon sandwich, it's clear that he's started at a rather less relaxing pace.

'We should have a lot of kids here today, so it will be a decent morning. It's going to get bloody busy, in fact, and it's not going to get any cooler either. I'm burning up already here. I must be mad.'

Tegg and his team have been running events like this all through the summer. Rough estimates suggest that they have managed to make contact with more than 200,000 people in the last few months, at local carnivals, festivals and anti-racist events. The total cost, thanks to a sponsorship deal Tegg obtained, was just over £7,000. When you hear the management of large organisations talking about their people 'on the ground', the group standing in front of me now is exactly what they mean. Oh, and the ground is continuing to get hotter by the minute.

'Someone said there was a game on later on?' Tegg jokes. 'I might get along to it if I can get the inflatable back in its box in time – get someone to save me a seat, will you? I must be mad, I really must, but this is what football's all about, isn't it?'

With a backwards grin thrown in my direction, he's off to carry on organising the chaos, all in a valuable cause. In an instant, Honor, my four-year-old daughter, has decided that Chris Powell might not be her number-one Charlton hero any more – after all, he hasn't got a bouncy castle and the sweaty man in the car park does. Amy, a year younger, throws a typical three-year-old tantrum when I try to drag her away. If it's as popular with other children as it is with mine, he might have a long wait before he can start to pack the giant goalmouth away.

As I stand in the stadium later that day, with kick-off just an hour away, the heat has risen further and it's now a genuinely hot afternoon. It's sticky, oppressive and the traffic fumes seem to hang in the air, while a digital thermometer by the side of the pitch shows that it's just below 100 degrees in the sunshine. Someone holding a clipboard walks past me on the touchline, determined to be important, but seemingly stuck for anyone to talk to. He settles on me, thus confirming that there truly can't be anyone important hanging around.

'I hope they make sure to drink plenty of water, because it's going to be very hot out there,' he opines.

'Mmm. Fingers crossed that the physios have thought of that, eh? They might not have noticed that it was getting warm,' I reply, tongue obviously not quite firmly enough in cheek to register with him.

'Yeah. We've got some really important people coming here today –

big clients, you know, so it's got to be right. Looks great, doesn't it? New advertising, new lounges. It's what football's all about. Anyway, got to go, people to meet. Bye.'

As he leaves, he clasps a hand on my shoulder, and strides off up the stairs. With our friendship still only ten or twelve seconds old, I'm thrilled to think that I'm worthy of such a warm farewell. I hope he was being sincere, but I still don't, to my acute embarrassment, have the slightest idea who he was. He wasn't anyone I recognised, so he wasn't all that important, but he obviously had designs on progress – the sort who wants to end up with a big car and a little phone.

It occurs to me that it's very difficult to describe exactly who markets a football club. I mean, the marketing department will, not unexpectedly, claim that they do, but they can't honestly say that they do it on their own. The players get involved through their actions on the pitch, the manager through his comments and the fans through their behaviour. Then, there are those who just get on with doing their job, allowing their actions to speak louder than words – the sort of people you bump into in car parks on Saturday mornings. Everyone has their place and their role, even if rolling your sleeves up, rather than doing your tie up, is sometimes the order of the day.

A fortnight later, and it would appear that Tegg has recovered from the exertions of the day and has finally been given some public recognition for his efforts, with a feature in the match-day programme. Rick Everitt, now the communications director, no less, has written a feature on the work done by the Community Scheme and seems to manage to put his finger on what it was that left me feeling so confused on that opening Saturday of the season.

'It's an oddity of football clubs,' he writes, 'that the most important marketing ever done on their behalf is nothing to do with those within the organisation who are professionals in that field.'

While there is obviously a distinction between something being important and it being physically exhausting, he seems to have hit the nail on the head. I think back to my Saturday morning trip to the supermarket car park and my lunchtime meeting on the touchline, and it reinforces the idea in my mind. Now I just need to discover why Tegg puts himself through such exertions.

As you stroll around Charlton with him, you become aware of two things. The first is that everyone knows him and says hello, while the second is that everyone who isn't saying hello to his face is only failing to do so because they're in the process of trying to phone him. A short, squat man, he seems to be living proof that if you try hard enough, you can survive on nicotine and nervous energy alone. I'm not much of a health expert, but I know that, in their own right, mobile phones, stress and cigarettes aren't meant to be good for you. Thrown together in the copious proportions Tegg manages, I'm starting to worry that he won't make it all the way through to the end of our chat.

Given the nature of his work, the stress seems unavoidable, but is he fighting a battle that he knows for certain can be won? Given the work that he does though, and the area in which the club is based, doesn't he ever feel that it's an impossible job?

> Never, no, I never think that, because we're up and running now. It was very hard in the early days, when I was still working for the national campaign, but now we're making progress. The important thing is that we were the first football club to set something like this up, and we wanted to be involved in the process of trying to change things a long time ago.
>
> This isn't something we've put together in five minutes in the very recent past just because it makes us look good. We were the first club in the country to seriously do anti-racism work and that was back in 1992. We set up our campaign a year before the national campaign was started and that came into existence a year later. There had been some work at Leeds and West Ham, but that was by supporters and not by the clubs themselves, so we lead the way in that regard.

Tegg and the scheme he represents have become a familiar sight around The Valley, and that in itself seems to be important. He doesn't turn up on a match-day, hand out a few leaflets and then disappear. That continual presence seems to be a key part of the thinking behind their work:

> There's a load of places that have said 'We'll have an anti-racism day, put a couple of posters up and it'll all look lovely and we won't have to bother with anything else.' Charlton have never done that, they've taken a long-term view and they've helped fund that long-term approach. Charlton spend five times more than any other club on this sort of initiative, in terms of community work and all that surrounds it, and the reward is there for all to see. We've got 21,000 season-ticket holders and people among them who maybe wouldn't have always thought of going to football.

If you talk to black people locally now, they want to come to Charlton. They might not all support Charlton themselves, they might support Arsenal or West Ham or someone, but they want their kids to come to Charlton. I know black dads who don't support us, but as their kids are getting more interested in the game, they want them to come down to The Valley to watch their football. That's because they think it's a safe and a good place for them to be and that's as it should be.

We approached it in three stages and although there have been a few run-ins with Greenwich Council through the years, in terms of our anti-racism policy, it's safe to say that without the Council, we wouldn't be doing all that we're doing now. They've pushed us, been involved with us and without them we wouldn't be doing as well as we are in this area – an area that gives us a huge amount of respect and good publicity.

Which is an angle I'd always considered obvious. Yet never seen explored. The money side of things and the community side of things at most football clubs remain firmly at opposite ends of the spectrum, with the traditional image being of one asking for more money and the other refusing and saying they get quite enough already. There are fairly clear reasons, about which they don't seem to be coy or embarrassed, why Charlton prefer to have them working in conjunction with each other.

There are two reasons why we do it. We do it firstly because it's morally right and also because there's no point in trying to run a business in an area such as this, and cheerfully cutting off 30 per cent of the people in your catchment area because they don't feel welcome coming along and giving you their business. There's no point in pretending that we do it solely for the moral reason, but at the same time, because of the long-term nature of the schemes, there's no question that it's not purely a business venture. That wouldn't stand up to scrutiny, because it takes a long time to come to fruition, and you can't project figures or give guarantees about things, because of the aim you're trying to achieve.

Other clubs should do it as well – there's no doubting that, not so much for the moral reasons, because it's not for us to preach to them about that, but for the economic reasons, because it's impossible to argue with them. The reasons other clubs don't is because football is so badly run it's unbelievable. I've heard clubs say that they don't want to run an anti-racist scheme because it will highlight the issue. Well, yes, of course it will highlight the issue, but then the issue might become a far smaller issue, and next thing you know, business will pick up because of it, but that seems to be financial planning and strategic thinking beyond a lot of clubs.

We started the campaign six years before anyone else, before it was a high-profile issue. Now it is high-profile, we've got past the stage of having to justify it on such a basic level and we can just get on and run it, and enjoy the benefits of it, on all levels.

Returning, though, to the question of the geographical location, and the nature of the problems faced by other clubs in the area, it struck me that Tegg must be in a prime position to provide an answer. He was working for the national anti-racism scheme before he came to Charlton and has worked with many other clubs in London and the South East, both the willing and seemingly those more resistant to the idea that change was required.

Returning then to the question of Millwall, and the points raised by their chairman, was I being hard on him? Do they have the commitment to change, in his opinion, that their public pronouncements suggest?

Millwall have got some decent people working for them, but their scheme isn't like Charlton's because Charlton invested in theirs and also had a number of people who had experience of being involved in the Valley Party, so were equipped to help the scheme get up and running. There were a load of people who were sound in terms of their opinions and morals and that experience and those values were passed on.

You can also look at the way the club is set up now and see that the same fundamental beliefs are being continued through. How many football clubs can you point to nowadays who have a chief executive who used to work in the charity sector? How many football clubs have a chairman who actually gets involved in the anti-racist work at the club because he sees it as being right, rather than because he sees it as a photo opportunity or a way of getting a couple of lines in the newspaper? There's a commitment here that isn't there at other clubs – especially where it matters.

The point about the experience of working in the charity sector is valid and one which, I confess, hadn't occurred to me previously. Before moving to Charlton, Peter Varney worked for the British Brain and Spine Foundation, and it's fair to say that his experience marks him out as approaching the role of chief executive from a considerably different slant to most of his colleagues. While it's obviously a contributory factor however, it can't be the whole story. Varney has been at Charlton for four or five years, and the scheme pre-dates him by about the same length of time.

The man who gets most of Tegg's praise, at least as far as hands-on support is concerned, is the same one who strolled out of Highbury on that glorious Sunday afternoon, red of face and broad of beam. Tegg sets great store by the importance of commitment and sheer hard work, and he appears not to have been let down by those at the top of the Charlton hierarchy.

> I look at the work of people like Martin Simons and that's commitment. He turns up at all sorts of events and doesn't care if there's a camera there or not, He's done big events, but he's done them with groups of four kids and no publicity as well, and been just as generous with his time. He's doing a thing in a couple of weeks with a group of kids from Brixton we've been working with.
>
> It's part of a scheme about jobs in football – not playing it, but working in it – and it's done to try and counter the lack of black people working in the game. Martin says without a second's thought: 'Bring them in, bring them into the boardroom, I'll have a chat, we can talk about what the director of a football club does.' Now, there won't be a camera in sight, but he'll be there and he'll talk to them and he'll enjoy it and be interesting and that's the sort of commitment I'm talking about. It doesn't cost anything, but it's not cheap, if you see what I mean.

It would be all too easy to fall into the trap of portraying Tegg as a bit worthy – a bit stern and serious – when it really couldn't be further from the truth. His work is serious, and he does something worthy, desperately so, but he does it, I suspect through necessity, with an almost constant smile on his face. He plainly loves what he does and his cheery disposition and readiness to roll up his sleeves and get stuck in appears to break down more barriers than the slickest piece of rhetoric. It's just another example, it seems to me, of the way in which Charlton have gone about tackling the issue.

People say to me that I'm working in a PR role, but that's wrong. Part of what we do is PR, sure, but if it's not backed up by decent community work, then it won't convince anyone. We try and tell people about what we're doing, which I suppose is PR. What we don't do is try and exaggerate what we do, try and convince people it's bigger and better than it is, or try and pretend it's an answer to all the problems in the world. If we did that, then, as far as I'm concerned, we'd be doing PR work.

If you look at our community work, it's on a number on levels. There are football training courses which involve the local community and then there's the stuff which involves them but doesn't necessarily rely on them playing football or getting coached or anything like that. It's community work for the parts of the community who might like football, but they don't play it, to put it simply. What we're saying is that we are a football club and we accept that means that there are some things we can't change. Just because we're a football club doesn't give us a magic wand to change things more easily than anyone else could, but it does give us both responsibilities and opportunities to do things for the community.

I think you can divide communities up in a quite straightforward way, and in this part of the world it's especially true. If you look at them as just one hundred people, there are ten active anti-racists, eighty decent, ordinary people, and ten racists, trying to convince people, in any number of ways, that there is something to be said for their views. We have tried to marginalise the ten racists, get rid of them, then start working and educating the other eighty, to carry on the work you've started. What we've done is worked on the other eighty better and more efficiently than any other club.

It's not the football club blowing their own trumpet and saying, 'We're great, listen to us', but it's community work delivered in conjunction with the football club, in partnership with other people – people who deal with the community all the time. We've provided a link that allows everyone to get the best out of the deal.

Having been a long-time fan of the club, Tegg has seen his fair share of downs, but it's his memory of one of the highs that dispels any lingering fear that he exists in some humourless, irony-free world, talking about 'issues surrounding' and seeking out offence wherever he turns. After an hour chatting with him, any stereotypes you might have carried around about people in his line of work are thoroughly shattered. There appears to be quite enough gratuitous offence in the world of football for him to deal with, without trying to invent any.

As for the humourless, I suspect that in order to do Tegg's job properly and remain sane, learning to laugh at things is about as important as learning to read. He is, at heart, a Charlton fan, and while he is passionate about his work, it's his football team that provokes the most vivid description he produced during our conversation.

> The play-off final was just the most amazing day. I arranged for more mates than I want to think about to get tickets, meet up and then go for a drink afterwards. I sent out maps and plans and timings, and then went through a game like that!
>
> We'd booked an Indian restaurant for the night, not a table at a restaurant, a whole restaurant and it turned into a right long night. I remember celebrating in a fairly liquid style and then everything goes a bit hazy. I do remember waking up though and I don't quite know what happened in the bits in between. When I came to, I was sitting outside the kebab shop in Charlton Church Lane, with a kebab sitting in my hand, un-spilled, but frankly, a bit past its best, if it had ever had one.
>
> It was about half past five in the morning and I was about as dehydrated as it was possible to be. I picked myself up, leaving my kebab to one side, and went for a little walk home. I don't think, on the evidence of what I saw in the streets around The Valley, that I was the only one who didn't make it all the way back to bed before crashing out for the night. It was a top day out!

The memory provokes much smiling and shaking of his head, which is probably more than he could comfortably manage when he first awoke on that post-play-off morning. If Charlton Athletic have moved on a long way in the last ten years, they can be as proud at their efforts to bring the entire community along with them as almost anything else. Back in the early days, shortly after the return to the club, everyone agreed that there was a need to improve the ground.

Convincing people that there was a need to try and educate the attitudes of some of the people within it was a trickier task. Charlton haven't earned their reputation as a community club lightly and when someone tries to put together a list of the heroes of the last ten years, the people who helped earn that reputation deserve a mention. If the job is difficult today, it must have been tougher back then.

When football's anti-racism campaign got started in 1993, it was 20 years out of date, but that was the way it needed to be, because you were dealing with overt racism. Football is now an excellent way of connecting and trying to change the views of racists. It wasn't always the way and there was a huge amount of work needed to be done before it become a vehicle for anything like that. Let's not muck around, racism is society's problem, but football has spent a long time being a vehicle for that problem and it let itself be used without putting up any form of protest.

Ten years ago, football was used as a tool, or a vehicle for racism. Now, it's used as a vehicle for anti-racism, and not just racism, but sexism and things like homophobia, which is appalling in football grounds. It's become a tool for good and from a commercial point of view, as the racism and sexism has died away, we've seen more ethnic minorities and more women at the ground. Now, they're all buying tickets to get in, so it doesn't take a rocket scientist to work out that it's been cost-effective and worthwhile, just from a business point of view.

Ninety per cent of racism is unwitting, it's just not thinking, or being lazy and generalising. Some of it borders on the deliberate and the unwitting, though. It's like when people talk about black players not being any good 'in December when it's cold' or on 'heavy pitches'. That's the sort of thing players had to put up with in the 1960s and '70s and it's still there so there's still obviously a job to be done.

So, having ascertained that the problem is one which we can overcome, and having concluded that the steps currently being taken are leading us in the right direction, how far do we still have to go? More importantly perhaps, given that we have made progress over the last ten years, and won some of the battles, in the decade to come, where will the battle take us?

There aren't as many Asian players as there should be and that's because we don't scout Asian leagues as well as we should. Asian players tend to play in Asian leagues over here, because when they try and play outside of those, they get abused and attacked. There used to be someone who worked with me at Charlton who was Asian and played in a multi-racial team and he ended up hospitalised because a group of lads from an opposing team beat him up during a game because of the colour of his skin. People trying to defend the situation try and suggest Asians keep to themselves because they don't want to integrate, but in my experience, a lot of times it's been because of concerns for their own safety.

People aren't born racist, but they pick it up as they grow up from those around them. If we can change the views of younger people, then slowly but surely we can help to eradicate the problem a bit further with each fresh generation.

The racists may have thought that they were winning on that sickening evening in Well Hall Road ten years ago and the killers who have evaded justice may still do so. The fight back, however, has been as intelligent and brave as their actions were Neanderthal and cowardly, and it's a battle that is starting to be won. As Tegg says, being a football club doesn't give us a magic wand – the problems lie somewhere deeper than we can go on our own. They might also, however, exist somewhere that can't be reached without us, and working together, we can, and will, make a difference.

Not all of the heroes at football clubs, it would appear, run around with their names on the back of their shirts.

12

NORMAL SERVICE HAS BEEN RESUMED

There were many ways of describing the first season in the Premiership and it's fair to say that we had a good go at using as many different ones as we possibly could. One view: it was a fantastic experience – a journey on which we saw places and played teams few of us would have thought possible not so long ago. Another view: it was depressing, as we were occasionally outclassed, frequently outwitted and regularly outscored on our way back to the First Division.

What made it worse was that we'd been roundly written off by virtually everyone you listened to in the build-up to the season and despite having done better than most pundits had anticipated, we'd proved them right – we weren't good enough. It was the sound of commentators preparing their 'Well, I hate to say I told you so' speech that left most of us really annoyed, and as we slid into the bottom three, it was starting to sound like our theme tune.

Once it had faded away, however, we found ourselves looking through the fixture list, trying not to become too depressed at the lack of 'big' clubs on it. We tried even harder to sound like hardened Premiership veterans, temporarily down on our luck, rather than people who'd just got back from a back-packing trip during their gap year, and started to assess our chances of winning a few games for a change. By the end of it, as history and the front of the book record, the very wildest expectation of the most optimistic fan had been dramatically and emphatically exceeded.

John Robinson, extraordinarily enough, was keen to point out the scale of the achievement:

It was always going to be hard on us when we landed back down from the Premiership, but the vital thing we did as a team was to get a really good start. That was so hard because with international games and everything else we found ourselves lagging behind everyone else in terms of the number of games that we'd played.

On top of that, everyone wanted to beat us because we'd just come down from the Premiership. That's a factor not many people remember, but it makes life that little bit more difficult for you. It certainly upset Forest and Blackburn because neither of them had the first idea of how to deal with it. You only have to look at the table to see who adjusted best.

We kept the bulk of the squad together and there was a quiet confidence amongst us. We knew we had the ability and also we didn't sell people all over the place, but strengthened the squad where we felt we needed to.

In the wake of the previous season's relegation, and despite the events of the pre-season – which had left us, on the surface at least, so confident about our prospects – we would have been forgiven for feeling a degree of trepidation. It wasn't so much a lack of faith in our own side, but more an appreciation of the sheer size of the drop into which so many clubs in our position had fallen over the years. Everyone talks about bouncing back when they leave the Premiership, and precious few manage it.

What we needed was something to settle our nerves – to make us feel a bit better about things and to leave us with the belief that everything was going to be all right. Not for the first time, Mendonca stepped forwards and did the trick. Having signed off the season before last with a Wembley hat-trick and opened his account at The Valley last year with another three goals against Southampton, he was becoming rather adept at starting and finishing with a bang. In between the injuries, he wasn't bad during the middle of the season either.

When Barnsley arrived in south-east London, also looking to return to the top-flight football they had been playing two seasons earlier, there was an unmistakable air of tension hanging around the place. It was as if we had watched a boxer get knocked out and suddenly were all at his comeback fight, wondering how he'd react the first time he got whacked on the chin. We needn't have worried, and to be honest, from about mid-December onwards, for three months at least, it was more like a sparring session than a real fight.

Mendonca volleyed us in front against Barnsley after a handful of minutes and then added a couple of penalties, just to keep his collection of match-balls freshly re-stocked. We won 3–1, and then just carried on winning matches, seemingly almost at will. Of course there were the occasional upsets, but generally speaking, from the perspective of a fan, it could hardly have been a more different experience to the one we had gone through the previous year. Back then, if we got a point in the dullest game imaginable, it got acres of coverage – now we were wiping the floor with teams week in and week out, and barely meriting a mention in the papers. Welcome to life outside of the Premiership . . .

By the middle of October, we'd won as many league games as we managed in the whole of the previous season and by the time the New Year came around, we'd scored more goals than in the last campaign, with the points target equalled by mid-November. We were all very aware of the need to treat this as a temporary stop, somewhere we were just resting for a year before getting back to the Premiership, but the sheer enjoyment of winning games every week was going to be a hard one to beat.

I've often wondered whether, if you left it to spectators, they'd object if their side turned down promotion some years, in favour of just staying where they were and going through another season of whacking everyone out of sight. Maybe you'd want to accept promotion every third or fourth year, just to make a few quid and see a few of the big grounds and famous players, but then you'd come back down and get back into the swing of the season-long goalfest and everything would be fine again.

There's no real point in trying to present the season to you in a chronological fashion, because Charlton fans know what happened and everyone else has got a pretty good idea, just because I've come across as such a smug sod up to now. We won the title by two points, having managed just four points from our last seven matches, as we slowed down to wave at the crowd, sign autographs and check our hair hadn't been blown about too badly before they started taking photographs. Alan Curbishley would stand there each week and solemnly tell the press how we 'hadn't taken our foot off the pedal', and how we were going to keep giving it our all 'right the way to the end'.

Despite all the effort he put into convincing us, the team might as well have stood behind him, wearing fancy dress and pulling funny faces, laying on sun-loungers and ordering cocktails, as they mentally disappeared off the beach long before the end of the season. If we'd approached the end of the season the way we'd gone about dealing with the middle part of it, the hundred-point mark would have been passed and we would have won the title by a ridiculous margin. That wasn't our style, though, so we tried to win it as narrowly as possible, too tired to raise more than a desultory gallop and with as inglorious a flourish as we could muster. We achieved that, at least . . .

Manchester City had spent the second half of the season not so much snapping at our heels as staring at our tracks, trying to work out where we'd gone. Like a trusty old bloodhound chasing a gazelle, they were determined to follow, but unable to keep up with the pace that was being set. As we stumbled and ground to a halt, though, they kept on plodding forwards, and while they couldn't catch us, they clawed back a lead that had almost at one stage reached 20 points, until we won the title by a margin of just two. City ended up drawing 11 games that season, and if they could have turned just one of those draws into a victory, they would have been champions and not us. Somewhere along the line, you can probably identify the dodgy offside, or the striking of a post, or the miraculous save that stopped them doing just that. Even in our hour of triumph, we had been trying to snatch defeat from the jaws of victory.

As well as I can remember, however, nobody really got too concerned, as the charge for the line became a stagger. We'd had far too much fun and enjoyed far too many good days during the course of the year to start moaning now, and anyway after the run we'd had, how could any of us start complaining?

Beating Crystal Palace on Boxing Day was obviously the way to ensure that the Christmas festivities lived up to their billing for once, but it was to be only the launch pad for an amazing spell of results. When we went up to Huddersfield a couple of days later, and became the first side that season to beat them at home, we had a feeling that things might just be starting to turn in our favour a little bit.

As it turned out, things weren't so much turning our way a 'little bit', as gathering momentum, ready to sweep everything else aside. Between Boxing Day 1999 and the middle of March 2000, we won everything. In fact, we lost once, in the FA Cup to Bolton, but the overall run almost beggared belief. We won 14 out of 15 games, including 12 league games on the trot, and between the start of December and the middle of April, we lost just twice.

It was fantastic and odd, all at the same time. It was as if the gods who had frowned down on us as we lost match after match the previous season had decided that we deserved a bit of a break. Maybe it was some kind of reward for taking the upset of the previous year so well and refusing to get too depressed about it. Personally, as far as evening out the balances goes, I put it in the same category as Paul Kitson, which isn't a sentence you find yourself typing too often.

It was plain to me: the footballing gods had extracted a belated debt from us for Kitson's winning goal against Crystal Palace, by allowing him a hat-trick against us when he returned to West Ham. Now, they were putting us back in credit for the bad-luck overdraft we'd run up while losing nine games in a row the previous year. It might not be a very precise argument, but it's a way of looking at the game that seems to suit me. Much as I'd love to have the energy to debate each and every point in huge detail, I really can't be bothered.

Sometimes it's not a bad idea to just sit back and let people carry on yapping away at you from all directions, throwing opinions from every available angle. When they ask you what you think, you can just affect an air of calm and suggest that things go in cycles, or they happen for a reason, or the old classic, 'that's football'. Sometimes, they just ignore you, but with worrying frequency they take your virtual silence as a sign of inner calm and certainty, and start to treat you as something of an expert. Try it – it works.

Some people, of course, didn't suffer such problems when it came to explaining how we'd put together such a record. Cue John Robinson, speaking at the time, and plainly rather impressed with what had been achieved:

> I'm not surprised that we're going straight back up, because we're good enough to do it and there has always been that belief running through every single player in the squad. If you ask me about the margin of our lead, the goals scored, the records and stuff like that, then I'd have to admit I'm a little bit surprised at just how big our lead is.
>
> Twelve games on the trot, whatever level you're playing at, is an amazing record. It doesn't matter if you're a professional, playing in the county league or in the park, twelve straight wins takes a fair bit of doing. I think the fans appreciate how good that run was, because teams make it as difficult as they can for you.
>
> To be this far clear, at this stage of the season, in a league as strong as the First Division, is a bit special. You only have to look at the results to see that everyone in the league is capable of beating everyone else.
>
> You get to a point where you know that sides are going to pack the defence, keep it as tight as they possibly can and maybe think

that a goal on the break is the best that they're going to do. When you're at the top, you're the team that everyone wants to nick a point off. People don't want to make it easy for you and that's what makes our run of victories a bit special.

Somehow, had Robinson sat there and mused enigmatically that it was all destined to happen and that the gods had meant it to be that way, it wouldn't have worked. Which is probably evidence that the slow, ponderous method of examining things isn't best suited to everyone – some people leave us expecting a bit of passion and some, like Robinson, rarely fail to deliver.

Elsewhere, while Robinson was happy to explain to the world exactly what we'd done and what a battle it had been, there were players quite prepared to show just why they were not cut out to be expert pundits. Earlier in the season, Andy Hunt had been the first to fall at the 'unduly cautious and modest' hurdle:

> Last year Sunderland ran away with it, but I don't know that anyone's going to do that this year. But there's still a fair way to go and when you look at sides like Blackburn, who've just begun to put a run together, you realise the number of sides that could really get into a roll and sweep through in the second half of the season. We have got the ability to be the side that sweeps everyone else aside, but it's too early to predict something like that happening.
>
> Expectation does turn into pressure when you're playing at home. It's been very hard, and it will continue that way, because when teams come to The Valley they know they're in for a hard time. They will end up doing what we did a few times last year away from home, and shutting up shop and looking to emerge with a point. If a team comes and plays with just one target man up front, it's not going to be easy to deal with and it's going to take a while to break them down.
>
> You have to accept the fact that you won't always end up breaking defensive sides down and it won't always go your way. Even the best teams in the world have days when they struggle to get past very packed defences. Just look at Manchester United – they have some of the best creative players in the world and they still have the odd slip up at home. Even when they win, they often have to wait until late in the game before finding the way through. If it's difficult for a side that's won the treble, it's even

more difficult for everyone else. Being patient and sticking to what you learned through the week on the training pitch is the key.

Hunt, who habitually gave more thoughtful answers than almost any other player, was acutely aware of the difference between the challenges provided by the last two seasons. He also left the distinct impression that he was being forced to review his opinion of what was 'possible' with each successive game. It wasn't only the fans who were amending their expectations:

> Last year we had some good results against some really big teams. Admittedly, in general terms we weren't good enough because we got relegated, but we got draws at some big grounds, and took four points from six against Liverpool. They went away saying 'How the hell did we get beaten by Charlton?', but the result speaks for itself. That was how far we'd come.
>
> Now this year we're walking round saying 'How the hell didn't we beat Port Vale?' That's the level of expectation that's been generated, but the truth of the matter is that you're always going to have the odd game like that. It's totally unrealistic to expect the team to batter everyone every week, because that's just not possible.

Hunt had arrived at the club in the wake of the relegation from the Premiership and proved to be a useful source of opinion about the nature of the club and the way he, coming to it as an outsider, had perceived the place:

> Charlton fans are really good and they seem to know their football. I've been at West Brom and Newcastle and the crowds at both those clubs can get really hostile if they don't like you. Fans at The Valley get right behind the team and they don't turn too easily, but expectations will change as we get more successful. People come along who weren't bothering to turn up before and that's a sign of progress, but the fans that turn up now are maybe expecting a lot more than the ones who have been coming to The Valley for years. That does add to the pressure.
>
> I wasn't here, obviously, but from what people say, it seems that when we went up it was almost a bit of a surprise and a real bonus. Now, with everyone expecting us to go up, every small

setback is a real disappointment. The expectation is very different, and that's a sign of just how far the club has come. People's views on what we're likely to do each week have changed dramatically.

Hunt scored almost a third of our goals in the league that season, despite being diagnosed with glandular fever halfway through the year. It was a spiral of illness that would ultimately lead to him having to leave the game early, midway through the second season back in the Premiership. He would come walking into the training ground, looking dreadful, doubtless feeling awful, and explaining how it felt a little bit like a very bad bout of the flu, but he just couldn't 'shake it off'.

Hunt was one of the nicest footballers you could ever hope to meet and if he never looks back at another image of his career, which in his case is entirely possible, he need never doubt his impact on the club. If he thinks back to a championship-winner's medal being presented to him on a sunny May afternoon, he'll know that he was up there with the best of them. Even when the team were in full flow, however, with results being notched up week after week, he didn't act quite like the typical footballer.

He would occasionally turn up to training in his girlfriend's car, which was a Fiat Uno or some similar machine, and had seen many better days. When questioned, he would explain that his car needed filling up with petrol and he was late out of the house and didn't have time to do it. Besides, it was only a three-mile drive into the training ground, why did he need to use a great big, flash car just to manage that? There was something very Charlton-ish about the sight of the star striker parking a car worth a couple of hundred pounds among the fleets of BMWs and Mercedes that make up a football club training ground car park.

He also did things most footballers consider deeply suspicious and troubling – like read books, discuss politics from a mildly left-wing perspective and play backgammon, rather than plugging into a Walkman or DVD player and disappearing off into a world of his own. You could often see him leaning over a backgammon board, usually locked in combat with Sasa Ilic – two men who had both been responsible for dozens of goals, desperately shifting counters around a board.

'He takes some right weird holidays,' Curbishley had observed earlier in the year, as Hunt had returned from a summer travelling around America in a camper-van. The previous year it had been Bangkok.

Different from other players, perhaps, but weird? For a footballer, extraordinarily so.

Hunt's illness was to change his life totally, but in its early stages at least, while he was still able to play the game during that championship-winning season, he was as potent a striker as anyone else in the division. His diffident manner when celebrating a goal, with the arm in the air and a slightly embarrassed lopsided grin, as people descended on him from all directions, just added to the illusion that he was fully aware of the slightly odd nature of his occupation.

At first, the fans failed to take him to their hearts, partly because of the difficulty of playing up front in a side which was busy getting relegated and partly because he didn't seem to be an overly emotional player. As the championship season wore on, however, Hunt won everyone over. His work-rate was huge, his habit of scoring goals was not a bad one for a striker to fall into and the way he conducted himself made him decent hero material.

During the course of that amazing run of success which propelled us back into the Premiership, Hunt was just about unstoppable. He claimed a total of 12 goals in 14 matches, including back-to-back hat-tricks against Norwich and Stockport and a last-minute winner against Premiership Coventry City at Highfield Road to put us through to the sixth round of the FA Cup. His hat-trick against Stockport went along with the one he'd claimed against them earlier in the year. Apparently he doesn't get many Christmas cards from that part of the world to this day.

After his hat-trick up there, they didn't even want to give him the match-ball, finally handing him a scruffy old plastic bag as the coach pulled out of the ground, following a request from Keith Peacock that tradition be adhered to. Halfway down the M1, and a quick look in the bag confirmed that it wasn't, of course, the actual match-ball, but an old training ball, stuck in the bag to keep the Charlton contingent quiet. Where was the real ball then and what did he do with the one they gave him?

> God knows where the one we played with is – probably still there, waiting to be used another day! The one I got was knackered, and I think it ended up in a service station, where we donated it to some kids hanging about in the car park. It's only a football, isn't it?

The run of success had to come to an end eventually and it was with almost perfect comic timing that we finally capitulated against the season's least-successful side. Swindon Town had no money, no chance of staying up and were sliding to the Second Division amid a wave of good humour from their supporters. They knew their side wasn't good enough and they knew they weren't going to survive the drop, so they just hoped to enjoy the ride and maybe claim a few scalps along the way. After we'd enjoyed 12 league wins on the trot, they turned up at The Valley and claimed a biggy.

It wasn't so much the loss, but more the nature of it, which caused so much amusement. We couldn't even really bring ourselves to be angry about it, because the afternoon had been so farcical. Any remaining doubts I had about the power of the footballing gods to predetermine the result of a game were banished, as the game wore on.

James Williams was the architect of Swindon's hour and a half of glory and a more unwitting architect you'll never meet. Just four minutes had gone when he whacked over a hopeful cross from the right touchline and saw Dean Kiely fall on the ball and somehow manage to elbow it backwards over his own goal line. The keeper had been absolutely solid all year long and when the mistake arrived, it was a belter.

From that point on, we set about launching a lengthy campaign of damage to the woodwork, as we smacked the ball against the bar, pinged it off the post and skimmed and shaved the outside of both of them. Frank Talia in the Swindon goal, who in the finest traditions of footballing humour must surely be nicknamed 'Jenny' by his colleagues, made saves the like of which he had plainly not managed all season. In fact, he obviously hadn't managed very many at all, as his side's league position testified. For Swindon, sitting on the rock bottom of the table, the only way might have been up, except for the fact that they were going down first. Before they got there, though, they were going to have one last party – and it happened at our place.

It was the way it was meant to end, I think. To have lost in the next game, against Manchester City, would have been far, far worse and we probably bowed out of our winning streak in just about the right way. Anyway, we were so far ahead by this stage, that had Swindon not beaten us, we may well have lapped them, which doesn't happen very much in football any more . . .

We actually got a draw up at Maine Road, beat Grimsby, Palace and QPR, and then shut down for the season and waited to see if anyone would catch us. I really wish I could pretend that it was a deliberate act, designed to string out the drama, or that we retained the capacity to start winning again if we really needed to, but I don't think we did.

Having gone flat out from the word go, then tried to accelerate hard all the way through Christmas and beyond, our legs had gone dead.

The bid to keep going to the end and get ourselves over the line was becoming desperate, as all the momentum we had built up during the season seemed to dissipate. The directors even paid for the fans to travel to Nottingham Forest, where a win would have sent us up, but a late equaliser from Chris Bart Williams ensured that the wait continued. I wonder where he ended up?

That was the fabled 'yellow day' when everyone was encouraged to wear a yellow shirt to send us up 'on a tide of yellow'. Cynics suggested that the club was simply trying to rid itself of a glut of away shirts which would be replaced the following year and the denials of the fact always raised a smile. Whatever the truth of the matter, as we slid back to London, like a tide of anti-climactic custard, we knew, or at least we sensed, that it was not going to be as easy as we had once hoped.

We managed to lose at home to Huddersfield, who had one shot on goal, while we repeated our Swindon experiment and tried to discover how much of a pounding the woodwork would take, before stumbling to a draw on Good Friday against Portsmouth. That left us just a fraction short of being ensured a promotion spot on the day, instead having to collect it the following day, when others played and failed to win. After 12 wins on the trot and having had a lead which was absurdly large, it was a splendidly understated way to return to the Premiership.

After a draw ensured that the title finally arrived with us while in the wilderness of Blackburn, we celebrated receiving the trophy in front of a packed Valley crowd, in style, by collapsing to a 3–1 defeat at the hands of Ipswich, who would go on to claim their Premiership place through the play-offs. It was a strange occasion, as George Burley's side went 3–0 up, with the Charlton fans singing 'we want four' and generally conceding the game in order to hurry along the presentation of the trophy.

Not everyone was in a party mood, though. I recall vividly sitting there in the press box at the final whistle and hearing two old men just behind me and to my right making their protest.

'I'm not hanging around to watch them flaunt that bloody trophy after that pile of shit. They should be bloody ashamed of themselves. They should get given it in the dressing-room, in bloody disgrace. That was bollocks.'

And with that, they stomped down the stairs and out of the stand, like the two old men who spent each week moaning about the acts in the Muppets. I don't think they had much trouble getting away from the ground – there didn't seem to be much by the way of traffic congestion – at least not until after the trophy had been presented. You hear people from time to time, muttering away about 'only at bloody Charlton'. Whenever I hear it now, I think back to that miserable, geriatric pair, and smile to myself. You can't please all of the people, all of the time, plainly.

In a last act of benevolence, we ended the season by going to the Hawthorns and losing 2–0 in order to allow West Brom to escape the drop. It was a bit like scoring a century at Lords and then waving to the crowd as you marched back up the pavilion steps, slipping, and twisting your ankle.

We had a second bite at the Premiership ahead of us, we were First Division champions and we hadn't won for seven matches. The confidence that had been there among the fans was ebbing away and we managed to surround ourselves with self-doubt, even before a ball of the new season had been kicked.

Maybe the miserable twins had a point. As I watched us collect a trophy, while moaning that we were going to 'get stuffed next year', that thought was the one at the front of my mind: 'Only at Charlton . . .'

13

MANAGING TO SURVIVE

It's a balmy Monday afternoon, with the thunderstorms that have been promised to us for the last week still stubbornly refusing to arrive. The air is unpleasantly heavy and every half an hour or so you find yourself dreaming of a cold drink, a cool shower and a breeze. This afternoon at Charlton's Sparrows Lane training ground, only one of the three is on offer, and it doesn't involve washing or wind.

The players are starting to disperse after their morning training session, with one or two hanging around chatting and mulling over the papers. One looks slightly more edgy than the others and it's obvious from his body language that he's waiting to see the manager. He hovers around by the foot of the stairs leading up to Alan Curbishley's office, as Curbishley calls down to me that he'll be 'just five minutes' and then we can sit down away from any distractions.

In response to a further managerial yell, the player plods upstairs and the door is closed. Half an hour later he emerges, the mood obviously lighter than when he went in and I hear Curbishley calling out, trying to find out where I am and if I'm ready. As I close in on the door, I'm beaten to it by the combined presence of Keith Peacock and Mervyn Day, Charlton's answer to Little and Large, who scoot out of Peacock's office next door and nip in for a quick word with Curbishley.

'Five minutes, Mick, I'll only be five minutes,' calls the manager and I go in search of one of those cold drinks. Another half an hour passes before Day and Peacock open the door and leave, Day grinning at the sight of me standing there and apologising for the delay after a 'You still here, Mick?' enquiry, laden with mock innocence. Getting time with the manager is never an easy task, it would seem, even if you're part of the management team. Even after a lifetime in the game, 'Merv' as he is universally known, still enjoys much of the schoolboyish competition of life at the training ground and putting one over on a former member of the press office is far too good a chance to miss.

Having become a well-known name in the game, throughout the course of a long and distinguished playing career, Day is now highly regarded, both by the players he trains, and his fellow coaches. It doesn't take long, while watching him on the training pitch, to see why. He has an ability to communicate with players that stems partly from having been a successful one himself and partly because he's highly adept at judging the mood and pitching his tone appropriately. He also reads the game with unerring accuracy, which is, I suppose, really what makes him a good coach, rather than just a nice bloke. He and Curbishley have been friends for a long time and the manager plainly trusts and relies on him.

Given their relative sizes, that's probably not a bad decision either. Day is a bear of a man, with the sort of hands usually seen on the end of earth-moving machinery. He's also extremely affable and easy to get along with, and it's not hard to see how handy the combination of physical presence and approachable demeanour can be in his work as a coach.

The third part of the trio is off looking for something to do – a game of table tennis to win or a ball to go and kick about. Keith Peacock is three years short of his 60th birthday, and looks like a man of about half his age. Having played 591 games for the club, he's a Charlton legend and looks like he could still get a game for the reserves today, if he asked nicely. I'm standing there, 31 years of age, and considering losing a bit of weight, as Peacock hurtles past, shouting a hello over his shoulder, on his way down to the gym. I don't feel any better about myself, quite honestly.

It's an infectious and perpetually cheerful atmosphere in which it's impossible to imagine that anyone could end up feeling too self-important. There are probably enormously expensive management consultants out there who will explain to you in huge detail why this type of relaxed yet focused environment brings out the best in people. It's also more than probable that they won't be arriving at Sparrows Lane at any stage in the near future. They don't require a surfeit of analysis to tell them that they're doing things the right way.

The light-hearted, yet unmistakably bustling and busy impression, is reinforced within 30 seconds of my arrival, when Curbishley's mobile rings. He takes a look at the screen, grimaces, and turns it off.

'Bloody agents, they've always got someone you "really need to have a look at".'

With a prod of his thumb, the mobile goes silent and someone, somewhere is trying to sell a player to an answer phone. I wonder if Nokia gets a consultancy fee?

At the relatively young age of 44, Curbishley has already clocked up 11 years as a football manager, with only Sir Alex Ferguson and Dario Gradi able to boast longer tenures. With the circumstances surrounding that period, it's hard to think of anyone currently employed in a similar role who has presided through a more tumultuous yet ultimately successful period. Every day of Charlton's rebirth at The Valley has been guided by Curbishley, as well as the tail end of their previously nomadic existence.

Over the last few years, he has started to receive the acclaim he doubtless deserves, but many of the early seasons were relegated to a couple of lines in the papers at the end of each campaign, talking about how he had done a 'solid job with limited resources'. As the success has started to arrive, there have been those who have questioned whether he has become too 'cosy' at the club and whether he needs to get out and 'stretch himself' a little bit.

Looking at him, and seeing the way his working week unfurls, it's hard to think that there's an awful lot more stretching to be done. Even with all the investment and hard work from a wide variety of people, Charlton's success will ultimately depend on what happens on the pitch and Curbishley has always ensured that his role in that has remained at a level almost beyond criticism.

The stresses and strains have started to take their toll a little, and the lines around his eyes have become noticeably more pronounced over the last three or four seasons, but he remains very much a 'hands-on' manager, in almost every aspect of the club. One of the first things you notice when you speak to him for any length of time is just how aware he is of the developments off the pitch.

Indeed, in order to keep relations between himself and his players on a strictly confidential, 'need-to-know' basis, he is almost happier to talk about the finances than the football. If getting the sums right is a priority, it's one he learned from an impeccable source:

> I've spoken to Alex Ferguson on many occasions and he maintains that his definition of a good football manager is one

that balances the books and keeps the house in order. That's what Manchester United have done over the years – it's only been in the last couple of years that they've splashed out and spent a lot of money, but they've always returned a profit.

I think Alex takes that on as his responsibility and I've learned from him, but I think I've always seen it as something that I've got to do as part of my job. Now, that's all well and good if everyone at the club is singing from the same song-sheet, but thankfully we are, and we always have been.

They say that perhaps the breed of managers being involved in all aspects of the club is over, because it's just too much to do. I think, though, that having been involved in nearly going bust and living off a shoestring budget and all that goes with it, stands you in good stead for what people might describe as the luxury of the Premiership. I learned a lot about the job through those years, and it's been invaluable to me over the last few seasons, when we're far removed from the position we were in then.

One of the fascinating things about talking to Curbishley for this book is that it gives a licence to ask questions about subjects he rarely has to offer an opinion about. In the current climate, football managers get asked about the forthcoming game, then about the game just gone, possibly about the referee in the game just gone and then about the forthcoming game again. It's a conveyor belt of almost interchangeable questioning, which continues through about nine months of the year.

Having sat, stood, slouched and occasionally snoozed through more of these post- and pre-match question-and-answer sessions than is good for one's mental health, I've started to sympathise with the managers as much as the media. Admittedly, their answers are not always overly illuminating, but the questions are hardly models of incisive enquiry either. When the manager gives a similar answer to a previous week, he stands open to ridicule, when an interviewer asks the same question as he has on a weekly basis for the last five seasons, nobody notices.

The end result is that managers rarely get the chance to put their point of view across in much more than bullet-point manner and they don't really get given the opportunity to say everything they want. They can hardly stop a press conference and say: 'I tell you what, I would like to discuss something else for a little bit, you know, just have a bit of a chat about it.'

This was never more clearly demonstrated than during the time when speculation floated around about the possibility of Curbishley going to

West Ham. The question of whether he was too comfortable at Charlton was often raised and circumstances dictated that the theory was dismissed with little more than a 'no, there's work to do yet'. The truth of the matter seems to be that, although he had more to say, he knew that to do it at the time would have fuelled more headlines and more speculation than were already being generated. After a break of several months, it's plainly something that's now safe to go into in greater depth:

> I know the press kept asking me if I was too cosy and I know it looked ridiculous, because of the nature of being a football manager, but it was definitely something that I had to look at as well. Because if you drive into work and it's not the same as it always was, then you know that something's wrong. You've got to start asking yourself if you're staying for the right reasons and you've got to start looking at whether you're where you are out of habit, or because you've still got things to do and a desire to do them.
>
> I think there's still things to do here and still things to get out of bed for, but I think you've to look at your situation sometimes and ask yourself if you're as happy as you should be. In all fairness, I'm in a profession where most of the people in it are happy doing their jobs and in most professions it's the opposite way round – it's just a means to an end. I do appreciate that I'm a lucky man, but I work hard too.
>
> I'm very conscious of getting caught in a rut, though, and of getting that sinking feeling before you go to Welling to play the first pre-season friendly. I don't want to be thinking to myself, 'Here we go again, another year down the line'. You have to be aware and watchful for that, but not only for yourself, but for signs of it in your players as well. The team has changed around dramatically over the last three or four years, though, so that's given things a bit of variety; but yes, it is something that I keep an eye out for.

It seems utterly absurd that anyone could worry about being 'cosy' in one of the most perilous professions around. There is no such thing as job security when you're a football manager. Many of the decisions are out of your hands, luck plays as large a part as planning and if you don't like it, striking is hardly an option, with hundreds of others ready to take your place at the drop of a chairman's hat. Given the state of the place when Curbishley and Steve Gritt first took over the reins, it's hard to imagine that 'cosy' was a word used too frequently when the words 'Charlton' and 'Athletic' were mentioned.

> Undoubtedly, the only reason we got the job is because they couldn't give it to anyone else. I think everyone appreciates that, and there's no point beating around the bush and not saying it. We already had players' contracts, so we were already here. I played 25 games the year before, Gritty had been involved too, and given the position the club was in and the state of things, I don't think there was any alternative.
>
> When I looked out of the window, there were about 14 players getting ready for pre-season, no ground to play our games at and no money to do anything about putting it right. We were going off to play home games at Upton Park for the first time and to be honest, a new manager would have been mad. He wouldn't have had a hope in hell of sorting out the whole thing, because it really was a mess.

The very best football managers don't despair and dwell on messes, though, or at least not once they've been dealt with and overcome. There are some, of course, who have made subsequent careers out of telling tales of the terrible clubs they were at and the chairmen they had to work with. They bluster on in the wake of a different sporting dinner every night, dodging the bread rolls as they tell stories they've told a thousand times before, with the promise that 'here's a story not many people have heard' growing increasingly untrue with each nightly airing. The best, however, look back and learn from the experience.

> That was one bonus of being here throughout those bad times, because I got to experience things like that and I don't think there's many other managers, and probably none in the Premiership, who have ever taken on a job quite that bad. It was decent timing and life's all about timing. Sometimes you need a bit of luck with that timing and sometimes you don't realise that you had a bit of luck until a few years down the line, when you look back at it.

Even the chronic lack of money at the club back in those days has ended up being viewed by him as a potential benefit. He appears not to feel nearly as much jealousy about the money now available at other clubs, as he might, and certainly doesn't speculate all that much over what he might be able to do with similar funding. Every now and again, he throws in a little reminder that we're not all equals, but he doesn't seem obsessed with what he hasn't got, as much as irritated by how much some of the others do. It's a difficult balancing act, because in order to tell the story of being in charge of Charlton seven or eight years ago it's impossible not to mention the relative poverty of the club, just to put things into context.

In a world where the media frequently seem fascinated by the personalities, rather than the system in which they work, it's interesting to listen to his thoughts on the way the game is run. When it comes to the way in which managers are employed, he chooses to look at the bigger picture rather than trip off a handful of stories about various quotable colleagues.

> As you progress along as a manager, sometimes it's easier to have no money, because money brings with it its own pressure. It raises the expectation levels; people expect wonders from everyone that you bring to the club and that just isn't always going to happen. Back in the early days, I knew we had a decent bunch of lads as well. I knew they were a group who could hold their own and would keep a decent spirit up and certainly knew that we were going to need that. So it wasn't all doom and gloom, although the pre-season was really poor that first year we took over.
>
> I think football's like no other industry. You wouldn't have the barman of the Hilton, with no disrespect, progressing overnight to becoming the manager of the whole hotel and without any other training either. That happens in football and sometimes it works and sometimes it doesn't – it worked with me. I was the reserve-team coach and then first-team coach for only a year before being given the big job. That only happens in football; it doesn't happen in any other walk of life.
>
> Some of the big jobs that have been taken by young managers are hard for me to work out, because they're not appointments made using business logic. That's perhaps because football clubs aren't run like any other business and that's perhaps why so many of them are in trouble. I might have landed the 'big job' fairly quickly, but I certainly didn't have any of the money that was meant to go along with it back then.

He speaks with considerable experience of managing a club in trouble.

When he and Gritt were first given the opportunity to manage the team, turning scouts from other clubs away from matches wasn't a huge problem for Charlton. The playing squad was as thin as possible, to the extent where even playing full-size practice games presented something of a problem. A couple of weeks after Manchester United spent £30 million on Rio Ferdinand, Curbishley smiles to himself and remembers the way it was just 11 years earlier:

> It wasn't until we bought Gary Nelson and Steve Gatting that we started to go somewhere. I begged Richard Murray for fifty grand and got hold of the pair of them, and then it just took off from there.
>
> We had some effective players and we had an enthusiasm that I knew was going to be vital, but I knew that above all the fact that they were good lads who would work hard and get stuck in for each other was really important. I knew Nelse and Gatts would come in and walk straight into the team and give us a bit of a lift, and obviously they did. Nelse ran himself everywhere for us, and I knew that Gatt had the ability to give us an extra dimension that we would have been missing otherwise.

As he says it, I'm looking over his shoulder into the car park, where a gleaming silver Mercedes is sitting, freshly delivered by a new car sponsor. Scurrilous rumours suggest that Curbishley is still deeply wary of the level of computerisation in the vehicle and the combination of satellite navigation and voice-activated gadgets have left him somewhat puzzled. One thing appears certain, and that is that his new car cost someone more than his first two players. Given the scale of the task he faced, surely there were those who queried his sanity?

> I don't think anyone thought I was that mad, because the people who knew me well knew that management was what I really wanted to do. That's why I came back here and I needed to progress, so when the opportunity came along, I had no option but to take it. I was up for it, and desperate to be given a chance, because those chances aren't that frequent.

That's a situation which appears unchanged over the last ten years, with the chances of a First Division player being given his first management job before his playing career even comes to an end now the stuff of *Roy of the Rovers* storylines, rather than back-page reports. We seem to have come full circle, where anyone getting a management job straight after they pack up as a player is only there because nobody else would take it and the club is close to being broke. As the game has grown more commercial and as the money has tipped in, does Curbishley feel irritated at the way it has been distributed? As soon as they drag themselves back to their feet, clubs all over the place take out huge loans and leap a few steps further forwards. Can the gap ever be bridged?

I'm instantly reminded of his habit of learning from experience, and rarely failing to spot an opportunity or a weakness in the opposition. In Curbishley's eyes, the current situation is playing nicely into Charlton's hands.

> We're in the position now where other sides might start to come back towards us, the really big Premiership sides that is. That will probably happen because the banks won't bail them out any more and they have to start selling and cutting costs, which will see them playing on the same sort of level playing field that we've been on before. The difference is that we've got used to living within our means and we know how to make the most of it, which gives us an advantage over them.
>
> We're also very wary of what happened to teams like Derby and Leicester, who stayed in the Premiership for four or five years, starting off with the 'this is a big adventure' approach and then, in the third and fourth years, realised that they were really in there. They were playing by big boys' rules and they were paying out some big old wages, and it wasn't quite the big exciting adventure it started out as. Real life was crowding in a little bit.
>
> They now find themselves in the Nationwide, paying out more in wages than they take in, and having been through that cycle, they know that the position has left them with some very serious problems that they've got to address. We've had the advantage of watching them and their progress and how they've gone about doing things.
>
> We've got to learn from it, keep a level head and see what happens. The clubs above us who are struggling with their debts, might start to come back to us and we could well end up overtaking them, because we've done things properly. We've not mortgaged our future and we stand a chance if the money dries up, or at least a better chance than a lot of other, bigger clubs. We've got to be in the Premiership for that ever to

happen, though, because otherwise we'll have blown that chance.

So, is he suggesting that we've got to a stage where, if we can stand still for long enough, and secure a solid enough footing, the others will, in the not too distant future, come tumbling back in our direction?

> Whenever there's any correction in the market, whether it be the housing market, the stock market or wherever, there are people who overreached themselves and ended up getting hurt. Take the housing market, for example, you borrow more than you can afford, the market corrects itself and the value of houses goes down and there are people left with negative equity – what they've got doesn't cover what they owe. I can think of plenty of football clubs in that position.
>
> As I say, I think football clubs are unique businesses. A year ago, everyone was euphoric about the Premiership and the Nationwide and football was the thing of the moment. A year later and it's doom and gloom for the Nationwide what with what's happened with the television companies, and everyone's expecting a little bit of it to rub off on the Premiership.
>
> I'm not so sure about that myself, but the people who are going along nice and steady, they can maybe afford to take a knock much better than some of the others who appear to be flying along, promising to pay the bills tomorrow or the week after next. We've got into that steady position and it might not be glamorous, but it's a good place to be. It might not be good enough for some of the fans, but we've worked hard to get here and we're where we are for a reason, and that's that it's the best place to be at the moment, in our judgement.

As he continues, it starts to dawn on me that, in the process of answering my questions, and cheerfully expanding on his answers, Curbishley is somehow sending me back to my initial, big question about the club. If it's so simple, why doesn't everyone do it like us?

> I think a few do, but I think people tend to want results immediately these days and in order to do that, it's a lot quicker if you manage to borrow a load of money and get on with it. Building foundations takes a bit of time, though, and as the situation gets a bit more fraught and a bit more pressurised, there

maybe aren't that many places left where they're prepared to wait that little bit longer in order to see if they can do it like we did. As the game stands, right at this moment, there might not be many clubs in the future trying to do it like us, but if it all changes suddenly, there might be a few taking a lot closer look at us and seeing how we did it.

It's not all sweetness and light at Charlton, though, and as the crowds have grown, the advertising campaigns and the need to fill seats have meant that some of the fans at the ground haven't been there all that long and don't subscribe to the long-term view. If you grab people from doing something else on a Saturday afternoon and then convince them that watching football is a good thing on which to spend their money, they are going to demand immediate results. Long-term fans have seen some dreadful sides and some shabby stadiums and appreciate the achievements of the last decade, but doesn't the manager feel the expectations, whether realistic or not, of those who have only recently arrived?

> I'm put under no extra pressure and I'm certainly under no illusions that the most important thing is to keep our status. I think about 15,000 of the fans at The Valley understand that, and I think they're the 15,000 who've been here for the last seven or eight years, while we've been back at The Valley and while we've been rebuilding things. I think they understand why things have been done a certain way, and why we have to follow a certain course.
>
> I think some of the new ones, the ones who have been here for the last couple of years, see it a bit differently and maybe think things should be done a bit differently, that there should be a few more risks taken. By and large, though, we've been all right in that respect. We certainly haven't suffered from the demand of expectations in the way that Sunderland have, for example.

There are, however, inevitably those who set their expectations at a level beyond the manager, or those who just expect an unrealistic level of performance every single week. The results at The Valley last year provided them with more than enough to complain about, as Curbishley's side failed to impress for virtually the entire season. The ground that had been a virtual fortress the previous year was getting breached with depressing regularity, and some of the fans were showing their discontent.

When Curbishley heard booing, did he, I wonder, after all that had been achieved over the last decade, ever think to himself: 'Sod this, I don't deserve this and I don't need it'? In his shoes, I would, and I don't think I'm unique in that regard. Not for the first time, I appear to have underestimated his capacity for taking it on the chin:

> I only really heard it once and that was after we got beaten by Walsall in the FA Cup last year and we deserved that. If we'd got our act together and done the job properly, we should have beaten them four or five, so I can't complain about that. I've heard it in little bits and pieces a couple of times, but people are entitled to voice their opinion, and this isn't a job to go into without a thick skin.
>
> I think that, in the main, although the club has come so far, up until the last season, the football team was ahead of the club in all sort of aspects. I think last season was maybe the first time that the club, that is what happens off the field, caught up with the team. I think staying up was a considerable achievement given the injuries we had, but I also think that the building of the new stand and some of the other things that went on meant that, if I'm trying to be as fair about it as I can, the club overtook the side for the first time. This year, it's our turn to put a bit of space between us once more.

It's the first time I've heard anyone at the club describe things in this way and it made me think. He obviously keeps a quiet tally in his mind, as to where his team are in comparison to the rest of the club. In a way, it's normal for someone to set themselves targets, but this seems a novel way of doing it. Then again, maybe it's extremely mundane, like the manager of the accounts department wanting his staff to outperform the people down the corridor in marketing? Maybe Curbishley has cut through the jargon, and uses very straightforward methods of measuring his own achievements? If that is the case, how does he feel the last couple of years have gone?

> That first season back in the Premiership raised the expectations up desperately high, and they were always going to be difficult to match. The Premiership is a difficult thing to predict and that was shown by what happened to Ipswich. We've got to be professional and sensible about what we do and how we go about it, but we know where we should be aiming. If we can

consolidate this year, finish well and stay safe, then I think we'll have the experience to push on next season and really start to set out our aims at something a bit more daunting than just survival.

It's a far cry from the early days, when even survival seemed to be a considerable achievement, and it's hard to believe that he never felt any pressure on himself to succeed. The image of a manager, secure to the point of almost being inextricably enmeshed with his club, has become the only version most of us care to remember, but things weren't always quite so unflustered:

> I've been very fortunate to survive these last ten years. We've come so far and I don't think people always appreciate that particularly. We've come from being bankrupt, playing on someone else's pitch and selling your best assets all the time, just to survive, to playing in front of 27,000 people in a sold-out stadium in the Premiership. What you have to realise is that it hasn't been given to us either, we didn't have some rich benefactor turn up and hand this all to us on a plate. Every single little component part of this has been worked for and earned, and when you look at the size of the jigsaw surrounding this club now, that's a lot of work in a lot of different areas.
>
> To survive the ten years has been an achievement in itself, because not many managers do that. Not many managers of really good and successful clubs manage that, so to do it against the background of what's been going on here is, I think, my best achievement.

The question of survival is one that is often raised during interviews with Curbishley, although rarely, if ever, in regard to him. The only way in which his departure from the club has ever been described, at least in the last few years, is if one of the 'big six' were to come in with a job offer. Similarly, survival has only ever been talked about in reference to the club's chances firstly of avoiding bankruptcy and secondly, of avoiding relegation. The idea that he might lose his job has never been a live issue, even when we were getting relegated from the Premiership.

As we looked back over the earlier years of his time in charge, though, I was keen to find out more about the nature of his relationship with Steve Gritt. Curbishley and Gritt had taken on what appeared to be an impossible job and then discovered a few years down the line that the board had moved away from the idea of joint managers and wished to return to a more traditional arrangement. As everyone now knows, Curbishley stayed and Gritt went, but the wounds are still apparent.

There's no question of ill-feeling between the two men – quite the opposite – but I was intrigued at what was disclosed. When interviewed, Curbishley is a model of self-restraint. I've never seen him really lose his temper in an interview, or even disclose more than the smallest amount of irritation, despite facing a barrage of enquiries, a matter of minutes sometimes, after the end of a game. The question of what has been said about Gritt, and the lurking feeling the current manager has that his old colleague hasn't received sufficient praise for his efforts, saw Curbishley get unexpectedly animated:

> I was close to going once, as well, when the board decided that they didn't want two managers, and either me or Gritty was going to have to leave. I didn't know if people wanted me, or they wanted him, or they wanted both of us to go and to start afresh with a totally new man at the helm. I think the job we did together was an impressive one, though, and I still don't think that it ever got the recognition it deserved. We kept the bloody club going, because if it got relegated that year, it would, or at least could, have gone out of existence. We were managing without a safety net, and learning as we were doing it.

Now in the grand scheme of things, 'we kept the bloody club going' is hardly swearing on an epic scale. Eminem won't lose sleep tonight over a word that has long since lost its power to shock, but coming from someone who prides himself on being reflective and calm when interviewed, it maybe showed the level of irritation that Gritt's lack of plaudits has caused Curbishley. They brought the club through some perilous times, and did it against a background where it still had to sell its best players on a sporadic basis – a situation Curbishley has now helped to ensure no longer exists:

> The first year at Upton Park, to finish seventh, and to have known that we should have made a play-off place was a real achievement, and about as good as anything I've managed. We had to sell Robert Lee, sell Anthony Barness, just to pay the wages when we were second in the table, and that was hard, so I suppose that time, when I just took over on my own, was the closest I came to being shown the door.
>
> The next year, we sold Lee Bowyer and we couldn't invest any

of the money in the side, and we came 15th or wherever, so I think that could have been close to being thank you and goodnight. The major one, though, the moment I know was the closest I've come to leaving the club, was when they decided they didn't want joint managers any more. At the very best, as far as I was concerned, I was only a 50–50 bet to stay in a job, and maybe worse than that.

As a tractor rolls by outside and the academy players come clacking their way across the tarmac back to the pavilion, he pauses to reflect a minute, before attempting to put it into perspective.

I suppose, strictly speaking, we didn't have to sell Lee Bowyer, but, being honest and realistic about it, we did, and that was a blow. The way things were, I couldn't have a penny of that £2.7 million to spend on the team and that sort of thing hurts you as a manager. Things have changed, though, and last year when we desperately needed to bring in some players because of an absolute injury crisis, I could go to Richard Murray and we could get Chris Bart Williams and Jorge Costa in on loan, who made a huge difference to us.

The board have been forthcoming whenever they can, but, in the early days, although we would have pushed on a bit quicker if we had, we just couldn't afford to bring in some of the players we wanted. We couldn't even hold onto some of the ones we needed to.

It's helped me not to change, as a person as much as a manager, and that's vital to your personal life. We went through things back then that make you stronger and better at what you do now. I wouldn't want to be in a position again where we had to sell Robert Lee to Newcastle when there were 15 games left, and they were first and we were second. I wouldn't want to be forced to sell anyone again, because it's not the way to build, but some of those were necessary, and there wasn't any other way around it.

The major part of his achievement at the club, and there have been many individual ones, is that there are now plenty of ways around the situations he encountered as recently as four or five years ago. The stability, as Richard Murray has been quick and generous to observe, has been gained in large part as a result of the work put in and results gained by Curbishley and his sides. As the club moves onto the next stage of their climb, the manager is, in turn, keen to point to the chairman as a vital figure and equal partner in its ascent.

> There are odd games when we end up all desperately disappointed, but Richard's not the sort to get down into the dressing-room and start ranting and raving and I think that's very important. He knows we're all trying our best and that we're all trying to make it right, and that helps.
>
> We can both trust each other. He knows when I'm setting out to bring in players or make new signings, and he knows that I've got the club at heart during all of that. The fact that I can look up and know that the chairman is approaching things in exactly the same way is a great bonus to me.

It's not a situation that exists everywhere:

> People look at football clubs and sometimes chairmen think that they're as big, or even bigger than the clubs. There's a few chairmen in London that spring to mind, but make no mistake about it, this club wouldn't be where it is at the moment if it wasn't for Richard Murray – and he doesn't stand and shout about what he's done from the rooftops either.
>
> His great strength is that he employs people and then he backs his own judgement that he's got the right ones, sits back and lets them get on with doing their job. Not all chairmen are like that. Obviously, he knows what's happening here on a daily basis and he deals with me on the football side and Peter Varney on the commercial side, but if you sit us all down together, we know what's going on and we know where we're all trying to get to.
>
> There's a great degree of mutual respect for each other and long may it continue, because there's a lot of clubs out there that aren't run properly.

Curbishley isn't an emotional man and he doesn't hand out praise lightly, but maybe most tellingly of all, he really isn't in a position where he has to be overly polite or effusive about his chairman, yet he still is. It may sometimes sound like any other manager at any other club saying a few nice words about his boss, almost as a kind of guarantee of future employment, but that's not the case at The Valley. The fans may continue to chant about 'Alan C's Red and White Army', but the subject of their affections is perfectly happy to direct the praise in what he feels is the appropriate direction. In fact, to the point of making a fairly bold suggestion as to how that thanks should be shown:

> There's no way you can spend any length of time here and not come away looking back proudly on what happened, and when Richard decides that enough's enough one day, I think we should do something about it. Whether that means a statue or even the Richard Murray stand, I don't know, but he's deserved it. He doesn't get involved in the publicity, he doesn't seek recognition, he doesn't hang around looking for reporters after the game and for me I've got the perfect working relationship with him.

As far as the fans are concerned, it's been the perfect partnership. Between the two of them, and with a loyal supporting cast, Charlton have become the sort of tale that Hollywood could write a really crass and over-the-top film about. They'd have to be careful about it, though, because every ten minutes something would happen which left you convinced that you'd just seen the grand finale. Five minutes later, as you were strolling out of the cinema, there would be a cheer from the auditorium behind you, as something even better happened.

The story has encompassed many highs and lows, and the manager is more aware of them than most:

> I think it gets forgotten quite easily what's been achieved here, because the story has been told a lot. Some of the new players don't really need to know, because, to be honest, it's not a part of the club that they're joining, in as much as it's not going to affect them. I've not had too many lows here to be honest. I've had frustrations, and there have been things which have got to me at the time, but there haven't been too many really bad lows.
>
> Relegation was very disappointing, but they gave me a four-year contract, told me to get on with it, and we got straight back up because we knew where we were coming from. You look at Ipswich, and they've kept faith with George Burley, and that's as it should be, because that's the way to get back on track quickly.
>
> The play-off was obviously a huge high, because it was an amazing game, a huge achievement, and everyone remembers it to this day, even if they don't support us. I think, though, that we deserved it, just because of the points total we got and the run

we put together to get to that final. In fact, it's hard to say that there was anyone in the top four that year who didn't deserve it, because we all sort of came across the line together.

Winning the First Division title was a huge achievement, although we ended up limping home a bit, just because of the way we recovered from the upset of going down, and did the professional thing and got back on with things.

The best of the lot, however, at least as far as Curbishley is concerned, is still ongoing. Football managers are meant to be able to see the big picture, to stand back and understand as much as possible about the situation, and he is no different. As the afternoon draws to a close, he pronounces judgement:

> When you've been where we've been, the highs are there all the time now. We're playing against Thierry Henry, David Beckham, Ryan Giggs and their sides are putting out full-strength sides against us, because we've given out a few bloody noses and teams know that when you play Charlton, you get a proper game. To have people saying that, when we're playing in the toughest league of the lot, after what I've been through here – the highs don't get any bigger than that.
>
> If I want a real high, though, I look ahead to that first game of the season. We're playing Chelsea, at home, in front of a sell-out crowd in a great stadium, with world-class players on display and not all of them coming from the other side. That's a real high and that's what makes the Premiership special.
>
> Right now, though, I need a cup of tea.

He turns on his phone, looks skywards in despair as it cheerfully announces half a phonebook worth of voicemail messages and strolls off to the kitchen to get that cup of tea he's starting to dream about.

A fortnight later, and Chelsea have just beaten us 3–2, thanks in large part to Paul Konchesky's highly contentious sending off early in the first half and two Chelsea goals in the last four minutes. An hour after the game, I bump into Curbishley, walking out of his room and down the tunnel on his way to the talking car, which you sensed was going to annoy him all the way back home.

'Unlucky. You all right?' I ask, probably winning the prize for the most stupid question of the day. After an afternoon of reasonably lucid discussion, it occurs to me that it had only taken the sight of a football ground to reunite me with the ability to make absurd and superfluous post-match enquiries.

'What can you do about that? That weren't a sending off and that's what's done us. And there's nothing anyone can do about that. That's a bit hard to take, that one.'

There wasn't much you could do about it and he isn't wrong – it was a hard one to take.

Once upon a time, there wasn't much we could do about many of the things happening to the club. The debts, the lack of a ground, the enforced departure of players, the troubles paying the wages – everywhere you turned, there was something that was hard to take and that we couldn't do much about. Those days are gone now and having shouldered much of the responsibility, Curbishley deserves much of the praise. We still can't do much about bad refereeing decisions, but the rest of it is, by and large, in our own hands.

It's not a bad way to be remembered if you're a football manager. It just didn't seem a good time to be making the point to the weary figure trudging across the car park, waiting for his car to start answering him back.

14

BACK AMONG THE BIG BOYS

Having restarted Premiership life with the mauling of Manchester City, it didn't take long for reality to come charging back. Before long, we'd settled back into a pattern of results all too similar to the ones with which we had bidden farewell to the Nationwide league, just three months previously.

There was a strange atmosphere surrounding the club, however, with a pre-season tragedy altering the way we viewed things and the extent, for a while at least, to which people felt they could get euphoric about something as trivial as a game of football. Just three days before the final warm-up for the season was due to kick off, with a game against Vicenza at The Valley, we learned that Pierre Bolangi, a left-back with the academy Under-19 side, had drowned on a pre-season exercise at a military base in Aldershot.

Bolangi had been born in the Congo, lived in Canning Town and had the ability to leave his mark on everyone he met, with his refusal to be ashamed or embarrassed at displaying his delight at the direction in which his dedication and determination was taking him. A few weeks earlier, he had been chosen by the management to accompany the first-team squad on their trip to the West Country, running errands and gaining a bit of experience.

I was down there with them and the sight of Pierre tearing around the place, fetching bandages for one and bottles of water for another, never for a second losing his seemingly constant grin, was a sight to behold. He kept up a running banter with Chris Powell, the first-team left-back, revolving around the fact that he didn't mind doing this now, because very soon he would claim his first-team place and Powell would have to do it for him.

In that sort of situation, football becomes quite primitive. First-team players either conclude that the youngster in their midst needs taking down a couple of pegs, or they take them under their collective wing. The mickey-taking handed out by a squad of footballers to an outsider can be particularly vicious, and acts as a device to stop youngsters, in particular, getting above themselves. They took to Pierre unanimously. Exuberance is very different to arrogance and nobody had a problem with him – his enthusiasm was a good thing to have around, especially during pre-season.

I last saw Pierre shortly after we played Bristol City, on a Friday night, as he ran across the car park to the Kentucky Fried Chicken shop to pick up a junk-food treat for the players. The deal appeared to be that Pierre could keep the change, if he got the chicken onto the coach before it left the ground. His frantic efforts had seen him manage to strike an individual deal with each player, rather than a simpler but less lucrative arrangement with the squad as a whole. Pierre, if he could remember 18 separate orders, was onto a nice little earner.

I called out to him as he ran off, and wished him luck with his challenge. He gave me a wave, shouted back that for this money he would run back home to get the chicken, and disappeared around the corner. Twelve days later, he was pulled from a pond, drowned. A non-swimmer, he had been sent across as part of a fitness exercise organised by the army. Dean May, an army fitness instructor from Aldershot, was later convicted of his manslaughter and fined £1,500. With further legal action entirely possible, even if one could find the words, it's hard to comment on the role of the army, before and after the incident.

The game against Vicenza was set to provide a testimonial match for Steve Brown, but he looked terrible. I had a chat with him and he just kept repeating that he didn't want to play, and it didn't seem right, but, at this stage, he'd been told that there was nothing we could do to change the fixture. The players struggled hard to come to terms with what had happened and although Vicenza turned out to be a nasty, spiteful side anyway, the tensions and underlying anger were hard to mistake. Powell was sent off and John Robinson ordered to be substituted, as the afternoon became a running battle. Even for professionals, there were times when wounds were still too raw to ignore personal feelings and just 'get on with the game'.

The following week, before the Manchester City game, The Valley stood for a minute of silence, in memory. The players formed an arc around one side of the centre circle, and arms around shoulders, tried to deal with emotions not normally prevalent in the minutes before a game. Especially not the first game of the season. Their performance that afternoon was their tribute and it couldn't have been more eloquently expressed. We would never forget Pierre. Being seen as a 'small' club might have been frustrating at times, but when tragedy struck, it could be strangely comforting. If we'd been 'close knit' before, after Pierre, we were, temporarily at least, more tightly intertwined with our club than ever before.

Life, however, as football fans understand better than most, is rather more complicated than a *Rocky* movie, and being a determined underdog, clenching your fists and making passionate speeches is no alternative for actually playing well. I remember hearing the story of a man sitting next to a priest, watching the Golden Gloves amateur boxing tournament in New York. One fighter got into the ring, crossed himself a number of times, and clasped his hands together in prayer.

'Will that help him, Father?' the man asked.

'Not if he can't punch,' came the short and brutally accurate response, as the man of the cloth watched and waited to see the man hit the canvas. All prayers and no punch, all determination and no finesse – we were starting to draw unpleasant parallels.

We went straight from victory over City, to Everton on a Wednesday night and got whacked 3–0, with Duncan Ferguson coming off the bench to batter two goals home. The following weekend, we went to Highbury, scored three goals, and managed to concede five, as Arsène Wenger's side always seemed to know where that extra gear was lurking, with which to accelerate neatly past us. That ominous feeling was starting all over again.

There we were, only a week into our latest Premiership existence, proudly clutching our three points in our sweaty palms and already, like the first cuckoo of spring, the first 'plucky little Charlton' of the new season had been heard.

Maybe there was more than I was prepared to admit at the time, in the theory about staying in the Nationwide, winning every week, and then politely refusing promotion in preference to a bit more carnage and another bulging 'goals for' column the following year. There were certainly times when I looked back ruefully at those golden days, and couldn't see anything wrong with them, particularly when the going was getting tough.

Throughout the course of the last two years, I think the one thing we've learned, whether we're fans, players or the manager, is just how difficult it is in the Premiership. I know, on the face of it, that's a statement of the most obvious sort imaginable, but I think you've got to experience it to understand just how good some of those sides are. In the First Division, you find yourself glancing through the opposing line up; it's a bit different in the Premiership. There's a couple of names that mean something, maybe someone whose dad used to play, two or three 'so that's where he ended up's' and the odd 'he was always a nasty sod when he was playing at . . .'

When a Premiership team sheet arrives, it generally tells the story of 16 threats to your team's chances of a happy afternoon and, depending on the opposition, three or four who you know, deep down, are almost certainly going to break your heart at some point in the game. It's an all-pervading fear, and it tells you with an accuracy that can't be disputed whether you're one of these people who, deep down, think their side is a big club or a small one. I spend ages telling myself how big we've got, and I'll argue with people and get upset with journalists who suggest otherwise, but my deepest-felt fears give me away as a hypocrite when the team sheet arrives.

I've always suspected that the goals were smaller in the Premiership, or at least the one we were attacking was, and you've got to be very careful not to allow rational thoughts like that to turn into paranoia. It's for that very reason that I've managed to ignore the fact that we always play uphill, into the wind, on a worse pitch than the opposition and with a referee who doesn't like us. The best thing about writing a sentence like that is knowing that there are people out there – worse sufferers than me, plainly – who are shouting out in agreement.

I might be suggesting that this is how it 'feels' to be in the Premiership, but there are a lot of people insisting steadfastly that this is the way it 'is'. It's the question of perception that, as a fan, really gets to you. In the Nationwide, nobody pays you a blind bit of notice and you don't expect them to either. You might get ten seconds of coverage at half past three in the morning on ITV Five as part of their Nationwide-extra sports pro-celebrity pop stars round-up show, but not a lot more. In the Nationwide League you can safely play Lord Lucan in goal, and as long as the people at the ground agree to keep quiet, nobody is going to find out.

Once you get to the Premiership, things change somewhat. Television cameras turn up looking to film everything from the club captain to the club cat, desperately filling up video tapes with clichés, out-takes and 'quirky bits' in a bid to ensure Sky Sports Eight doesn't run dry halfway through its late-night Tuesday-evening show. In the Nationwide, you've got to keep looking hard to find yourself on the television – in the Premiership, think of it as wallpaper.

The irony is, and this has always made me smile, that the moment we got into the Premiership, we started complaining that everyone else was on television more than we were. Now, granted, our coverage on ITV's imaginatively titled *The Premiership* qualifies for flash-frame status on a weekly basis, but we do sometimes get on in the background, if we're lucky enough to be playing a really big, proper team. Similarly, although we're not on Sky all that often, we do like to stand up for ourselves, firing off a letter every now and again in complaint.

It's obviously a tactic that's struck fear into the hearts of the match planners there, because, for the first half of this current season, our complaints saw them decide to come to The Valley three times, and not once follow us away from home. A triumph of sorts, with any coverage being better than no coverage at all, but useless for those who were coming to The Valley anyway, but didn't want to travel miles to an away game. The idea of sitting there at the ground while one of our 'viewings' is being used up back at home, on a television with nobody there to watch it, is clear evidence to me that the schedulers are playing a game with us – and winning, sadly.

In that first season back, however, we were slowly but surely showing ourselves to be potentially interesting television fare, not least because of our habit of beating other London sides. With all the glamour surrounding the capital's Premiership sides, it was us, easily pigeon-holed as unfashionable and meek, who kept popping up and raining on their collective parades.

Having endured that terrible thumping on Boxing Day at Upton Park, we recovered and set about the challenge of London derbies with relish. Having opened the second half of the season with a win over Arsenal at The Valley, before grabbing draws with West Ham and Spurs, we finished the year with another win over Chelsea, our second of the year. As the campaign rolled onwards, we recovered from the shaky start and started to look more like the side we remembered as having won the league and less like the one which finished the year trying to lose it.

Just as we feared that the Manchester City result had been a false dawn, the London derby win against Spurs seemed to set us back on track and then the following week we made the journey up to the North-east to face Newcastle at St James' Park. Old Trafford might be slightly bigger and Highbury might boast about its marble halls (not that you'll ever get to see them) but there's only one winner for me. St James'

Park is, as far as I'm concerned, the single most impressive ground in the country (note to self: remember to put 'apart from ours' lest you annoy everyone).

Obviously there's the fact that St James' Park is the total opposite of The Valley, perched on the top of a hill rather than the bottom of a pit, but it commands the skyline for miles around. The rest of the town may, strictly speaking, have been there before, but I still think it makes more sense to think of the entire place being built on the slopes, paying homage to the ground at the top. From about noon on a Saturday, the roads to the ground are packed with black and white shirts, many bearing the legend 'Shearer' and the Number 9 on the back.

Far be it from me to make suggestions which could be advantageous to criminals, but it doesn't take a genius to work out how a Saturday-lunchtime bank robber might best mingle in with the crowds in that particular part of the world. If he threatened to use his elbows or tried to kick someone in the head, the bloke wouldn't even need a gun – and he'd get off on appeal, but that's a different story . . .

It's also a fantastic place to be around in the run-up to a game, with a fervour for what's about to happen evident to the point where you start to get caught up in it through the midst of the thickest hangover. It doesn't matter whether you intended to have one or not, if you got there the night before, believe me, you'll have a horrible hangover come Saturday morning.

Newcastle is one of those places where alcohol is advertised and sold purely on a volume basis, rather than any other particular merit any one drink might enjoy over another. Each pub and bar you pass seems to have a competing offer, enticing you in to collect more beer, spirits or alcopops for your money – sometimes with interesting side-effects. I went for a Saturday morning stroll along the Quayside and found the Tyne a mass of bubbles. What, I asked a passer-by, was going on?

He explained that they were hosing down the dance floors of the party boat, moored opposite, and that this was a fairly familiar sight every Saturday morning. As the dark depths of the river started to develop a creamy head, I watched the world's biggest pint of Guinness float gently under the Tyne Bridge and knew it was time to get ready for the game.

Within five minutes, the supposedly impossible had happened and we'd opened the scoring, with Graham Stuart pouncing on a slip in the home goalmouth to stab home from about three yards out – he's always been deadly from that range. From that moment on, it was a siege. I sat in the press box at the front of the main stand, with about ten storeys and 40,000 Geordies behind me. Up and away to my left, at the very top of the stand, were the rest of the Charlton fans, still recovering from their trek to the summit of Mount St James.

They cheered themselves hoarse at the goal and scarcely made a dent on the wall of noise that greeted it from the home fans, as if they could cancel it out if they all screamed loudly enough. We clung on though, until finally it appeared our luck had run out, when Carl Cort equalised on the hour mark. The noise sweeping down from behind got so loud, so quickly, it left me thinking I'd been punched in the back of the neck, as relief mixed with elation saw the crowd explode. Inside a second, the goal was ruled out for a push and we were back in front, without having to score further, if you see what I mean.

We held on, claimed our win, and set about coming to terms with what had been achieved. Whenever I'm asked who the 'big' sides are, I'll have to include Newcastle, just because of the sense of wonderment I was left with when we beat them. I confess to having been more than a little daunted when I walked into the ground, but the Charlton players showed no such sense of stage fright. As I sat outside the ground and burbled into my mobile to everyone I could think of that we'd come here and won – at this bloody great big place – I knew we'd arrived. I think I knew, deep down, right at that precise moment in time, that there was no future in my wonderfully clever 'stay in the Nationwide and win every week' idea. A season-load of 4–0s over Grimsby doesn't come close to winning at Newcastle.

The only problem with beating Newcastle is, firstly, that their fans are as good as any in football, staying loyal and passionate, even after their chairman was caught in the sleaziest of circumstances trying to belittle them about the prices they were prepared to pay for their shirts. As luck, and an undercover reporter from the *News of the World*, would have it, he ended up looking like the gullible one, but it's still hard to see what the fans had done to deserve him. Secondly, though, you risk upsetting Bobby Robson, and he's without doubt the most entertaining and passionate manager in the game.

Now Sir Bobby, he'd yet to earn his title when his side came to The Valley for the re-match and saw the margin of defeat doubled, as we beat them 2–0 on a chilly February afternoon. If the Palace had heard the outburst that followed, he might still be waiting for his gong (that's Buckingham, not Crystal – pay attention at the back).

He stormed into the press conference and sat there like a ticking bomb, waiting for the first person to fiddle with the fuse. As protective clothing was handed out and sandbags piled up around the room, someone reached for the detonator and cut all three wires at once, by asking him about his side's impending training trip to La Manga. He went off in spectacular style.

> I don't want to go to bloody La Manga. I want to go back to bloody Newcastle and run their bloody legs off because they're a bloody disgrace, the bloody lot of them. They don't deserve La Manga. They made me ashamed, ashamed to be their bloody manager and ashamed to look into the eyes of the decent people who paid good money to come and support them and who they let down. God, I'm pissed off with them, the bloody lot of them.

It had been a bad morning for Robson, with a piece appearing in a Sunday paper suggesting that he had offered an opinion as to the suitability of David Beckham as England captain, which he vehemently denied. I, for one, believed him. Firstly, it was much too dangerous to disagree with him on the evidence of his current mood and secondly, he didn't seem to be in the mood for shying away from home truths. He proceeded to offer a scathing assessment of the journalist he held accountable for the Beckham story, thanked us for our time, and stormed off, presumably to 'bloody La Manga'.

Experienced journalists came out of the room on the brink of crying with laughter, not so much at Robson, who was treated with considerable affection, but at the passion he plainly still has for the game. I was slightly taken aback – we had seen managers turning up looking annoyed at press conferences before, but back in the First Division it really wasn't anything to write home about. They were hardly household names and as we were winning games on a ridiculously regular basis, everyone tended to sit there in a foul mood anyway. Suddenly, we'd upset Bobby Robson by outplaying his side. This was progress.

From that point on, the season, despite having only three more wins waiting us, seemed to go from strength to strength. In the days after the Newcastle win, we learned of Powell's selection in the England squad and suddenly anything really did seem possible. I remember the morning of Powell's selection well, simply because it was so unexpected. It had been vaguely predicted in that morning's *Daily Mail*, but people were very sceptical. Powell arrived at the training ground, had to say a few words to the gang of reporters gathered there and went off to try and get his head round the news while preparing to play against Coventry the next day.

At about midday, a friend who worked for a national newspaper got a copy of the squad leaked to him and called me to say Powell was in. I went downstairs from the press office to the main hall and tried to tell him quietly, but the news slipped out everywhere in an instant. I then went upstairs to let Curbishley know what I'd been told. He was immediately calm, as he always is in any new and unusual situation, and went through the options.

'Can you go and get him to come up here, Mick, but don't tell him. I think I should tell him.'

He was, of course, right, and if I'm being honest, I'd been acting like a star-struck kid, dazzled by this sudden turn of events. The problem was, that while I had intended to say, 'Bit of a problem there, Curbs, you see, I've just told him', it seemed to come out of my mouth as 'OK, no problem, back in a minute.' Well, it was a slip of the tongue . . .

As I marched back down the corridor, towards the stairs that led to the sports hall below, I heard someone running up them towards me. As England's new left-back came bounding towards me, I was forced into trying slapstick to save myself. 'He doesn't know you know,' I mouthed dramatically, putting a finger to my lips to say 'play dumb'. I did the whole thing with the sort of pathetic facial expression adopted by a puppy who's just done something disgraceful on the sofa. That sort of 'I'm shit, but please don't hate me for it' face.

Whatever was said in that office, either Powell made a plea in mitigation for me, or managed a performance of Oscar-winning standards in feigning shock, surprise and delight. He even kept up the charade, by doing a bit in a local paper about how Curbs had broken the news to him, much to several people's amusement. Either way, I owe the man, although I've no idea how I'll face Curbishley again. Maybe I'll get his car to start arguing with him again and distract him that way.

Looking back at it now, the draw at The Valley with Manchester United was probably the game we'll all remember in years to come. Goals came in all directions and Robinson's manic, screaming run around the north end of the ground after his equaliser stands as a testimony to the wisdom of keeping the gates locked until the end, lest one of your players runs into the Thames in celebration. There were an absurd number of alternative candidates, however, with Chelsea, Arsenal, Spurs and many others being beaten.

Slightly more detailed consideration, however, leaves little alternative than to conclude that the whole season was something of a highlight. We were only meant to survive, finish fourth from bottom, live to fight another day, hang around and collect another year of television money

– we described it, a hundred different ways, meaning exactly the same thing. What we did was to prosper – prosper – and set ourselves an almost impossible act to follow in the season ahead.

Apart from the obligatory loss of the last two games, there was to be one last blot on the end-of-season mood. It came with the announcement that, having failed to recover from the illness which had kept him out for most of the season, Andy Hunt would be retiring from the game on medical advice. Hunt had been diagnosed as suffering from post-viral fatigue syndrome and, despite a number of attempts to return to action, the illness was never to allow him to get anywhere close to the physical condition he had been in at his prime.

The physical change in him was dramatic and immediately noticeable, as he went from being a gaunt yet extraordinarily fit young man to a hollow-eyed, fatigue-ridden figure within about six months. The exertions of everyday life were beyond him, and the idea that he was ever going to be fit to play football again were, despite a couple of falsely hopeful signs, plainly wildly misplaced.

I spoke to him a few weeks after he made the announcement and while he might have been physically a shadow of his former self, his balanced and happy outlook on life was the same as it ever was:

> I'd love to be able to play football again, but it's not going to happen and that's something I've got to get used to. I need to concentrate on getting well again and there's no point in moping around and feeling sorry for myself, because that won't help me get better or make life any easier for any of the people around me. I've got a few ideas about what I want to do next, but we'll have to wait and see what comes of them.

Somehow, I knew he wasn't going to sell insurance, run a pub or become an agent, but I must admit, I was left smiling when the announcement was made. Hunt moved to Belize, into a remote area of semi-jungle, and started a business, Green Dragon, producing medicinal herbs and organic produce. He also runs a non-profit organisation, dedicated to developing recycling operations and educational projects in Belize. He reads a lot, studies the language and waits for his girlfriend to give birth to their first child.

He never was the most conventional of footballers and his choice of occupation post-retirement stands up there with the best of them. I spoke to him recently and mentioned I was writing a book. He wished me luck, said it was a shame we couldn't sit down and have a beer and a chat, but that he had no plans to come back to 'Blighty' in the near future. I don't blame him. I hope he has a bumper harvest – he deserves it. If Charlton are a slightly unusual football club, Hunt's actions after his retirement show that he was playing at exactly the right place.

We had, of course, previously been considered a slightly unusual 'little' football club, but the ninth-place finish in our first year back in the Premiership was endangering the continued use of the word 'little'. Curbishley had shown that his men could compete at the highest level, if not comfortably, then at least to a level beyond which our critics and maybe even we had believed possible.

It would only have required a couple of results to go the other way to find ourselves in contention for a European spot, something eventually claimed by Ipswich. We waited to see how much further they would progress the next year, having spent the season listening to them being showered with the type of plaudits we thought belonged exclusively to us. Ipswich were like a little brother, who had come along and left all the people who used to make a fuss of us infatuated with the new arrival. To be honest, we were getting a bit jealous and fed up with them.

We spent a summer dreaming of how much further we might go than last time around and stopping occasionally to pinch ourselves that all this was really happening. It only seemed like five minutes ago that Michael Gray was stubbing his penalty into the waiting arms of Sasa Ilic, and now we were being treated like an established Premiership side. That old show-business line about stepping out in the chorus line and walking back a star might be a bit hammy and far-fetched, but I bet I wasn't the only one at the time who could relate to it.

We even strengthened the squad, just like big clubs tend to, rather than selling people to help pay the bills, which is how we used to spend the summer. We bought Jason Euell for a club record sum of £4.75 million and Luke Young for a fee which could, so we were told, reach £4 million. We also finally signed Shaun Bartlett for £2 million, who had been with us on loan for much of the previous season, as well as building a new stand, which brought the spending up to £20 million. Oh, and I think they put some new carpet down in the lounge as well, which not so long ago would undoubtedly have been the summer's largest outlay. There's probably a joke in there somewhere about the outlay on underlay, but you'll have to find it for yourselves.

In hindsight, we might have been better signing the cast of *Casualty*, such were the injury problems that were to plague us through the year. Richard Rufus damaged knee ligaments in the second game of the season, at Ipswich, and didn't return until there were only half a dozen matches left. Matt Svensson collected his obligatory pre-season injury, writing himself off until the New Year, and Claus Jensen hurt his foot in January and didn't stop hopping until the last game of the season. Almost everyone in the squad picked up a knock of some sort, as the concept of picking an unchanged team became an ever more unfamiliar one to Curbishley.

There were, however, a few laughs along the way, starting before the campaign even began properly, on the pre-season tour to Sweden. A group of journalists came along with the squad and watched with stunned expressions on the second day, as Peter Varney firstly agreed to a challenge five-a-side game against the coaching staff and then set about trying to take side bets on the result. Within five minutes, Mervyn Day had kicked the club's chief executive in the air more times than anyone cared to remember, to a chorus of hysterical laughter from the players who had stayed behind after training to watch. Varney, who had somehow procured himself the position of referee as well as player, then disallowed a 40-yard Curbishley lob, on the grounds that it was 'a bit too flash for this game'.

We repaired, later that night, to the only bar in town to discuss events. In fact, it wasn't the only bar, there were two, but the other one had bouncers on the door with leather caps, black leather waistcoats and large, handlebar moustaches. The general consensus seemed to be 'each to their own', but a group of a dozen men going in there without the benefit of speaking the language was always going to be a little bit too open to a well-meaning, yet incorrect, interpretation. Instead, we sat there while Curbishley tried to illustrate a point about overlaps or offside traps, or some other technical point, with a variety of cutlery and beer bottles, while a Bon Jovi tribute band played at full volume about six feet from our table.

The bar, for some reason I didn't want to know, looked like an operating theatre, covered in white, ceramic tiles, on the floor, walls and ceiling. I didn't dare order the liver – it's very remote in northern Sweden, and if there was a serial killer lurking around, I wasn't helping him dispose of the evidence. It meant that the noise was deafening already, with every slight scrape of the chair reverberating around the room. If you dropped a knife on the floor it threatened some form of hearing impairment and by the time he'd got halfway through 'Living on a Prayer' (the tribute bloke, not Curbs), I wondered if I'd ever be able to hear anything again.

As we left the bar, one of the journalists stopped, stared around at the surreal scene in front of him, and tried to sum up what had happened.

> The chief executive gets cut in half by the coach, while all the players laugh. Then the management team go out with the press and the chief executive to the loudest, strangest bar in the world. They sit there, trying to argue 4–4–2 over 3–5–2 while a skinny blond bloke dressed in black leather imagines he's playing a concert in a stadium, and then we all walk back to the hotel, as if nothing unusual has happened. This isn't your normal Premiership football club. It's great, but it's not normal.

He was right, but it hinted that there wasn't all that much wrong with the mood in the camp either. Then again, the squad hadn't started dropping like flies by that stage.

Actually, the idea that we weren't like a normal club could easily have become the theme of the season. It was early in the year, during a home game against Leicester, when the fans first joined in to stake their claim to the crown. Referee Mike Dean sent Steve Brown off in marginally dubious circumstances, but managed to upset the crowd a hundred times more by flourishing the red card theatrically, just as Brown departed proceedings on a stretcher. Before the game, someone at the club had taken the decision to place a copy of the new merchandise catalogue on each seat and once one person decided to throw theirs in protest, the rest was inevitable.

About 15,000 airborne catalogues later, and you could scarcely see the pitch. When questioned about it after the game, Curbishley took the very shrewd decision to try and make a joke out of the matter.

'At least it was only catalogues. At some places it's seats and bottles!'

The press chuckled along, the headlines next morning were humorous and supportive, rather than prissy and outraged, and we heard no more about it. Far be it from me to suggest they are swayed by such things, but if the media had made an issue out of it, I'm sure I'm not alone in thinking that the FA might have come down on us a bit harder. Dean later sent off Junior Lewis of Leicester, presumably for wearing a blue shirt in a built-up area, in a shocking display of trying to even things up. Leicester lost the game and Peter Taylor lost his job because of it. On balance, it wasn't funny and justice was far from done.

We were doing all right, especially considering the injuries, but it hadn't been nearly as exciting as the previous year. Someone said to me at the time, 'You've not been flirting with relegation though.' Why, I wondered, would you 'flirt' with relegation? Surely you'd only flirt with something you wanted? Why does everyone in football use phrases that mean nothing, yet still get passed down from generation to generation?

Why do we laugh at the irony of the man on *The Fast Show* talking about jumpers for goalposts and then say 'at the end of the day' without feeling silly? Why didn't these questions occur to me last year? Probably because it was more exciting and I was too wrapped up in the football.

This time around, it just wasn't a season to capture the imagination. It was, as it transpired, more about determination than flair – maybe there was something to be said for just clenching our fists and being passionate. We had loads of injuries, we clung to mid-table with all our might and set about the process of 'finding our feet' or 'going through a transitional period' depending on whom you spoke to. Every silver lining seemed to have two clouds claiming ownership of it and the home form, which had been such a source of excitement the year before, had collapsed. Last year, nobody wanted to come to play at The Valley, but a year later they were willing to swap their own home games for the right to come to SE7 and play us twice.

The rumours that all was not well in the camp still seemed to be wide of the mark, but they weren't helped when Andy Todd was transfer-listed and suspended for a fortnight, after an 'unsavoury incident' at the training ground. Nobody officially admitted what had gone on, but judging by Dean Kiely's two black eyes, it wasn't, despite the rather prim description of his offence, that Todd's table manners had fallen to an unacceptably low standard.

I suppose even that was progress, of a sort at least. When I first went down to The Valley, there were people getting chinned in front of a paying audience during the game – at least now it was all behind closed doors. As if there weren't enough already, it's just another example of how professional the game has got.

The low point of our time back in the Premiership, from a footballing point of view, was the announcement that Clive Mendonca had been forced to retire. He had been a hero of quite extraordinary proportions at the club and it's hard to believe that any player at any other club has ever done so much to cement himself into the affections of the fans in just one afternoon. There will be those who argue that he had a marvellous season and it's wrong to think of his career as just being that day at Wembley, but they're not kidding anyone – you can't be a Charlton fan and mention the play-off final without Mendonca.

The years after that season for Mendonca had been wrecked by injury, though, and it slowly became clear that he was never coming back, which did nothing to lessen the impact when we finally heard that he'd retired. I saw him a couple of days later at the training ground, and asked him to sign a shirt for me.

'Who's it for?' he asked.

'Me,' I said. 'It's going on the wall in my study.'

'Ah, stop taking the piss, Mick. Who's it for?'

It wasn't false modesty and I wasn't 'taking the piss'. Mendonca was a hero, and the inside front cover of this book doesn't lie. I do live at home with it proudly looking down at my desk. On the final day of last season, he received an award from Richard Murray, on the pitch before the game, shortly after a video montage of some of his goals was played to the crowd. It probably won't be the last time the 'Super Clive' song is heard in SE7, but it seemed like the loudest rendition yet. The season might have slumped to a reasonably disappointing conclusion, certainly when judged against the absurdly high standards set the previous year, but the man who sent us into the Premiership enjoyed a fitting farewell. If he'd stayed fit for a few more years, who knows how things might have turned out?

The growth of the club was still impossible to dispute, however, and the figures supported that. In the previous year, they'd enjoyed a turnover of £28 million, which was up from £12 million the year before. We were just 16 years along the line from almost being wound up for debts of 'almost £1 million', and had just coughed up £20 million in the close season for new players and facilities. The overall graph of the club was still heading upwards at a rate of knots and I was reminded of something that Ben Hayes had said:

> Every year since we got back to The Valley, something has happened to the good of the club. We've built a stand, or paid off a debt, or increased the training ground. They're not really very striking things for the average fan, but without them the club couldn't have made the leaps forward that it has. If we went down next year, which is always a possibility, it wouldn't hit us the same way as it hit, say, Barnsley. We wouldn't go into freefall because of it, and that's a very important position of safety to reach.
>
> We won't have to sell players to meet the bills again and that means we can think about life from a footballing point of view. If we go down, it's because we lost too many games and that's what football should be about. We had to immerse ourselves in a load of financial details most supporters don't care about, because our future was in among those details. Because we spent so long pondering the finances, now we can concentrate on the football and that's a huge advantage.

He's right, I think, but it's not a considered standpoint that tends to find sympathy from football fans in the heat of the moment. Even when things are going extraordinarily well, and the overall picture is undoubtedly positive, we still manage to find things to trouble us and convince ourselves that the temporarily bleak outlook is set to stay for far longer than is likely to be the case.

We wound up in 14th place in the Premiership last season and managed to feel fairly miserable about it, yet less than two years earlier we had been promising street parties if we ended up fourth from bottom. In that time we'd strengthened the side and built a huge new stand, yet our expectations had changed dramatically. I'm divided on whether that's a good or bad thing.

In moderation, I can see that expectation is the fuel which powers a club like Charlton onto the next stage of their journey. The trouble is that you never get expectation in moderation, just as you don't get social crack users or occasional, 'only at Christmas' meths drinkers. Expectations grow out of control quicker than the Argentinian rate of inflation and soon leave you, depending on your position, either daunted at their size, fed up at your failure to meet them or furious at people's inability to be more realistic.

Soon after the start of the current season, the club sent fans into a state of near shock by announcing that they had sold Mark Kinsella to Aston Villa. The man who had saluted the north stand, lifted the Play Off trophy and First Division Championship trophy, and generally been our hero, was gone. The fact that we accepted a bid of only £1 million did little to assuage people's anger.

Once upon a time, it would have rattled on like thunder for months, and there would have been calls for either the manager or the board to go – and maybe both. This time, however, things were a little different. There was genuine and deserved affection and thanks for Kinsella, not just for what he had done, but for the way he did it. There was also, however, especially after the fuss of the first few days had abated, a realisation that we were having to move on, and maybe we couldn't afford to keep someone around on big wages who couldn't command a first-team place.

The emotional side of me was fuming, but the rational side could see not just the logic, but that the people who had made the decision had not served us so badly so far. Kinsella wouldn't stop being a hero just because he'd gone to another club, and it certainly wouldn't threaten his place in Charlton history. His knees, by all accounts, were giving him problems, possibly accounting for the meagre fee, and, anyway, I'd always pleaded with my heroes to go out at the top. If Mark Kinsella was going to be unable to perform as he had done in the past, I didn't want to see it – I wanted to remember the extraordinary player of two or three years ago.

It was, in a way, a summary of the battles Charlton had faced over the last few years. Once we wrestled with accountants and the taxman, and now we wrestled with our past. How much of it could we carry forwards with us until it became baggage and slowed us down? How much of it could we shed before we were 'selling out' and forgetting where we'd come from, making the journey pointless?

I wish there was a simple answer, or even a definitive one, but I don't think there can, or even should, be. Just as Keith Peacock had said after the play-off final, the club means different things to different people, and what it means to you tends to be reflected in how much emotional effort you've expended on it over the years. To some, being in the Premiership and selling Kinsella was like winning the lottery and having nobody to share the money with. To others, it merely represented the price of the ticket.

When I'm thinking with my head, it's a difficult dilemma with which to come to terms. When I'm thinking with my heart, it's impossible. We all knew that being in the Premiership wasn't meant to be easy, but we thought that just related to the teams we had to play against. If there's one thing we've learned over the last couple of years, it's that it also means the decisions we've had to make.

Who said it was only a game?

15

AND FOR OUR NEXT TRICK?

It's hard to write about anything close to your heart, and Charlton Athletic, as you may have spotted, are certainly close to mine, without entering into the project laden down with preconceptions. It's a subject you think about and discuss on an almost daily basis, and in the case of a football club, a subject with which you go through the most emotional of ordeals. If you experienced the same highs and lows in any other relationship that you do with your football team, they'd be queuing up to get you onto daytime television. You'd sit there, looking uncomfortable, with a studio audience clapping away at the good times, and sighing, crying and offering words of support as you painfully recounted the bad ones.

Putting aside all the words of warning about keeping things in perspective, and remembering that it's only a game, as soon as your team step out onto the pitch, logic deserts you and semi-primal fears and celebrations step in. Trying to collect the memories of these events subsequently, and committing them to paper, should, you'd imagine, be fairly simple. After all, most of the memories, for better or worse, are burned into your mind and almost all the details are held in crystal-clear form somewhere a lot closer to the front of your brain than the back, pathetically enough.

Whatever you try to pretend to outsiders, and people who don't share your passion for either the game or the club, you won't manage to convince yourself that you're not addicted. If the bit of your brain dealing with emotional memories, both happy and sad, is kept separate from the rest of your mind, then much of the available space has probably already been taken up with football. As a Charlton fan, though, I've never felt, at least not in the last ten years, that I'm doing something too illogical in making the trek down to The Valley for my fortnightly fix.

Some fans aren't so lucky, having been chosen at birth to follow clubs that were going nowhere, and even then, doing it in a dawdling and chaotic manner. The average man on the terrace, or in the stands as he has now become, can't see any way in which his side are going to break out of their torpor. While there might be the odd bit of excitement along the way, a few late winners and a couple of shocking defeats, it's mostly going to be fairly mundane fare.

About 15 years ago, and probably much more recently than that, Charlton fitted that description quite well. It seemed that the price we paid for avoiding financial extinction was to spend our days roaming around the league, playing at other people's grounds and never really doing anything all that spectacular. We had a history as a big club, which was becoming more and more remote with each passing season, gradually being written out of living memory by the passage of time. You would have been hard pressed to find more than a handful of people who would have been prepared to announce publicly that they could see a way of us getting back there again. The dull nature of our day-to-day existence proved to be an unlikely place from which a visionary was suddenly going to appear and, in any case, we'd had experience of visionaries and still bore the scars to prove it.

The problem with the preconceptions you have about your football club is that it's very difficult, because of the ludicrously intense nature of your relationship with them, to know when you're being reasonable, and when you've turned into a hyperbolic bore. To tell the truth, that's the problem with football itself, but when you've gone through what we have in the last decade, you've less chance of approaching the subject in a sane and rational way than almost anyone else.

What is certain is that the fortunes of Charlton Athletic have been picked up and spun through 180 degrees over the last 12 or 13 years, with the return to The Valley acting as the starting gun for the most dramatic period of growth and progress. On top of that, about four years ago we 'kicked for home', accelerated off the bend and found another gear. We might have only been progressing at what seemed like a reasonable rate even then, compared to a lot of other clubs, but we seem to have done it in a far more sensible and sustainable way. I said we were predisposed to start sounding smug, didn't I?

While loans were obtained and debts piled up all around the league, we've learned from our previous near-misses and seem to have accepted, mostly at least, the value of playing the tortoise, rather than the hare. Having said that, there aren't many analogies you can draw which end up with us being portrayed as a tortoise, so maybe it's not the best example of what we've achieved.

What did strike me, as I looked back over the last decade, was the extent to which the progress has been meticulously planned and the way in which the plans of tomorrow have very quickly, as time has moved on, become the working practices of today. If Charlton were to be viewed as a skyscraper, no sooner would the next floor up have been completed, than someone would be moving into it, while the next storey was still under construction. Learning to live and thrive through the middle of a major redevelopment has become an art in itself.

There had to be something more, though, and something that wasn't necessarily in existence at other clubs. If it were really that simple, then everyone would be doing it. It's possible to present the progress as a straightforward example of not spending more than you earn, but as with any such attempt to make a complicated achievement seem simple, the key to it all seems, to me at least, to be in the small details. They don't get mentioned when you start trying to summarise things neatly and concisely, but the longer you look at the club, the more obvious it becomes.

Almost all the arguments and disagreements in football, or at least the ones which cause real damage to the clubs, come about when the fans fall out of love with the people running the club – more specifically, when the fans stop trusting them. Whatever is happening to you, no matter how unkind the referees are being to you, how much bad luck you're having with injuries, indeed, how much bad luck you're enduring generally, if everyone stays united behind the cause, you'll probably be fine. Indeed, with a few wise words and clever quotes from someone senior, you can make the most terrible setback sound like a blessing in disguise.

When the fans lose faith in the way the club is being run, though, you just can't move forward. Lots of teams have had great results while everyone is complaining about the ineptitude of the referee, but very few have ever done well while blaming the way their own club is run. We haven't heard much by way of complaint in the last ten years, nor does it feel like we've been given reason to want to, as everyone seems, most of the time at least, to be happy to push in the same direction in pursuit of the same purpose.

Martin Simons, as far as I was concerned, summed it up quite well:

> I'm amazed that other clubs in the country haven't followed the
> lead that we started when we got involved with the fans. There's
> a chain running from the Valley Party to the patrons scheme, and
> the common theme is obviously keeping the links with the fans
> not just alive, but thriving.
>
> We all feel at this club, that it's our club, it's the fans' club. We
> listen to the fans, we listen to the supporters' club on the pricing
> of season tickets and issues like that, and that's what makes us
> special. It is unique, but I'm surprised that it's stayed unique,
> because I'm surprised other clubs haven't followed the example.

Simons is right, of course, not only in his belief that a chain runs
through the club as far as the involvement of the fans is concerned, but
also to express surprise that other clubs haven't adopted, or apparently
even investigated, a similar approach. With a financial crisis seemingly
set to sweep the game, you suspect that there might be a number of
clubs wishing that they had done things rather differently. It's too late to
change the way your club is run suddenly, just because times are hard,
because the fans will spot the air of desperation about you from a
hundred paces. The key to making it work is to convince people that
you are a club that is being run differently from the start. It won't work,
as we see on a daily basis, if you are seen as inviting involvement from
the fans in the hard times, and then banishing them from the boardroom
again as soon as the good times reappear.

Returning briefly to the idea of tomorrow's plans becoming today's
working practices as soon as they're completed, which is probably a
complicated way of saying 'turning dreams into reality', the essence of
what Simons is saying simply underlines that idea. It was used to me in
a different context, but to make broadly the same point, by Ben Tegg,
when talking about the work the club does in the community.

> It's a programme of work – it's not an individual thing, a one-off.
> It's no good doing a one-off thing, because they don't work.
> They're only good for media opportunities and nice photos. This
> is more than that.

In a way, it's exactly what Simons was saying about the fans – whatever
system you run, stick to it, plan for the long, rather than short term,
have a bit of faith in yourself to have made the right decision, and then

stick to your guns. The vast majority of plans instigated when we first returned to The Valley still hold firm, at least as far as their sentiment is concerned, although the detail has obviously changed as the scale of the matter at hand has grown. That in itself is a matter of some confusion, as Ben Hayes observes:

> You can tell people that you're a Charlton fan and they don't say 'Who?' or 'What division are they in?' But they recognise the name and they sometimes talk about how they used to go to The Valley in the old days but they stopped for one reason or another. It's hard to put your finger on it, but there's something there that makes them view the club in a different light all of a sudden. Now I meet loads and loads of people who don't go to the games, and maybe don't particularly want to go to the games, but they're happy to call themselves Charlton supporters. I suppose because not so long ago that would have been seen as embarrassing, and now it's not.
>
> I think we're still being remembered for what we were a little bit. You speak to people and one of the things mentioned about us a lot is this idea that we're punching above our weight – and I don't think we are. I think that they're remembering the Charlton side of a few years ago and not the one we've got at the moment. Mind you, I think there's a lot of our own fans who haven't caught up to that either.

There is certainly some truth in that, but it's not just the fans who are a little confused – the club itself is still occasionally to be found struggling to find a steady path towards commercial advancement, while balancing the demands of its history and the changes required for its future. Charlton isn't like anywhere else – nobody else has travelled to the Premiership down the route we've gone and, as a result, we don't fit into any neat business models or development plans, so we've had to create our own.

The greatest single force at the club is generated by the degree of harmony between the board of directors and the fans in the stands. It's the fuel that powers the whole thing, and it is in evidence to a greater degree at The Valley than anywhere else in English football and has enabled the club to perform a miracle over the course of the last ten years.

People might think that Charlton harp on a bit about how well they all get along, that we play on it just to make us look a bit 'special', but that's not true. It's there and it allows us to operate on a level quite possibly greater than the sum of our parts. The degree of trust apparent makes it easier to resist the temptation to react in a knee-jerk fashion whenever a problem comes along, and that, as Alan Honey acknowledges, is part of our strength:

> The key nowadays is planning, planning and not panicking when the plan doesn't work perfectly first time out. We didn't panic when we got relegated and, as a result, we were able to bounce back and get on with things. If we'd panicked and sacked the manager and sold a load of players, we wouldn't be back here now. You look at clubs who have panicked and sold everyone and they never come back. Well-run clubs, who don't suffer knee-jerk reactions – they come back, because the things that were done properly before, stay being done properly and they stick to the plan and weather the storm.

If we do nothing else over the course of the next decade, it occurs to me that we should, at least, keep trying to stand back and look at the bigger picture, the wider view of what has been achieved at our club. Football is a game of passions and tempers and things are blown out of all proportion, but we shouldn't allow short-term frustrations to cloud our view of what has been done and the scale of the journey that has been undertaken.

We can't sit on our laurels and keep telling each other how clever we've been, because that would mean a return to the comfort zone and celebrating 'being mediocre for so bloody long' that Honey had complained to me about, as well as the lack of ambition. 'It was as if the people who ran the club didn't believe we could ever do anything all that special. Well, if they didn't, then why should anyone else think we could?'

It's a two-way thing, though, as with everything else at Charlton. If the fans stop looking at what's happened and stop appreciating what's been achieved, then they're blinkered and our forward progress is at an end. If, on the other hand, the board stop appreciating what the fans have done, how they've stayed loyal, and how they've remained convinced that we're a bit 'different' to other clubs, then they'll lose the respect of the fans and, again, our forward progress will have come to an end. Both sides of the equation have their role to play and both appear to be willing to keep their side of the bargain, for the foreseeable future, at least.

I was reminded of something that Alan Curbishley had said to me, which just about sums up the dilemma facing us at this stage of our development:

> That's the great thing about this football club – we don't forget. If we start forgetting, maybe we'll end up just like any other football club. While we mustn't forget where we came from, though, we've got to remember to keep looking to see where we can go next.

Considering the public perception of a football manager is of a man unwilling to converse about the game to a level deeper than 'man on' or 'keep it tight at the back', Curbishley certainly confounded expectations with his analysis. It's as good an attempt at summing up the challenges facing us as any other I've read or heard, as it wraps up the secret of the last ten years and sets out the task to be met in the next, all within forty-eight words.

The interesting thing is that he says it with no sense of wonderment or amazement, just a hint of pride. There's an understated quality about him, which stretches out to encompass much of the club. We don't boast about our triumphs as loudly as we might and we don't wail about our failures as morosely as some. Having looked like they were slowly disappearing from life as a football club, Charlton have discovered the merits of just getting on with things a day at a time.

When I was first discussing this book, I met with the publisher and having got the business of the book out of the way, we soon found ourselves chatting about the club in general. Within a couple of minutes we'd scooted through play-off finals, penalty shoot-outs, losing your ground, winning it back, centre-halfs going in goal, last-minute winners, European superstars and boats full of rubber. We glossed over London derbies, coming five minutes from bankruptcy, rebuilding grounds, anti-racism initiatives, building a squad and balancing the books. All the things in fact, that only Charlton seem to be able to discuss, at least by reference to things we've actually experienced.

'Bloody hell,' he exclaimed, 'it's never quiet there, is it? I'd not even heard of half of that.'

We may not realise it, or at least we might sometimes forget it, but the continuing rise of Charlton Athletic is an amazing story. In fact, it's a long string of amazing stories, all stitched together to provide a recent history more amazing than any other club in the land.

Richard Murray could hardly have dreamed that any of this would be possible when he first came to the club. As recently as five or six years ago, he was expressing the dream that we might one day become as big as Norwich or Leicester. It's safe to say that he's achieved that particular ambition, along with a host of others along the way:

> I look around now, at the north stand and the development around the ground, and, yes, it really does give me a sense of achievement. It gives me a tangible example of what we've done over the last ten years. I don't want to sound trite, but at Charlton I really believe, and I always have, and this is why we only have fans on the board, that we have to do as good a job as we possibly can for the club while we're running it. Then, when we run out of steam or energy or whatever, we've got to be in a position to hand over the baton with the club in the best position possible for the next generation.

It seems safe to assume that the preparations for the eventual handing over of the baton will be made as thoroughly as just about everything else Murray and his colleagues have done and it also seems likely that the fans will be kept extraordinarily aware of exactly what's going on. If you're running things in a straightforward and honest way, it's a lot easier to be open with people about what you're doing. As far as their dealings with the fans are concerned, cloak and dagger have never been the order of the day.

It's been an amazing decade through which to support my club and I can honestly say that there isn't anywhere else in the country where I'd have experienced more drama and elation. At least, nowhere that by rights shouldn't still be here, where I could have watched it unfold.

When I think back to that evening, when I trudged my eight-year-old footsteps across the car park and along the road, just as the middleweight championship of Charlton was being decided, I think I was probably a bit hard on my uncle. If I'd sat there, watched the whole of that fairly turgid encounter and then seen it culminate in two of the home players battering each other, I might not have come back. It would have been easier to go and support one of those 'big' clubs, who were on the television on Sunday lunchtimes. As it was, the old theatrical maxim of 'leave 'em wanting more' seemed to come into effect, and I was hooked.

Without him, I wouldn't have experienced any of the events mentioned in this book and a thousand others beside. Without him, I wouldn't have watched Super Clive at Wembley on That Afternoon, or seen Claus score at Highbury, or Powelly play for England. I wouldn't have seen Browny go in goal, Robbo equalise against United, Jason win it for us yet again against Chelsea, Jorge wave us goodbye in the sunshine at Old Trafford or Kins punch the air in front of F-block a hundred times over. The nicknames just wouldn't have the personalities to go along with them.

From Portakabins to Porto captains – it's been quite a journey. Maybe it's time to forgive him?

POSTSCRIPT

So, now the disappointment of defeat against Chelsea at the start of a new campaign has faded, another Premiership season is over and our status as a top-flight side has been maintained. On this sunny June afternoon, football seems to be both far enough behind and in front of us to allow a considered opinion as to how the club's tenth season back at The Valley unfolded.

Where, back when the memories were still sharp and vivid, we might have looked at each contest with excruciating detail, and worked out why points were dropped and performances wavered, the break allows even the most obsessive to relax a little. Now, with the dust settled and the excitement passed, we can look upon things in a more considered manner. To be honest, the season itself really didn't warrant terribly much by way of detailed analysis in any event.

We started by playing a string of 'big' clubs at home, and got turned over with monotonous regularity. Of the eventual top four in the Premiership, we donated three away points to three of them before September was out. By the time Newcastle arrived in SE7, despite it being mid-March, we remembered our manners and gave them all three as well.

Our first home win of the season, against Middlesbrough, lifted us out of the relegation zone, but all around there were voices suggesting that this was going to be 'the' year – the one when we got 'found out'. The season Charlton were brought back down to earth, and dispatched off back to the Nationwide league, where so many pundits thought we belonged. In truth, while we can all get offended and demonstrate a bit of mock indignation at the very mention of the possibility, as far as I remember it, this seemed to be a fairly widespread fear at the time, even among the most determined of the faithful.

Visits to The Valley were not exactly treated with trepidation by opposing sides. Indeed, children head off for Disneyland with expecting less delight than the teams in the top half of the table who sauntered down to SE7. Apart from Dani Behr's flat, it's hard to think of one place in London that caused so much delighted screaming and shouting among so many Premiership stars. A couple of years ago, we called our end-of-season video 'Fortress Valley'. It wasn't all that good a gag at the time, but now, it seemed, someone was definitely slapping us back down into place.

Being Charlton though, nothing was ever quite as bad as it seemed, as we came through in fine style, winning an impressive clump of contests throughout the middle of the year. It took a late equaliser for Manchester City to stop us claiming five successive Premiership victories before Christmas had arrived, although we went on to achieve that particular target by the end of February.

Winning all of that month's league contests earned Alan Curbishley the Manager of the Month award and, in keeping with the finest traditions of the game, this was the signal for an end-of-season belly-flop, as we lost to anyone and everyone the moment March arrived. Our seasons were beginning to take on a distinctly familiar look, as despair gave way to hope, which flirted with the possibility of developing into expectation, before building dramatically into, well, what can only be described as an excruciatingly dull anticlimax.

At the time, and to be honest, there were few who would have considered us to be over-reacting, misery and gloom reigned almost unconfined. We'd been on the brink (ish) of European qualification, only to throw in the towel in dramatic style. Looking back now, however, with the benefit of hindsight, it's difficult to reach a conclusion anywhere near as damning.

Upon regaining Premiership status, Curbishley had spoken of a 'three-year plan', designed to see our position set upon proper foundations and safe from the vagaries of a one-year wonder scenario, which had seen so many sides take a catastrophic turn for the worse. Ipswich, who had long been held up as a bastion of financial prudence and long-term planning, had gone into administration. It went deeper, however, than just the clubs who had been surprised by the 'big time'. A quick glance around the Premiership revealed clubs of the magnitude of Leeds, Chelsea and several others who had enjoyed years of success, recording losses that only the most optimistic of gamblers could ever hope to see recovered.

There had been members of what has almost at times felt like a family, who took the chance to move on as the season wore on. Steve Brown, as brave and scruffy and loyally committed to the cause as anyone, finally, after three seasons of limited appearances, accepted the inevitable and moved to Reading in search of first-team football. The signs are that the Reading fans love him, and that comes as precious little surprise to anyone. Some players exist to generate respect and affection from the stands, and Brown fits the blueprint more accurately than most.

John Robinson was another from the same mould, granted a free transfer at the end of the year, in order to move to Cardiff and enjoy more regular first team appearances. Having spent a decade wearing the red shirt with a snarl and a grimace, contesting every challenge and chasing every lost cause, squeezing every ounce of ability from his frame, Robinson stood for something. His heart had been on his sleeve from his first game for the club through to his last. Both of them deserved the plaudits they received – both had played a huge part in the club's development, and the fans knew it.

Replacements had to be obtained, however, and when they were, there was an unmistakable 'Charlton' air about the deals which brought them here. As the season came to a close, Hermann Hreidarsson arrived from the troubled East Anglian outfit, followed shortly afterwards by Matt Holland, for a combined fee of £3m. Just eight months earlier, they had been lined up for moves to West Brom and Aston Villa respectively, for fees totalling £9m. Suddenly, financial common sense seemed less starchy and more attractive. We might have thought we were at the end of our tether as far as being sensible and careful were concerned, but we were wrong. The thought of having £6m more in the coffers than would otherwise have been the case, was a very persuasive argument against joining the transfer trail with the manic profligacy of so many other clubs. Being boring was back in fashion.

Not too boring of course, because to become predictable would fly in the face of everything Charlton have managed to do for the best part of the last 20 years. As if to remind us that he still had a few tricks lurking up his sleeve, Alan Curbishley pulled off maybe the most surprising transfer move of his Charlton career in the days before the new season, when Paolo Di Canio joined the club.

Having earned, during spells at Sheffield Wednesday and West Ham, the sort of reputation Curbishley normally steers clear of, Di Canio, on the face of it, could hardly have been further removed from what we thought was the stereotype of a Charlton player. Things have moved on at the club though, and maybe his arrival was a sign of just how far.

He spoke of passion, and desire, and a host of other adjectives which had the fans grinning and blushing in equal measure. We understood our history, Paolo told us, and he could see how much work had been done. More to the point, he understood how much more we still wanted to do. Outside our immediate world, there were people who respected us, and respected the quiet way we had gone about developing our club to ever greater heights. Above all, they admired us for doing it properly.

And that, maybe more than anything else, summed up quite why we had managed to reach the position we had. Once the resentment of another end-of-season slump had faded, it was hard not to look back at a wider view than the immediate post-match reaction had encouraged. Maybe we weren't, through our own actions, racing to close the gap on the teams at the top at quite the same rate as our earlier progress had suggested we might. However, as predicted by those dictating how the money was spent, maybe the fact that financial mismanagement was forcing several of the more glamorous names to retreat, was leading to a closing of the margins nonetheless.

Most millionaires are able to call upon a string of tales about the difficulties of life back when the money was far from plentiful, and only a fool could fail to see that our club was moving into a position where a similar boast could be made. Having made mistakes in our past, and plenty of them, we had learned from our errors, and set about ensuring that they never happened again. If the newspapers dictated that spending more than you could afford was a benchmark of progress, then we had failed. As the debts spiralled out of control elsewhere, however, and the transfer market crumbled, it was hard to agree with their reasoning.

The real fear when writing a postscript to a story such as this is that the progress cannot be maintained, and that the sense of anticlimax becomes inevitable. Looking back, even through admittedly rose-tinted lenses, it's impossible to reach that conclusion. In a footballing world gone mad, Charlton have allowed the mistakes of their past to put the problems and pitfalls of the present into perspective. For more than a decade, nothing has knocked them out of their stride.

Since deciding that they had to do something positive about their future or die, the foundations have been thoughtfully constructed, and the continued development intelligently and meticulously enacted. By rights, we shouldn't have a club left to support. Through the intervention of determined, talented and visionary individuals, spread throughout the management structure and all across the fan base, things are different.

English football, in its pursuit of swift reward, has damaged itself beyond all recognition. The league structure is cracked and collapsing from the foundations upwards, and the effects have begun to impact upon several gilded follies at the very top of its pile. When the rest start going backwards, steady progress becomes more attractive than ever before, and sustainable development, as businesslike and dull as it sounds, even more essential.

It's hard to resist the thought, even from a position of glorious and unapologetic bias, that the rise and rise of Charlton Athletic has not yet, by some considerable margin, run its course.

Long may it continue.